LUCY CALKINS ✦ MARJORIE MARTINELLI

LAUNCHING THE WRITING WORKSHOP

This book is dedicated to Kate Montgomery.

DEDICATED TO TEACHERS

FirstHand
An imprint of Heinemann
361 Hanover Street
Portsmouth, NH 03801-3912
www.heinemann.com

Offices and agents throughout the world

Photography: Peter Cunningham

Library of Congress Cataloging-in-Publication Data

CIP data on file with the Library of Congress.
ISBN: 0-325-00863-9
ISBN-13: 978-0-325-00863-9

Printed in the United States of America on acid-free paper
10   09   ML   5   6   7

ACKNOWLEDGEMENTS

This book is dedicated to Kate Montgomery, who has edited all the books in both this series and in the series *Units of Study for Primary Writing*. Kate has been my closest writing partner for the past decade. She's written sections of each of my books. More than this, she has trimmed and tailored every book, making each one more graceful as well as more explicit and more helpful. Kate has also managed the multi-faceted organization that has formed around these books, keeping the contributing authors, co-authors, production crew, editors, teachers, and publicists in close communication with each other. She has been my North Star and my compass, helping me steer a path.

I also want to thank Marjorie Martinelli, the contributing author of this book. Marjorie was a support in *Units of Study for Primary Writing* as well as in this book. I thank her for her generous efforts throughout both these writing projects. She contributed to many of the extensions in this book and in the *Launching* section of the CD-ROM. Marjorie is a wizard with classroom management, and her years as a staff developer made her especially helpful at thinking through ways we could provide additional supports for teachers who will first encounter the writing workshop through this book. Marjorie helped locate specific samples of children's work, obtain permissions, and fill in gaps in the manuscript.

I want to thank all the children whose work has been featured in this book, and their wonderful, generous teachers. I specifically want to thank Teresa Caccavalle and Lis Shin from PS 116 in Manhattan, Mollie Cura from PS 28 in the Bronx, Larry Neal from PS 18 in the Bronx, Kathy Doyle from Smith School in Tenafly, and Mary Chiarella from PS 57 and, before that, from PS 199 in Manhattan.

Tasha Kalista took almost unreadable manuscripts of this book and all the others, and, like the fairy godmother at work at her spinning wheel, transformed the flax into golden threads. Those of us who have had the chance to work with Tasha are convinced that she is magic. Her skill comes from understanding this work so much that she could co-author any one of the books.

The teaching that is described in this book and throughout the series is only possible because of the extraordinary leadership that New York City principals and superintendents have provided to their schools. I am especially grateful to a few of these New York City principals and superintendents who have supported the process of developing these units of study. These include Liz Phillips, Melanie Woods, Arlene Berg, Nora Polansky, Donald Conyers, Lillian Druck, Eileen Reiter, AnnaMarie Carillo, Daria Rigney, Leslie Zackman, Peggy Miller, Carol Wertheimer, Carol Stock, Anthony Inzerillo, Jack Spatola, Elsa Nunez, Maria Ciccone, Adele Schroeder, Cynthia Hunter, Joan Ratner, Jacqueline Jones, Peter MacFarlane, and Janette Cuban.

LAUNCHING THE WRITING WORKSHOP

Welcome to Unit 1

WELCOME TO THE UNIT

LAUNCHING THE WRITING WORKSHOP

About the Unit

We start the year by teaching children some of the biggest lessons they'll ever learn. First and most important, we teach them that their lives and their thoughts are worth writing about. We help children realize that the small moments of their lives can be compelling stories, and we help them feel committed to capturing the truth of their experience in words.

The first lessons in this unit center on topic choice. We teach children a number of strategies they can draw on in order to generate their own ideas for writing, and we set them free from a dependency on the teacher. Children will benefit from knowing that writers think of a person, then brainstorm moments they've spent with that person, choose one moment, and write the story. Writers similarly think of places that matter to them, brainstorm moments that occurred in those places, choose one moment, and write the story. Writers know that objects and photographs from their lives hold stories and that by listening to the stories of others, they can recall their own stories. Naomi Nye's beautiful poem "Valentine for Ernest Mann" reminds writers that "poems hide . . . in the shadows of our room they are hiding." Stories hide too, and with just a few minilessons we can be sure that all our students know where important stories are likely to hide.

Many teachers find that in this first unit, it helps to celebrate the fact that stories of significance can be found in the smallest and most ordinary occasions. Perhaps after children throng back into the classroom after lunch, we will want to help them choose one small story

from all the many that occurred while they were eating and tell that story as well as possible to their partners. In this fashion, we can teach students to reexamine the everyday routines of their lives in search of stories that have humor, beauty, and drama.

Meanwhile, during this unit children learn the essentials of narrative writing. They learn that narratives are just that—stories. In a personal narrative, one character (presumably the writer) experiences one thing, then the next, then the next. These texts are usually chronologically ordered. Children also learn that their narratives will be more effective if the writer has zoomed in on a small episode, written with detail, expanded the heart of the story, made their characters talk—and above all "made a movie in the mind" and then recorded that movie on the page. As children learn to write in ways that reflect all that they have already learned about focus, detail, strong leads, and so forth, their writing will improve in very noticeable ways. The improvements in children's writing should prove to them that learning to write well matters and thus launch them into the year.

One of the few nonnegotiable qualities of effective narrative writing is the hard-to-describe (and hard-to-achieve) quality that some teachers refer to as "writing in the moment" or "making a movie in your mind." If a child talks all about an event—summarizing it with sentences like "It was a good baseball game. We won 6 to 2. I got a lot of hits."—then the child is *commenting on* the game rather than *telling the story* of it. The child has not yet grasped the idea of writing in a storyteller's voice. If, on the other hand, his piece begins, "I grabbed a bat and walked up to the plate. I looked at the pitcher and nodded. 'I'm ready,' I said," then the child is writing a story. Most children need to be reminded to make movies in their mind and to write so readers can picture exactly what is happening. As the year unfolds, we will let children in on the fact that stories are not shaped like those we teach children to write in this unit, but for now, children find that they've got their hands full.

During this unit, many children will profit from learning a very simple form of focus. For example, a child might initially plan to write a page-long piece depicting his whole day at the beach, but because of our teaching, he'll write instead about body surfing on one wave. Another child will decide that instead of retelling the entire trip to Grandma's house, she will focus on how she accidentally let the pigs loose. As children narrow the time span of their stories, it is crucial that they then elaborate on the portion of the event that remains in their spotlight. In other words, the main reason to "zoom in" or to "write about a little seed story, not about a big watermelon topic" is that this makes it more likely that the writer will relive an episode with enough detail that the reader, too, can experience the event.

As children learn about narrative writing, some of the lessons will be explicit, taught in minilessons and conferences. But some of the lessons will be implicit, gleaned as children are immersed in texts that sound like those we hope they will soon write. It is not always easy to find published personal narratives, so we also share realistic fiction, especially picture books and short stories that resemble the stories about small moments the children will write. Even just one dearly loved and closely studied text can infuse a writing workshop with new energy.

This unit of study is designed to launch a writing workshop that is well-managed enough that children can proceed with some independence. Children learn the structures and rituals of a writing workshop. They learn to gather for a minilesson, to sit and listen throughout most of it, to "turn and talk" with a partner at the designated moment. They learn that they can get themselves started on writing, work past the hard parts, rely on one another as well as on themselves, share their writing, and so forth. Soon children will be able to get themselves started writing new entries without needing any input from the teacher; this means that during one day's writing workshop, they'll write one entry after another, working with independence.

The Plan for the Unit

During this *Launching* unit, most children write two focused personal narrative stories and then select one for further revision, editing, and publication. The major "bends in the road" of the unit are as follows:

- Children learn a variety of strategies for generating entries and begin to live like writers, collecting lots of entries in their writers' notebooks. We hope these entries are focused, detailed narratives (or "Small Moment" stories.)
- Children choose one of these entries to function as a "seed idea," and they write various lead sentences and storytell as ways to rehearse for rewriting this entry, this time as a rough draft, outside the notebook, in a story-booklet.
- Children collect more entries, drawing on strategies they learned earlier and on new strategies, and they again select a seed idea.
- This time, children rehearse for drafting by making and revising a timeline as well as by writing and selecting between leads and storytelling.
- Children write a draft of their second story. Hopefully each child makes a movie in his or her mind, envisioning the story as it unfolds, and each child writes in a step-by-step fashion.
- Children select the piece they like best and revise it. One way to revise it is to locate the heart of the story and to stretch that section of the text out, writing it in an even more step-by-step fashion. Another way to revise is to bring out the internal as well as the external aspect of the story.
- Children edit and recopy the draft they select as their best, checking especially their use of end punctuation, capitals, paragraphs, and spellings of high-frequency words.

GETTING READY

- Your own filled writer's notebook
- Daily schedule with plans for a distasteful subject, which you'll replace with a writing workshop
- Memories of people who matter to you, for use in demonstrating strategy
- Chart paper and markers
- Notebook and pencil for each child
- Sheets of paper, each with the names of two children numbered 1 and 2, to place on the floor to indicate partners' spots
- See CD-ROM for resources

STARTING THE WRITING WORKSHOP

Years ago, the poet Lucille Clifton gave me some advice that I've cherished ever since. "Nurture your sense of what's possible," she said. "We cannot create what we cannot imagine."

This advice has changed how I work in many ways. As a staff developer I now realize that before I help teachers with the brass tacks of implementing a writing workshop, I need to show them what a whole writing workshop sounds and feels like. I encourage teachers to visit effective workshops, immersing themselves in the workshop environment.

Children, too, need to imagine what's possible in a writing workshop before they begin writing. Today you'll nurture children's sense of what's possible. You'll describe the writing workshop to them, helping them imagine what this time in their day could be like and helping them anticipate its rhythms.

Children need not only to imagine the workshop, but also to imagine themselves as writers, and so in this session you'll show them they have important stories to tell. You'll teach children to take small, true stories of their lives and tell those stories in ways that strike a chord in their readers. During the first week of this unit, you'll help them collect a dozen focused, detailed personal narrative entries. Children will write these in their writer's notebooks. Then they'll select one and eventually a second of these entries to develop, then draft, and then revise. Finally, they'll choose their favorite to further revise and edit, publishing it. Today, you'll teach writers to recall an episode, quickly sketch a sequence of events within that one episode, and then write the story as an entry in their notebooks.

You will find that your work flows beyond writing time. Throughout the day, you'll want to listen with rapt attention to children's stories. Say often, "You'll definitely need to write about that!" You'll also want to immerse children in the sort of literature you hope they will write. Read books and poems about writing, and read books and stories that resemble the first-person narratives your children will write. Say, "This story by Eloise Greenfield reminds me of the stories you wrote earlier today!" Draw from our list of recommendations on the accompanying CD-ROM or from any texts you love. Read to them, read to them, read to them.

MINILESSON

Starting the Writing Workshop

CONNECTION

Build your children's identities as writers by exclaiming over the stories they've told.

"Class, can I have your eyes and your attention? I want to tell you something very important. I have been listening to the stories of your summer—to stories of helping your grandma shuck the corn and stories of building model trucks and stories of learning to whistle—and these stories are so extraordinary that we can't let them float away. We have been together for only one day, one hour, and twenty minutes, but I'm already awed by all of you. You have amazing stories from your lives!"

Build your children's enthusiasm for writing and explain writing workshop.

"You have such extraordinary stories to tell that I'm thinking that this year I should teach you how to write like professional writers! We need to save these stories forever! We need to hold on to them so that as we learn how to be better and better writers, we can make our stories better and better too! To be writers, you need the tools that real writers use, and the most important tool is this: a writer's notebook. I've been learning to become a writer, too, and so I keep my own writer's notebook." I held up my own well-decorated and much-used notebook and turned through a few pages so the children could see my pages filled with writing, sometimes also containing a sketch or a photograph.

"We will also need to spend time writing every day, just like professional writers do. Our writing workshop will be at the heart of our whole year. Starting right away, I am going to change our daily schedule so that every day we give a big chunk of time to writing." On the daily schedule, I erased "ditto sheets" and wrote "writing workshop."

COACHING

If you pattern a minilesson after this one, you'll want to name the true stories your own children have brought to school. As you read all these minilessons, remember that they are not meant to be a script for your teaching, but rather, they are meant to convey the story of my teaching, providing one example of how your teaching could go.

Often, children enter the classroom in September not believing they have anything to say. "Nothing happens in my life," they'll say. Our first job is to help children see that they do, indeed, have stories to tell. We want each child to think that, as Faulkner puts it, "my own little postage stamp of native soil [is] worth writing about and that I [will] never live long enough to exhaust it" (Cowley 1958, p. 141).

In this minilesson, I act as though it is because the kids' stories have given me goose bumps that I want them to have writer's notebooks and an hour-long writing workshop every day. The truth is that I approach the start of a new school year planning to be astounded and amazed by the great things that kids do. I try to approach each year with that mind-set, expecting to be touched and awed by my children and their stories. I know that it is all too easy to spend the first weeks of school mourning the loss of last year's kids. I know, too, that my responsiveness to these kids is vastly more important than any lesson I could teach.

"Our workshop will be like all sorts of other workshops. Usually workshops begin with the artists—they might be writers, they might be painters—convening to learn a new strategy. The teacher says, 'Let me show you a strategy, a technique that has been important to my work,' and then she models it. After about ten minutes together, everyone goes to work on his or her own project, and the teacher becomes a coach."

Name the teaching point. In this case, tell children that you will teach them a strategy for generating personal narratives.

"For now, let's write true stories, personal narratives. Today I want to teach you a strategy I use to help me decide which story to write (because writers aren't usually given topics; we decide which stories we will tell). If I can't figure out what to write, one strategy I use is this: I think of a person who matters to me and then I list small moments I've had with that person. I list moments that, for some reason, I remember with crystal-clear clarity. Then I sketch the memory and write the story of that one time." I turned to the chart paper and wrote:

Strategies for Generating Personal Narrative Writing

- Think of a person who matters to you, then list clear, small moments you remember with him or her. Choose one to sketch and then write the accompanying story.

TEACHING

First teach your children the contexts in which a writer might use the strategy you are about to teach. Then teach the strategy: one way to generate personal narrative writing.

"So let's say it's writing time, and I've got my writer's notebook in front of me, open to the first blank page. I *might* pick up my pen and think, 'I already know what I want to write,' in which case I'd just get started writing an entry."

"But, on the other hand, I *might* pick up my pen and think, 'Hmm . . . What am I going to write about?' When I don't know what to write, I think, 'What *strategies* do I know for generating narrative writing?' and I use a strategy to help me generate an idea for a story."

You'll notice that I explicitly teach children how the writing workshop generally goes. During the next few days, I plan to teach children specifics. If I see a child waiting for a personalized nudge to get started, for example, I'll say, "In a workshop, whether it's a painting workshop or a writing workshop, after the short lesson, the people go back to their workplaces and figure out what their painting needs next or their writing needs next, and they just get started on their own."

Notice that every minilesson begins with a section titled Connection *that is patterned like this first one. Every* Connection *ends with the teacher naming precisely what it is he or she aims to teach. We call this the* teaching point. *Some people refer to this instead as the goal. Usually the teacher embeds this teaching point in a sentence that literally says, "Today I will teach you that . . . ." You will notice that the teaching point is reiterated often throughout a minilesson.*

Intonation is important. I use my voice to suggest that if I think, "I already know what I want to write about," then today's strategy wouldn't be relevant or necessary. On the other hand, if I'm stuck over what to write, then today's strategy will be useful indeed. A strategy is only a strategy if it helps you past a challenge, if it is a tool you select to achieve a goal. When something that could have been a strategy is assigned, and done for no purpose except because it is assigned, then it is no longer a strategy, but merely an activity. You'll notice that often, before I demonstrate how I use a strategy, I set up the context in which the strategy will be useful.

Demonstrate the step-by-step process of using the strategy. In this case, think of a person, list focused memories related to the person, choose one of these stories, then sketch and storytell it.

I gestured to the chart that now contained one strategy. "Using our strategy, I'll think of a person who matters to me and list small moments connected to that person, moments I remember with crystal-clear clarity. So watch me while I use that strategy."

You'll notice that when we want to teach children how to use a strategy, we often teach by demonstrating. We role-play that we are a writer, and then we use the strategy in front of children. Your role-play is meant to function as a how-to or procedural guide, so act out the sequence of steps you hope children will undertake. You are showing them how to proceed when using the strategy. In your role-play, show children the replicable steps to take whenever using the strategy.

Picking up my marker and turning toward the chart paper, I said, "The person I write down should be someone who really matters a lot to me, because if I just put down any ol' person, like, 'the man at the checkout counter at the deli,' I'm not going to want to write about my list! So let me think . . . hmm, I'll write, 'Dad.' It's a good choice because my dad matters a whole, whole lot to me, and also because I have a zillion tiny stories I remember with crystal-clear clarity that I could tell about him."

Here I am teaching kids a strategy for coming up with a topic in a way that directs them toward writing personal narratives. The strategy will yield personal narratives only if each item in the list represents a small moment or an episode the writer experienced with the special person. If I had abbreviated my description of the strategy so that children simply wrote about a special person, they'd be apt to produce informational, not narrative, texts.

"I'm thinking of my dad. The first thing that comes to my mind is that last Saturday I woke up, and he said, 'I'm going to make breakfast for you,' and so I sat and read my book while he went into the kitchen. I heard him get out the bowl, and pretty soon I started to smell bacon." I wrote on the blank chart paper:

I could have pretended that I almost dismissed this story as too insignificant. That would have helped me make the point that writers tend to shove memories aside as unimportant, but that they should try not to do this. You'll decide how many minor tips you can tuck into your lesson.

Dad

When dad made me Saturday breakfast

"What else . . . oh, I know! A moment I remember is the first time I saw him cry. It was kind of shocking and scary to see him cry, but I learned that he has deep feelings inside him, just like I do." I added to the chart:

Dad

When dad made me Saturday breakfast
First time I saw my dad cry

Notice that both entries represent stories of common, small episodes that could easily be written chronologically. Both entries have personal meaning to me, the writer. They are the sort of stories that children could conceivably write about—I try to steer clear of ideas that will resonate only with adults. I'm aware that the stories I tell provide models for children, and therefore I try to tell stories that will set children up for success.

"And I remember a basketball game I went to when I was your age, when my dad embarrassed me by walking right into the gym and sitting with me." I added to the chart:

Dad

When dad made me Saturday breakfast

First time I saw my dad cry

When my dad walked into the basketball game

"I've got a lot more moments to add to my list, and I can add them anytime! But for now, I'm going to choose one moment from my list—I'm going to write about the basketball game because I really remember it! In all our lives, there are some moments that imprint themselves onto our memories, and they are ones worth writing about because they often have special, sometimes hidden, meaning for us."

"Watch how I go about picturing the memory in my mind, and then start telling the story of what happened in a step-by-step way."

Tuck bits of advice into your demonstration. In this case, tuck in pointers about envisioning your story and sketching quickly.

Switching into the role of writer, and speaking in a musing sort of way, I said, "So which part of that basketball game do I especially remember? (I need to zoom in on the part I remember most.) Well, what I really remember is that I arrived just before halftime and I didn't know where to sit. I'm going to make a movie in my mind of exactly what happened, in a step-by-step way, and sketch what I picture in my mind. I walked along the basketball court, looking up at the bleachers full of kids. I worried because all the kids were already sitting with other friends and there weren't any open spots for me. Then Sarah signaled for me to join her group. I was relieved!"

"I'll sketch this so I remember it: Here I am, walking alongside the court, looking up at the bleachers." I made a rapid sketch. "Here is Sarah, in the crowd, signaling to me." I drew a box in the top half of my page and sketched inside it.

Then, as I talked, I moved to the lower half of the page and made a second sketch to show what happened next. "So I clambered up the bleachers and sat with that group. Everything was fine until my father came to pick me up. He didn't wait in the car like all the other parents—instead he came marching right into the gym." Turning towards the chart

---

Three examples are plenty. Notice they are varied; they are meant to illustrate a range of possibilities so that students will realize a wide range is open to them as well. It is important to teach children that listing topics involves a few minutes, not a few days, and to show them how to shift from gathering to selecting and writing.

This first unit of study could have encouraged children to write in their choice of genre rather than channeling them toward personal narratives. In fact, my book The Art of Teaching Writing *describes a curriculum that welcomes a huge variety of writing at the start of the year. You, as a teacher, have choices to make! I have come to believe that the lessons writers can learn through shared work around personal narrative writing are so foundational that it's valuable to channel children toward personal narrative writing right from the start. But some of my colleagues still prefer to begin the year by inviting children to write in a wide variety of genres. There are compelling reasons for starting the year either way.*

Notice that for now I demonstrate (but do not discuss or draw attention to) a few qualities of good personal narrative writing. I've "zoomed in on," or focused, the narrative. I "make a movie in my mind" and retell what happened in a step-by-step way to help me recall and record tiny details. Before long, I'll devote whole minilessons to these qualities of good writing.

I deliberately decided to write about an episode from my own childhood, one in which I worried about fitting in and being judged. I want to create a community of trust, one in which we can leave behind our armor. I know that by telling stories of my own troubles, I can make the classroom into a safer place for others to share their vulnerabilities.

paper, I said, "I'm going to sketch that. (Here I am sitting with Sarah. Notice I'm sketching really quickly.) Then I saw my father come walking into the room. (Here he is, with his silly red hunting cap that he always wears!) I remember that he walked in front of the bleachers, scanning the crowd of kids. Then he saw me and called, 'Lukers!' and started climbing up toward us. I wanted the floor to open up and swallow me."

"The memory is really clear, so now I am ready to write. I need to go back and remember what happened first." I looked at my first sketch, then dictated to myself: "When I arrived at my first basketball game . . ." Returning to the chart paper on which I'd made my sketches, I fast-wrote, repeating my text as I scrawled down the page.

> When I arrived at my first basketball game, all the other kids had already found seats. I walked in front of the bleachers hoping to find an empty seat but everyone seemed ensconced with a group. Then I saw a hand wave. Yeah! I thought, as I climbed up the bleachers, flattered that popular Sarah had signaled for me to join her. When the game was almost over, I glanced toward the doorway and saw my father striding across the gym floor toward me, his red plaid hunting cap perched on his head.

"And I'll keep writing . . ."

Debrief. Help children recall the situation in which writers would use this strategy and the sequence of actions the strategy requires.

"So writers, I want you to know there are lots of ways to come up with stories to write. One strategy I use often is I think of a person who matters to me and write that on my paper. Then I list Small Moment stories connected to that person. I take one of these, one I remember with crystal-clear clarity, and zoom in on the part I remember most. Then I sketch and write what happened first and later."

When you are coming up with your own story to sketch, keep in mind that the simplest way to help children improve their stories is to teach them to focus. One way to focus a narrative is by writing a story that occurs within a tight time frame— retelling an episode that occurred in an hour or less. Writing about small episodes encourages writers to enrich the moment by writing with details.

Be sure to retell the first thing (and then the second thing) that happened in the story so that the children will feel the chronological structure of this genre.

This may be the longest story I'll ever write in front of the class. Minilessons need to be brief so that children have lots of time for their own writing. The last thing kids need to do is to watch us write on and on. Still, I think this one bit of public writing can give children an image of the way we hope they shift from drawing to writing and a sense for the genre. Notice I've zoomed in on one episode and written it almost as if this was a bit of fiction. You'll want to substitute your own story.

You will notice that I tell my story in more detail than is necessary for the teaching point I am trying to make. I do that because on this, the first day of the workshop, I am trying to build a relationship of trust with the class, and also because I know the power of shared stories.

ACTIVE ENGAGEMENT

Set children up to try the strategy. First, help them imagine themselves in the situation that calls for the strategy. Then, lead them through the steps you've demonstrated.

"Class, let's practice this strategy. Pretend it's writing time and you open *your* notebook," I opened an imaginary notebook, "and you pick up *your* pen to write and think, 'Hmm, what should I write?'"

"If you aren't sure what to write, try the strategy we've been learning." I pointed to the chart I'd begun.

Notice the rhythm of a minilesson. First I tell children what I'll teach, then I teach it, and then I give children the chance to practice the strategy with my support. You'll see this in all of our minilessons.

> **Strategies for Generating Personal Narrative Writing**
>
> • Think of a person who matters to you, then list clear, small moments you remember with him or her. Choose one to sketch and then write the accompanying story.

Before I set children up to use this strategy, I establish the conditions in which the strategy would be useful. First a writer sits in front of the blank page, unsure what to write. Then (and only then) the writer reaches for a strategy that can help her generate a story. I am not only trying to teach kids a strategy—I am also trying to show them when, in their lives, they can use the strategy.

"Right now, sitting here, think, 'Who is someone that matters to me?' Now, try listing across your fingers two or three little moments you and that person had together, moments you especially remember." I gave them a minute to do this. "Now choose *one* moment, one time. Give me a thumbs up when you've done this."

Notice that when I give directions, I word them in a very sequenced, step-by-step way.

"Think back to the event. Which part do you want to tell? Zoom in on the most important part." I bring my hands together to contain a smaller area. "Remember that I didn't tell *everything* about the basketball game—getting ready, getting there, the start of it. I just zoomed in on the middle of the basketball game, when Sarah signaled me to join her group, and the end, when my father embarrassed me by climbing up the bleachers to join us!" I gave children silence in which to think. "Thumbs up if you have thought of how your zoomed-in story begins."

The most important part of this may be the moments of silence. Don't skip past this! Give children a chance to think . . . watch their brains work.

"Make a quick thumbnail sketch of whatever you did first." I watched just a minute while children sketched their opening action. "Now make a second quick sketch to show what you did next." I whispered with a few children to learn what they were sketching.

"Now tell the person beside you the story, starting with what you did first. Tell it with tiny details."

This Active Engagement portion of the minilesson provides children with scaffolding as they try a new strategy. You'll notice that I don't just assign the work; instead I guide kids step-by-step through the process of using this strategy. In a few minutes, they will try the strategy again in their writing places, this time without scaffolding.

I am channelling children towards stories in which the first-person narrator is the active agent, not the passive recipient of events. "Sketch what you did first . . . next . . . ."

Debrief. Share the good work one child has done in a way that provides yet another model.

The room erupted into talk, and I circulated among the children, listening to their stories. After two or three minutes, I said, "Writers, can I have your eyes and your attention please?" I waited an extra long time until there was absolute silence. "Thanks. Next time, could you give me your attention a bit more quickly so we don't waste one precious minute of writing time?"

"I heard amazing stories, just as I knew I would with this class. Jessica told about riding her bike through her neighborhood one evening. First one kid joined her, then a bunch of little kids from across the street joined, and the group kept growing until there were ten of them riding bikes together! These are the stories of your lives, the stories writers put onto the page."

LINK

State your teaching point. Remind children that whenever they want help thinking of a true story, they now have a strategy they can use.

"So writers (with stories like these, I need to call you *writers*), without wasting another second, let's start putting these amazing stories onto the pages of your writer's notebooks."

"As you work today, and every day for the rest of your lives, remember that as writers we *choose* the stories we write. If we aren't sure what story to tell, we sometimes use a strategy to get us started. One strategy is to jot down a person and list small moments connected to that person. Then we take one Small Moment story that we remember with crystal-clear clarity. It often helps to ask, 'What was the most important part?' so we can zoom in on that part of the story and sketch or remember it with a lot of details. After we make thumbnail sketches of what happened, we write the story!"

Send children off to write, reminding them of your expectations for their independent work.

"As you work, I'll come around to admire your amazing stories, and later we'll share them with a friend or two."

"When you write today, the room will be totally quiet because writers need silence to be able to think and remember and sketch and write. The only sound will be pencils or pens on paper. When I call your name, you can come to me, get your writer's notebook, and go quickly to your seats. Antonio. Samantha." I gave each a notebook. "Don't you love how they are going quickly to their seats! Let's watch them while they get started. Look how well these writers get down to business."

Notice the example I highlight is a sequential story of a single brief episode—one that retells a rather ordinary, everyday occurrence. The writing that I make a fuss about will tend to be the sort of writing I hope kids will produce at this point in the year. For now, I am steering kids toward sequential, detailed personal narratives.

During the link, I articulate again what I have taught, reminding children that this is a strategy they can use for the rest of their lives. You will see my closing words "As you work today, and every day for the rest of your lives," end many minilessons.

Over the next few days, you will want to develop and practice a system for getting students from the meeting area to their workplaces smoothly. You might say, "Table monitors, will you please get the tools your table needs for writing?" Or "Supplies managers, please check that every table has supplies for writing." Each table will need a toolbox containing writing utensils and, soon, a box containing the writing folders for that table. Usually children carry writer's notebooks home each night and therefore have their notebooks in their backpacks at the start of each day, but you won't institute that ritual for a few weeks.

During this first week of writing workshop, you'll want to establish a serious working tone by pointing out behaviors you want to reinforce: "Let's admire how quickly that group got to their seats to write!" or "I love the way you have gotten straight to work. It feels like your minds are on fire!"

WRITING AND CONFERRING

Using Table Conferences to Reinforce the Minilesson

Listen to your children so you learn what they know. Donald Murray, the Pulitzer Prize–winning author widely regarded as the father of the writing process, describes teaching writers this way:

> I am tired but it is a good tired, for my students have generated energy as well as absorbed it. I've learned something of what it is to be a childhood diabetic, to raise oxen, to work across from your father at 115 degrees in a steel drum factory, to be a welfare mother with three children, to build a bluebird trail . . . to bring your father home to die of cancer. I have been instructed in other lives, heard the voices of my students they had not heard before, shared their satisfaction in solving the problems of writing with clarity and grace.

> I feel guilty when I do nothing but listen. I confess my fear that I'm too easy, that I have too low standards, to a colleague, Don Graves. He assures me I am a demanding teacher, for I see more in my students than they do—to their surprise, not mine.

> I hear voices from my students they have never heard from themselves. I find they are authorities on subjects they think ordinary. . . . Teaching writing is a matter of faith, faith that my students have something to say and a language in which to say it. (1982, pp. 157–160)

I was one of Murray's students, and I can still recall the great hope that welled up in me when he leaned

MID-WORKSHOP TEACHING POINT   *Writing More*   After ten or fifteen minutes of the workshop, you may feel that your students' attention is waning. This is a good time to intervene. You will probably stand in the middle of the room gathering students' attention. It could simply be that you say, "Writers . . ." and wait until they freeze, eyes on you. Then you can proceed to talk. You can use this mid-workshop time whenever necessary to teach additional, smallish points. Today, you might want to teach your students ways to write more.

"Writers, can I have your eyes and your attention? (When I say this, that means stop what you are doing, pens down, and all eyes on me, please.)"

continued on next page

toward me, listening with spellbound attention to my stories of growing up on a farm, struggling to find my place among the brood of nine Calkins children. If you can give your children just one thing right now, it must be this: your unconditional faith that each one has a story to tell, and your rapt attention to these stories.

Once the writing workshop is well underway, your conferences won't always reinforce your minilesson; but for now, you need to make sure your minilesson affects kids' actions. So go to a table full of writers, crouch low, and say something like, "I am just watching to see if you are looking at your sketches, and remembering your stories, and then writing these stories down, like your minds are on fire. Oh, look, Christina's looking back at her sketch and getting the whole story down!" When you go from one table to another like this during a writing workshop, we call these interactions "table conferences." In a table conference, you don't select kids who need specific help and gather them as you'll do for strategy lessons. Instead you blanket the whole table and often the whole room with support. For now, your job is simply to rally the group to do what you just taught.

Shifting from extolling what one child is doing to rallying them all to follow suit, you might say, "Don't stop working because I'm here. I am just researching to see if any of you are finished writing about your first sketch and are about to make a second one to show what happened next. Oh my goodness! Look at what Antonio is doing! This is so spectacular!"

Once a child has sketched or written a bit of a story, it can be helpful to set the child up in such a way that he tells his story to you, starting at the beginning and proceeding in a step-by-step, sequential fashion. Show your interest in the story. "Oh my goodness! Did you really go to the SPCA and choose your own puppy? How did the story start—with you opening the door? With your mom saying, 'Let's go?' Or what?" Don't hear the entire tale. You need to move to other children, but also, once the child has told the entire story, he or she will often lose interest in writing it. So help the child tell the start of the story well, then say, "Before you do anything else, you need to get that down!" Wait while the child gets started and then slip away.

> continued from previous page
>
> "I want to teach you one more thing. Some of you are telling me that you are done. Writers have a saying, 'When you're done, you've just begun.' That means that when you think you are done, there is a lot more to do. One thing we writers do when we're done is think, 'What's another Small Moment story that I've experienced—maybe about the same person, maybe about someone else?' Then we leave a little space on our page (or move to another page) and we think, 'How did it start? What happened first?' and we sketch and then write another story. Or we simply think, "What's another true story I could tell, another memory that for some reason lingers for me?' How many of you think you are done with your first story, your first entry? Thumbs up. Okay. Well, for the rest of writing time I am going to admire what you do now that you know the saying, 'When you're done, you've just begun.' Return to your work."

For now, I also want to teach students that during the writing workshop, there is no such thing as finishing early and then doing something else—drawing, reading, or just waiting. When a writer finishes one entry or one draft, he or she starts the next. You may wonder why I don't encourage revision. In the end, I will expect many kids to sustain work on a particular entry for much longer than ten minutes. But at this point, I anticipate that children won't find it easy to sustain work on a single text. It is easier to write several underdeveloped stories than to write one good one—and for now, my first goal is simply to have children work productively, putting the stories of their lives onto paper.

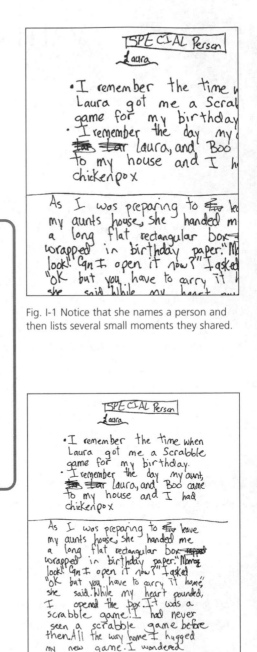

Fig. I-1 Notice that she names a person and then lists several small moments they shared.

Fig. I-2 Notice how quickly the writer shifts from listing to writing.

SHARE

Establishing Writing Partnerships

Convene children in the meeting area. Establish the seating arrangements and systems that underlie partnership conversations.

"Writers, can I have your eyes and your attention? (I love the way most of you stopped what you were doing as soon as you heard me say that! Thank you.) Let's gather in the meeting area because I need to talk with you today (as I will at the end of nearly all of our writing workshop times)."

"When you go to the meeting area, you'll see a paper that has two names on it—your name and another child's name—and a number, 1 or 2, next to each name. Sit where I've put the paper containing your name and your number. You and your partner will sit facing each other, knee to knee, and each hold two corners of the paper."

"Writers, these papers are really important because they signify that the two people whose names are listed will work together as writing partners for our first unit of study in our new writing workshop. You won't write the same stories, but you'll sit alongside each other in your designated place every time we gather and you'll help each other write really great stories. The numbers 1 and 2 are just a management system to help us know who will talk first or share first. If you are partner 1, give me a thumbs up. If you are partner 2, give me a thumbs up. Terrific."

Set children up so they name some qualities of effective writing partners, then plan with their partner how they can assume this role for each other.

"As partners, you'll help each other write well. In my life, I've had a few people who have helped me as a writer tremendously. Would you each think of a person who has helped you in your writing life. Partner 2, will you tell partner 1 what that person did that helped you?"

After the children talked for a while, I added, "Now would you and your partner make some plans for how you can be effective writing partners for each other? (Some of you were

Share sessions often involve children convening in the meeting area, but when you want to expedite things, you can simply stand in the middle of the room and call for children's attention. For now, however, your children's stamina for writing probably isn't especially strong, and you will want to create a sense of solidarity among writers. So for the next few days, you'll probably convene children in the meeting area for all your share sessions.

You'll see that I institute partnerships. You could, of course, simply have children talk with whomever sits beside them in ever-shifting talk arrangements, waiting a few days before you establish firmer partnerships. I establish partnerships right away because I know that before the next unit of study, I'll have a chance to tweak these arrangements.

Notice that we generally ask for a thumbs up instead of asking children to raise their hands. This is less obtrusive, a signal rather than a call for attention or a claim on the teacher. You'll need to demonstrate. When you do so, keep your hand low, at knee level so that thumbs up is not a way to raise one's thumb (instead of one's hand.)

Notice that only one partner spoke and the other listened. This wasn't a typo! Children benefit from both roles, and another day I'll reverse the parts.

talking partners and some listeners today, and we didn't reverse roles. That'll be the case often in our workshop.) Again, will you talk together about how you two can be really helpful to each other?" The partners talked together for a few more minutes, making plans.

Bring closure to today's workshop: Recall and share one thing that was learned.

"Can I have your eyes and your attention? I wonder if writers like Walter Dean Myers and Cynthia Rylant and Patricia MacLachlan can remember back to the day they began keeping *their* writer's notebooks or the day they first had a person who really helped them as writers."

"We are lucky because all year, we will remember today, the day when we launched our writing workshop. Right now, will you each think of one thing that you did today or that a friend did or that you learned—one thing that you are going to remember—and tell it to your writing partner."

The children spoke in pairs, and I listened in. After a moment, I convened the group. "I heard you say so many smart things! Tiffany said, 'I learned I can write any story from my life that I remember.' And Abraham said, 'Sketching helps me picture my story like a movie video.' And Christina said she learned that writers can ask, 'What's *another* story I can write?' so that when we're done, we've just begun."

Notice that we try to teach children how the workshop tends to go. Transparency is a good thing in classrooms, just as in government. Today I have two conflicting goals. I want to bring children smoothly into a writing workshop, conveying to them that this will be easy and rewarding. On the other hand, I want to help children understand that the writing workshop in general and the work they began today is a very big deal. I want to rally their energy by saying, "This will be hard work, but it's worth it!" I do this in part by likening children's work to the work done by beloved authors.

HOMEWORK *Decorating Notebooks and Collecting Ideas for Tomorrow's Writing*
Tonight, at home, would you decorate the cover of your writer's notebook? You'll see I laminated pictures that I love onto my cover, and Marjorie did the same thing, only she used dried flowers and blades of grass. If you decide to paste a collage of pictures onto the cover like I did and want to borrow our rubber cement and contact paper, bring the pictures in tomorrow and I'll have the materials ready for you. One way or another, you will need to personalize your notebook, to make it special, because it will hold your writing, it will hold your stories—which means it will hold your life.

And as you decorate your notebook at home, keep in mind that tomorrow you will have another chance to write in it. So tonight, when you are home with your family, be on the

You may wonder why I suggest that you and your students take time at the start of the year to decorate your notebooks. This may seem excessive or extraneous, but I don't believe it is. If you think about it, we outfit our children for the roles they play as soccer players, Scout members, and cheerleaders. We do this, I think, because we know that something as simple as a new T-shirt can help a child assume the identity of being a soccer player, an athlete, and a team member. Isn't it just as important to help each child assume the identity of a writer?

lookout for stories. Listen for stories. When things happen at home, let them jog your mind so memories surface. When you feed your cat, maybe you'll remember the day you picked her out from a litter of kittens. When you take out the garbage, maybe you'll remember the time you saw a big raccoon on top of the garbage can. Tomorrow, come to the writing workshop already remembering some stories you could write.

TAILORING YOUR TEACHING   We call each component of this book a *session*, not a day, because we know that you may want to devote several days to one session. We also know that it is likely that this book will support teachers across two or three years, and that in each grade, teachers will teach variations of the same minilessons as well as invent new ones. There are many ways you and your colleagues can teach the concepts in this session. The following are a few suggestions. More ideas are included on the CD-ROM.

If your students are having difficulty thinking of stories from their lives . . . you may decide to weave storytelling into your days so that each child is simply bursting with stories before you hand out writer's notebooks. Perhaps you'll want to begin or end each school day (at least for a while) by suggesting children storytell to a partner. You'll find that if you create conditions that welcome stories, one child's story will remind every other child of a story she too has to tell. You might start storytelling time by simply letting the children know that you are dying to hear their stories. "Let's tell stories from times in our lives that for some reason are very clear in our memories," you could say, and then choose your own story to tell. I recommend telling a story from your own childhood, ideally a story of a small moment in which you were vulnerable; this helps bring you and your class together quickly. I might tell the story of when I was given the role of Abraham Lincoln's mother Sarah in a school play. "I'll need an old-fashioned dress," I said. The teacher looked me up and down and said, "You can wear the one you have on!" I can still feel my cheeks burning in shame over my hand-me-down clothes.

If your students need help listening well and responding respectfully to each other's stories . . . you can teach students to wait until they have the listeners' full attention before they continue to tell their stories. You can teach listening also by modeling this. When a child tells a story, listen in deep, responsive, respectful ways and rally the rest of the class to do the same. Be vigilant, too, for even the tiniest shows of disrespect, and be ready to shift from teacher to preacher when needed, espousing your absolute commitment to helping everyone listen to the stories told in the room.

ASSESSMENT

I remember taking my sons, Miles and Evan, to our local public pool in summers past. I was struck time and again by the cheerful, energetic scene at the pool—the packs of children in their bright swimsuits like the colorful plumage of birds, and the packs of moms and sometimes dads lounging on the grassy sides of the pool, reading books and magazines. Those parents always maintained peripheral vision. As they read, they were picking out their own precious children from among the dozens of others, surveying the situation, ready to rise at any instant should there be a safety problem. I noticed two important truths about how kids and parents act at swimming pools and I wondered if one begets the other: The children never tired of trying new stunts in the water, getting braver and braver by the day, and every time, they begged Mom or Dad, "Watch me!" For their part, parents consistently shouted back, "That's great!" And some even commented on some aspect of the dive or swim stroke that was improving.

Why does it seem that in schools, children seem to slouch, sigh, and give up trying to improve things like writing? I think it's the way that schools assess children. When a person is trying to learn how to do something, nothing squelches courage and enthusiasm more quickly than criticism.

I believe that writing assessment can be just as loving, constructive, and vigilant as the assessments at the pool in which parents watch their children and admire their energetic efforts. And it begins the same way, with kid-watching. In the classroom, we watch how kids get started with their writing and how they procrastinate. If our children self-select spots to write in, we watch where they sit, and with whom they sit. We notice when they use tools to write, such as the word wall and our instructional charts. We see them rereading and making changes to their texts. And we watch for signs of risk-taking and growth, making note of them so we can give feedback to

individual children. Pretty soon, children learn to trust that we are watching with loving, interested eyes, and they begin to perform for us, almost shouting, "Watch me!"

Since we are not parents watching only one or two children, but teachers who are responsible for twenty to thirty children, it becomes necessary to track in writing what we see and hear kids doing. Methods of record keeping range from checklists to rubrics to anecdotal note taking, and the best system is the system that works for you. I scrawl notes as fast as kids talk, so there will be times in the year when I write down everything they say to me in conferences. But I also devise checklists based on what my hopes and expectations are for a unit of study and these checklists help me keep an eye on goals that are important to me. For example, during this unit of study, it is very important to me that children learn their lives are worth writing about, and that in time they find it easy to generate ideas for writing. It is important to me that children learn one very simple and concrete way of focusing a narrative—that is, that they zoom in on a relatively small period of time. Therefore, as I confer with writers in this unit, I'm apt to carry with me a checklist that reminds me of these and other goals. If a child is generating focused narratives, the checklist will remind me to compliment the child on this and to record the child's success. If the child needs help focusing his or her narrative, the checklist can remind me that this might be something to teach, in which case I'll want to record that I did this teaching so that in a later conference, I can reinforce the teaching point. No matter what kind of records you keep, the key is to be sure that your record keeping improves your teaching. You will find your system changes as your goals change.

GENERATING MORE WRITING

Today you will teach children a second strategy *for generating their own topics for personal narrative writing, and you'll encourage them to write with stamina, self-assessing their volume and devising strategies to keep themselves productive. These will be the explicit lessons you spotlight.*

Meanwhile, however, you will implicitly teach children the norms of a writing workshop and continue to help them develop identities as writers and cohesiveness as a writing community. Throughout today's session, you'll tuck in comments that socialize children into the culture of your workshop: "Remember to check the board, because every day it will tell you what to bring—that way, we won't need to waste one precious minute of writing time." Because you want to teach children that what they learn in one day's workshop applies to other days, you will repeat any ritual you established on day one. For example, you'll use the same attention-getting phrase today that you used in the previous session, and the same means of sending children off to work on their own writing. You'll also rely again on the partnerships you instituted in Session I.

You'll want to convey high standards around each of the rituals you've established. For example, wait the necessary time for quiet so children learn that when you ask for their attention, you expect nothing less. Expect children to gather for the meeting quickly; you may need to help them practice this so they "don't waste even a second of writing time."

You'll notice that my minilesson reminds children that they are developing a repertoire of strategies from which to draw for the rest of their lives. My message today is, "When you are stuck on what to write about (and are hoping to write a true story), draw on yesterday's or today's strategies."

As I teach particular strategies for finding a topic, I am also conveying some very basic expectations for narrative writing, showing children their stories will probably involve a character who progresses through a plot line. I choose stories that celebrate everyday life moments. Continue to read to the children; marinating them in writing that resembles what they'll write. Don't hesitate to reread texts, and to show children that you savor them. Gasp over writers who put the truth of their lives onto the page. Say things like, "She writes with exact, honest words, just like so many of you did today!"

IN THIS SESSION,

IN THIS SESSION, YOU'LL TEACH CHILDREN THAT WRITERS SOMETIMES THINK OF A MEANINGFUL PLACE, LIST SMALL MOMENTS RELATED TO IT, THEN SELECT ONE AND WRITE ABOUT IT.

GETTING READY

- Instructions on chalkboard telling children to bring their writer's notebooks (pens tucked inside) and sit with their partners in the meeting area
- Donald Crew's *Shortcut* and *Bigmama's* or other texts children know well
- Strategies for Generating Personal Narrative Writing chart from previous session
- Chart paper and markers
- Storage baskets or boxes for children's notebooks on each table
- Tool containers on each table with sharpened pencils
- See CD-ROM for resources

MINILESSON

Generating More Writing

CONNECTION

Establish the systems you will use every day to convene the writing workshop.

Before the children convened, I said, "Please remember to check the section of the board that says 'Writing Workshop,' because every day it will tell you what you need to bring to the meeting area. That way we won't waste one precious minute on logistics. Today it tells you to sit beside your writing partner on the rug spot I gave you yesterday, and to bring your notebook with a pen tucked inside."

Build your children's identities as writers by celebrating that they live like writers, paying attention to the stories around them.

"Writers, can I have your eyes and your attention?" I waited for them. "I had a chance to peek at many of your writer's notebooks as you were coming in this morning, and you did a beautiful job making them your own by inscribing and decorating them. And many of you told me stories of what happened last night! I could tell you lived like writers—you paid attention to the stories that were around you. Some of you even went ahead and wrote them in your notebooks! Donald Murray, a Pulitzer Prize–winning writer, once said, 'Writers see more, hear more, think more because we are writing,' (1968) and I could tell that was true for you. Evan took one tiny moment and wrote this entry." [Fig. II-1]

> It's 8:30 and Dad's not home. I walk upstairs, me and my book. I lay in bed listening but Dad doesn't come home. "Turn off the lights," Mom calls. I switch the switch. I drift away. The garage door opens. Dad opens the door, walks upstairs to kiss me good night.

"Isn't that an amazing moment Evan caught?!"

COACHING

I introduced these rug spots and partnerships during Session I. Therefore, I must refer to them again today. I need to teach children that lessons they learn on any one day make a lasting impact. It is important to set up and maintain everyday procedures so these become automatic and free us to focus on other teaching. For now, don't hesitate to devote teaching time to management issues.

Minilessons generally begin by contextualizing the lesson by referring to the previous day's lesson, to children's related work, or to the prior instruction upon which the minilesson builds.

> It 8:30 and Dads not home
> I walk up stairs
> Me and my book
> I lay in bed listening
> but Dad dont come home
> "turn off the lights Mom
> calls I switch the
> switch. I drift away
> the garage door opens
> Dad opens the door
> walkr upstars to kiss me good night

Fig. II-1 Evan

Remind children that writers draw on a repertoire of strategies for generating writing.

"Although we did great work in writing yesterday, it was also hard work. At the start of writing time, some of you sat with the blank page in front of you and thought, 'Nothing happens to me. I don't have anything to write.'"

"This happens to *every writer*. So today I want to teach you that writers do not have just *one* strategy for coming up with ideas. We need a whole repertoire of strategies for generating writing." I gestured toward the chart I had started the preceding day. "Yesterday we learned a strategy writers use to generate ideas for personal narrative writing."

> Strategies for Generating Personal Narrative Writing
> • Think of a person who matters to you, then list clear, small moments you remember with him or her. Choose one to sketch and then write the accompanying story.

Name the teaching point. In this case, tell children you'll teach them a second writing strategy—think of a place and list small, memorable moments linked to it.

"Today I want to teach you that writers sometimes think not of a person but of a *place* that matters; then we list small moments that occurred in that place, moments we remember with crystal-clear clarity. Then, just like we did when we thought of the person, we choose just one Small Moment story from our list. Sometimes we take a second to sketch what happened first; sometimes we just go straight to writing."

TEACHING

Name the context that might lead a writer to use today's strategy. Give an example of a writer using the strategy.

"Donald Crews may have used this strategy when he came up with the idea for his Small Moment story, *Shortcut*," I said, holding up the familiar book. "I think that for a moment, he wasn't sure what to write. Then, probably, he decided to use the strategy of thinking of a place."

It is important to teach the kids that first a person has a need for a strategy, then that person reaches for the strategy. Writers who approach the desk already knowing what they want to write about don't need to rely upon a repertoire of strategies for generating topics. So I first help kids recall times when they have been stuck, unsure of what to write about, and then I introduce the idea that writers profit from having a repertoire of strategies. This is important because throughout the reading and the writing workshop, we will often use minilessons as a time to demonstrate new strategies or more effective ways to use strategies. In these early minilessons, we need to teach kids the whole concept of having a repertoire of strategies that one draws upon when the situation demands.

At the start of a minilesson teachers are apt to say something like, "Today I will teach you another strategy for generating narrative writing." I urge you to include a follow-up sentence in your teaching point as well, so that you name exactly what that strategy will be. This means that by the end of the connection, kids have a good grasp of what they will be learning. When we have already named the strategy before we even enter the teaching component of a minilesson, we are less apt to confuse naming the strategy with teaching it.

Whereas in my first minilesson I used demonstration as the method in the teaching component, here I use the teaching method I refer to as explain and give an example. This is not a demonstration because I do not reenact a sequence of actions; instead, I simply talk about an example—I talk about how Crews probably used the strategy.

"Crews decided to write about his grandma's place—Bigmama's place—down south, because he spent every summer visiting there." I held up the book *Bigmama's*. "I bet he probably thought to himself, 'What Small Moment stories do I remember that happened to me at Bigmama's place?' He probably remembered lots of different times and then decided to choose just one story to tell. Crews did what writers often do. Instead of writing about 'my summer vacations at Grandma's,' he wrote about when he and his friends were walking on the train track, and a train came bearing down on them. He thought of a place that matters (his grandmother's place down south) and then of episodes that have happened in that place. Then he chose just one episode to write."

ACTIVE ENGAGEMENT

Set children up to try the strategy you've just taught. Scaffold children through the first step by brainstorming together a place they care about and a small moment related to that place.

"So let's try this together. Pretend you were stuck and not sure what to write about. You might look up at our list of strategies," I gestured toward the chart, "and decide to think of a place and then list episodes we recall that happened there. So let's think of a place that matters to us." I paused to let them begin thinking on their own of a place. "Hmm, how 'bout . . . the playground? Thumbs up if the playground is a place that matters to you."

"So now let's make a list of small moments that happened on the playground. Think for a moment about a small moment that has happened to you on the playground, a memory from the playground. Give me a thumbs up when you have remembered one thing that happened on the playground. Okay, now turn to your partner and share the story that came to your mind." As students talked to each other, I leaned in to listen to one pair and then another, each for only thirty seconds, so that I had some stories to bring back to the whole class.

I actually do not know how Crews came up with his topic. This is why I tuck the words "I bet he probably thought . . ." and "He probably remembered . . ." into my speech about Crews. You'll see that when I ask kids to learn from an author, I often speculate on how that author probably went about doing the writing. I do this because I don't think it's enough to show an example of good work and urge children to do likewise. We need also to show them or tell them how to proceed.

In the Active Engagement, I could have suggested each member of the class think of a place that matters to him or her and jot that down. Then I could have prompted each child to list a couple of small moments connected to that topic. I could even have asked children to star the one Small Moment story that they particularly care about and tell this story to a classmate. That active engagement would have started each child on that day's writing. Try this if many children are staring at blank pages during writing time, or if you are teaching a class full of struggling and reluctant writers.

There are advantages (described above) and also disadvantages to having kids work on their own pieces while in the meeting area. One disadvantage is that once kids go back to their seats, they have already used the strategy you've taught—they miss the opportunity to try the newly learned strategy on their own while it's fresh in their minds. Therefore, I often use what I call an exercise text in the minilesson—a group piece of writing. For example, here I help the kids try out the strategy of thinking of a place and then recalling moments that occurred in that place by doing it together on a place I select. I definitely do not expect children to write about this exercise topic—it exists just as place to practice and I intend for children to transfer the strategy (not the topic) in their independent writing. I know in advance some children will need reminders about this.

"Writers, can I have your eyes and your attention?"

I waited for silence. "I loved hearing your tiny moments from the playground! Like hearing about yesterday when Christina, Yazmin, Abraham—oh, a lot of you—crowded up under that one puny tree in the schoolyard to get out of the sun! Or the time last year when Gabriella finally got a group of girls to agree to play soccer with the boys." As I spoke, I made a list:

The Playground

- When we crowded under one puny tree
- When the girls joined the boys' soccer game

Debrief. Remind children that when stuck for a writing idea, they can use the strategy of thinking of a place and listing and selecting moments in that place.

"Now that we have this list of moments that all fit under the bigger topic of the place we've chosen (the playground), you could go back and write the story of one of these times. Of course, the strategy that you have learned today is not, 'Write about small moments that happen *on the playground*.' We just *practiced* this strategy using the playground—but Donald Crews used his grandma's place down south, didn't he? The strategy is, 'Take *any* place—a big chair in your bedroom, the school bus, your grandma's apartment—and then list moments that happened there, like we did with the playground. You will choose your own places, and make your own lists of small stories."

LINK
State today's teaching point and set it alongside the previous session's. Remind children that whenever they want help thinking of a true story, they can draw from their growing repertoire of strategies. Send them off to write.

"So writers, from this day forward and for the rest of your lives, remember that whenever you are sitting in front of an empty page feeling stuck over what to write about, you can take a place, and then list Small Moment stories that happened in that place, like Donald Crews did when he wrote *Shortcut* and like we did today, when we thought of stories we could write that occurred on the playground. You could also think of a person," I said, gesturing to the item from the previous minilesson. "Either way, you might jot a list of Small Moment stories you could write and then choose one that you remember really well."

"Today, you'll go to your writing spot, and you'll open your notebook and pick up your pen, and then you will decide what to do." I had already added the new strategy to the chart.

Strategies for Generating Personal Narrative Writing

- Think of a person who matters to you, then list clear, small moments you remember with him or her. Choose one to sketch and then write the accompanying story.
- Think of a place that matters to you, then list clear, small moments you remember there. Choose one to sketch and then write the accompanying story.

"I'm going to circle among you, noticing and recording what I see you've chosen to do."

"Let's watch how quickly and quietly the writers in the back row get started writing. Oh, look, Joe is rereading what he wrote yesterday to decide what he wants to do today. That's smart. Writers in the front row, you can disperse and the rest of us will watch to see how quickly you get started." I stage-whispered to the remaining kids, "Do you see how everyone is walking so quietly and quickly to their tables! That's great. Let's watch the rest of you get started just as beautifully."

A fiction writer once said, "The hardest thing about writing fiction is getting a character from here to there." The same could be said for teaching. It is very important that, at the start of the year, we purposefully teach kids how to use every minute of the writing workshop productively. This send-off is one way to do so. Even with very young children, transitions do not need to be full of dilly-dallying!

WRITING AND CONFERRING

Using Table Compliments and Small-Group Strategy Lessons to Address
Predictable Problems

Eventually, while children work, you will pull close to one child and then another, conferring with writers individually. But for now, one-to-one conferences probably don't suffice because too many children still need you in order to work productively. If this is the case, you will probably want to divide your time between table conferences and small-group strategy lessons. For now, your table *conferences* may actually be table *compliments*.

The concept of table compliments originated from the recognition that it is sometimes best to use fragments of conferences rather than entire conferences when we interact with kids. If you study some of the transcripts of our conferences in our book *One to One,* or our CD-ROM *Conferring with Primary Writers,* you will see that conferences typically begin with time for research. This is our time to figure out what it is that a writer is trying to do, to think about what is already working for that writer and what the writer might benefit from doing differently. Then we usually give the writer a compliment, using this as a time to make a fuss over something the writer is doing well that he would benefit from doing other days on other pieces. For example, suppose in one conference we encounter a child who began by writing about his trip to the Dominican Republic, then realized the topic was too large and shifted to writing about when he first saw his dad. We might say, "I love the way you realized your topic was so, so huge, and you zoomed in on a more focused one. It is brave of you to not feel as if you need to tell everything, and to realize that if you zoom in on a smaller topic, you'll actually see more treasures! For the rest of your life, whenever you write narratives or stories, always remember that writers are like photographers. We zoom in on the specific story we really want to tell."

> **MID-WORKSHOP TEACHING POINT**   ***Generating More Personal Narrative Writing***   "Writers, can I have your eyes and your attention? We already learned that, as writers, we can take a person or a place that matters to us, then list small stories connected to that and write one of those. But I want to also teach you that we can look at the stuff of our lives and let the *things* around us remind us of memories. Sometimes writers look at the things near us, and let those *objects* jog memories."
>
> "For example, right now I am noticing my shoes. I'm going to let my shoes jog a memory. Hmm . . . Now that I'm thinking about it, they remind me of one time I've never forgotten when I saw a homeless man walking onto the subway on a cold day with no shoes on at all. His feet were very dirty and callused. I've always wished I'd given him some money to get some shoes, but for some reason, I just looked at his feet, and then he got off the subway before I could react."
>
> "Can you all try the strategy of taking an object and letting that object remind you of a Small Moment story? Just for a sec, look at something in the room or something you're wearing or something in your desk. Let what you see remind you of a story." I gave the children time to think. "Tell that story in your own mind." I again paused. "Thumbs up if this strategy worked for you. Did you find that not only a person or a place but also an object could remind you of a story?" After the children nodded I said, "The good news is
>
> *continued on next page*

In a usual conference, after we give writers a compliment, we decide upon a teaching point and then teach it, rather like we would teach a minilesson. Although ideal conferences contain all these components, early in the year, when we wish we had roller skates to get to every writer ASAP, we often forgo the research and the teaching parts of conferences and just use compliments to rally writers' enthusiasm and channel their energies toward habits we know will serve them well.

You will probably go from table to table, watching what writers are doing. At one table, then another, you'll watch for a moment and then convene that small group's attention. "Writers, can I have your eyes and your attention please?" Then you'll name what one child has done (or what the group seems to be doing) that is exactly right. For example, you might say, "I love the way the group of you has gotten started. You didn't wait for me to come around and help each one of you, one by one. No! Instead you've done exactly what real writers do. You've picked up your pens and gotten started. I can tell, some of you came to the table already knowing your topic and you just started zooming down the page. Others of you used a strategy to help you generate a story to tell. That is so, so smart. You are doing what writers do. Get back to work, and I am just going to admire what you do for a minute."

In a similar fashion, you could extol the way some writers have remembered to record what they did first in the small moment, reliving an episode starting at the beginning. You could make a fuss over the fact that some writers didn't tell *everything* about their trip or their day, but instead zoomed in on just one small moment. Or that writers selected small ordinary events, or invented their spellings as best they could and kept going, or filled one page and then moved on to the next, or ended one entry and began another.

The very things that you could compliment are also things you could teach in small-group strategy lessons. If you see a handful of kids having problems with something, beckon for them to pull close in a circle around you, and teach them what they need to know. Be direct: "I pulled you over here because it seems like you are having trouble with . . . . Sometimes I have the same trouble. One thing that helps me is . . . . So let's together help Sasha do this, and then all of you can try it."

---

continued from previous page

that now you have another story you can write. More important, you have another strategy for generating personal narratives."

"Let's add this strategy to our chart, because now we know that writers can look at (or think about) *objects*, and then let an object (as well as a person or a place) spark memories." I added this strategy to the chart:

- Notice an object, and let that object spark a memory. Write the story of that one time.

"Remember that when you finish one entry, you can use any of these strategies—or make up a new strategy that works for you—just so you are able to get yourselves started on some good writing. Now you can return to your work." I watched as Alexa looked over her jacket, noticing her badges and buttons. She took one from a gymnastic meet and put it in front of her, then wrote an entry about a memory that object sparked. [*Fig. II-2*]

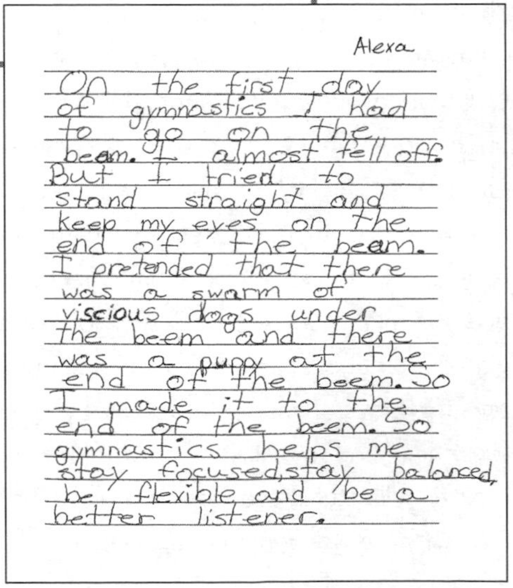

Figure II-2 Alexa

SHARE

Building Stamina for Writing

Convene children. Rally your children's enthusiasm for writing more and for a longer time. Set children up to self-assess and to set goals with partners.

"Writers, can I have your eyes and your attention? Nice work today. You really seemed to push yourselves to get a lot of writing done, and that is important. I think it is hard to write well unless a person writes quickly and can sustain writing for a long time."

"I have been thinking that we, as writers, can take some lessons from runners. I have been trying to jog every day. I have strategies that I use to get myself to run farther and faster. I keep records of how long I run and compare what I do one day with what I do the next day. Sometimes I set goals for myself. I say to myself, 'Yesterday, I ran for a mile, today I am going to try to run a mile and a half.' I not only set goals for myself, I also have strategies for meeting those goals. If I get tired, I have ways to keep myself going. Sometimes I give myself a break halfway through the run so that I have a second burst of energy. Have any of you ever pushed yourself to run farther, or to do more in gymnastics or swimming or some sport? What did you do to keep yourself going? Would partner 2 tell partner 1?" They talked.

"What I am wondering is this: If we have all these ways to push ourselves as runners and soccer players and gymnasts, might we use similar techniques to push ourselves to write longer and more? For starters, could you look back on the writing you've done since the beginning of our writing workshop and ask yourself, 'Did I write more today than on the first day?'"

"Then look at how much you usually write, and ask yourself this question: 'What could I do to push myself as a writer, like some people push themselves as runners?' I'm going to give you some time to just think about this." I paused.

Ask writers to talk with partners, listen in, then reconvene the group and list what you overheard.

"So, please talk with your writing partners. Show each other how much writing you've done today and the day before, and talk about plans you have for how to push yourselves to

At the start of the year, you need to induct children into the norms and mores of a writing community. Unless your children are accustomed to a writing workshop, you'll find they are probably accustomed to doing a bit of writing, then stopping for the day. You need to explicitly teach them to keep going. It is crucial for them to learn that when they finish one entry, they start the next one, which removes any incentive to finish entries quickly by writing in a cursory fashion. When you push for volume, you push for making the workshop a place for productive work, and this helps with classroom management.

Be sure that children date each day's writing, and that one entry follows the next, gradually filling the notebook. If they jump hither and yon, you'll have a hard time keeping track of their progress and their volume. (Perhaps they are onto this and this explains their propensity to jump around!)

write more." They talked. "Writers, here are some of the thoughts I heard from you":

- When I finish one entry, I should start the other one because some of mine are little.
- I think I worry about making it really good even if it is an entry, and that slows me down.
- One day I wrote a lot and a different day I did not. I think I gotta talk less.

"Writers, these goals (and others that you haven't had a chance to say aloud) are really, really important. Starting tomorrow, we are going to work harder to make sure everyone gets a lot of writing done every day. For today, leave your notebooks in the box or basket on your table, because I'm dying to read them tonight."

You'll see that I haven't collected these comments in a chart. My decision was that they're worth saying, but not worth taking the time to record. I am conscious, however, that sometimes I am orally constructing a list. I usually lift one finger, then another, to give children a visual scaffold that helps them to recognize that I'm listing.

HOMEWORK *Noticing Stories Like Writers Do* Writers, the poet Naomi Nye once said: "Poems hide. In the bottoms of our shoes, they are sleeping. They are the shadows drifting across our ceilings the moment before we wake up. What we have to do is live in a way that lets us find them" (1990, p. 144). I think that stories, like poems, hide. Tonight when you are at home, writers, will you pay attention to the stories that hide in places of your life? Think about the places in your life that hold stories, and come to school ready to talk about lots and lots of ideas you have for Small Moment stories you can write during writing workshop. You should find yourself living differently because you write. Be like a magnet, pulling story ideas in to you.

TAILORING YOUR TEACHING The minilessons in this book were tailored for a class of children that's different from your own class. Borrow whichever parts of this model work for you, but substitute your own life stories and your children's own drafts. You may decide to slow down the teaching we describe, spending two days on concepts you think merit more time. And next year's teachers may return to these sessions, bringing a new twist to them. These ideas and the others that you will find on the CD-ROM can help you develop extension minilessons as well as small-group strategy lessons, mid-workshop teaching points, and share times.

You'll need to decide when to institute the ritual of the children taking their writer's notebooks home. Eventually, it will be crucial for your children to write at home, as this will double the amount of time they have to write each day, and it will allow parents to see and celebrate children's progress. If your children already carry reading books between home and school, you may decide they are able to carry writer's notebooks as well. If you worry terribly that the notebooks won't return to school, you might make little portable notepads so your writers can become accustomed to carrying those between home and school without the risk, yet, that the notebooks will be left at home. If your children record in notepads, at the end of a week they can tape pages from the notepad into the writer's notebook. You may, however, postpone writing homework that includes actual writing for now. If you institute homework, you need to provide a great deal of follow-up. If you assign homework and aren't prepared to address the fact that some children don't do it or don't bring it to school, you are allowing children to develop problematic habits. You'd be better off to postpone assigning it until you are ready to be vigilant.

If it seems that most of your students are struggling to stay focused throughout writing time and if you are overwhelmed with management concerns . . . it is important to remember that a host of challenges are to be expected at the beginning of the school year, especially if you or your students are new to writing workshop.

In general, if your kids are having difficulty, it helps to first specifically name the difficulty. Try not to say, "Writing workshop doesn't work," or "My kids have no stories to tell." Instead, ask yourself, "What exactly is the problem? When does it occur? Who is having this problem?"

For instance, if your room is too noisy during writing workshop, you need to ask why. Instead of just saying, "My room is too noisy during writing workshop," and spending time reminding kids to whisper or banning talk altogether, you'll want to get at the root of the problem. Perhaps the noise is a symptom of another issue. Maybe your students need more strategies for generating notebook entries. Maybe they need a specific time to talk with a partner to help them plan what they are about to do.

Another question to ask about any problem is, "When does it mostly occur?" Maybe it seems like it's noisy throughout writing workshop, but it is more likely that the noise happens in patterns. Perhaps your children are only noisy when they are trying something new or only when they are revising. Maybe your students need a shorter writing workshop for a couple of weeks because it's chaos in the last ten minutes. Perhaps you'll want to build the length of writing workshop gradually rather than beginning with a too-ambitious expectation.

You'll also need to figure out exactly who in the class is having the difficulty. It usually isn't every student, although at first glance it can very often feel as if everyone is struggling. Watch for a day or two to see exactly who is having the problem so you can get to the bottom of the problem while also addressing her needs as a writer. Notice children who are not having the particular problem. If we notice a table of students who work quietly during a writing workshop, we can find out how they do this and then teach the rest of the class the strategies they use.

You could also choose to let the whole class in on the problem and brainstorm with them a strategy to help the problem go away.

ASSESSMENT

A great treat lies waiting for you—you can spend some time poring over your students' work. Gather up their notebooks and give yourself a block of time so that you can really take in what these children are telling you about their lives and their literacy.

When you first read their entries, try to use them as a way to know your children. The author Avi was wise when he said, "If you can convince a child you love him (or her), you can teach that child anything" (1987). Of course, falling in love with children is tough in September, when you're still mourning the loss of last year's group. Remember, you'll be a much more powerful teacher for your kids if you find ways to fall in love—fast!

Try to see past your children's errors and past their writing skills to their content—to what is important to them, and to what they are trying to say and do. If you are able to do this, you will go a long way toward understanding and supporting the children as writers and toward creating a community conducive to writing. Your children's errors and skills matter—but now is not the time to focus on either. Jane Yolen, author of *Owl Moon,* (1973) once told a story about a child who came to her and said, "I love *Owl Moon*. I like your metaphors." Jane was pleased, of course, that the child responded to her book but sorry that it had been the *metaphors* that the child loved most. "I want children to open my books and fall through the rabbit hole of the story," she said, referring to Alice's adventures in Wonderland. Children, too, want and deserve to have readers who listen *through* their attempts at descriptive language and high-frequency words, to hear and care about their content. If we can give children readers who really listen to the content of their stories, we enable children to feel how powerful it can be to write the stories of their lives.

So begin the year by trying to use your children's writing as a way to become an expert on the little ones you teach. Learn what each one knows and cares about, and then make specific, individual plans to let children know that their writing has gotten through to you. Prepare to tell them, "I had no idea you have a beagle! I've always loved those dogs," or "Someday you need to bring in pictures of your town in the Dominican Republic."

Meanwhile, however, you may also want to make some mental groupings of your children according to the support you want to give them right away. You may, for example, plan to convene the children who have not done much writing of any kind for a strategy lesson in which you help them get more down on the page. You may make another mental group of children who are writing all about a topic rather than telling a story in narrative form (this will probably be a huge group). You may also notice a few children who are writing focused narratives that could be exemplars for other children.

Hopefully, some of your more struggling writers will be among those who have zoomed in and told a focused story—this is something even kindergartners can do, so prepare yourself to find focused stories hiding behind problematic spelling and penmanship. A writer need not have accurate spelling or a sophisticated control of syntax in order to zoom in and tell a story in a chronological, step-by-step way. If you can find some exemplar texts among the writing your strugglers have done, and make a big fuss over the smart decisions those children have made, other strugglers will see children like themselves meeting with your approval, and their expectations for themselves will skyrocket.

QUALITIES OF GOOD WRITING:
FOCUS, DETAIL, AND STRUCTURE

IN THIS SESSION, YOU'LL TEACH CHILDREN THAT WRITERS FOCUS THEIR STORIES, AND THAT THEY TELL STORIES IN SCENES RATHER THAN SUMMARIES.

GETTING READY

- Instruction on chalkboard telling children to bring their writer's notebooks (pens tucked inside) and sit with their partners in the meeting area
- Qualities of Good Personal Narrative Writing chart
- List of story topics, some watermelon-sized and some seed-sized
- See CD-ROM for resources

You are still at the very start of the school year, and you and your students have months still stretching ahead of you. You could argue that it's not urgent to lift the level of student writing right now, that instead what's needed is to teach students to proceed independently through the writing process. I argue, however, that it actually is important to teach children what they need to know so their writing becomes dramatically more effective, quickly. Ultimately, children will invest themselves in learning to write if they see their writing becoming stronger—and you will invest yourself in teaching writing if your hard work pays off!

In this session, you'll explicitly teach some qualities of good writing. First, you'll teach some ways writers focus. Children are much more apt to write organized, detailed pieces if they closely focus their writing. The easiest kind of focus is temporal focus—writing about a short span of time. For now, help your children to do this. Eventually, you'll acknowledge that good stories need not fit into twenty minutes, but for now, encourage children to "zoom in" and to write with detail about brief episodes.

In this session, I point out that writers often think first of watermelon topics and then focus on a story the size of one tiny watermelon seed. The metaphor of a watermelon topic is one I will revisit later, pointing out, for example, that there are lots of seed-sized stories in a single watermelon topic. After teaching about focus, I remind children that writers use specific details. It is impossible to overemphasize the value of detail.

There is another quality of good writing that I do not overtly address in this session but that matters tremendously: significance. When we write well, we convey that we are invested in our own stories. It is important to write in such a way that readers do not read our stories and shrug, thinking, "So what?" Steer children toward writing stories that matter to them. As Robert Frost said, "No tears in the writer, no tears in the reader." (1963, p. 32) Whereas E. B. White can take a subject like warts and write well about it, most of us will have an easier time writing well about moments that bristle with significance. You'll notice, then, that the stories I spotlight in this session are ones in which everyday events (a goodbye kiss before the school bus arrives, decorating a classroom for the first day of school) carry emotional resonance.

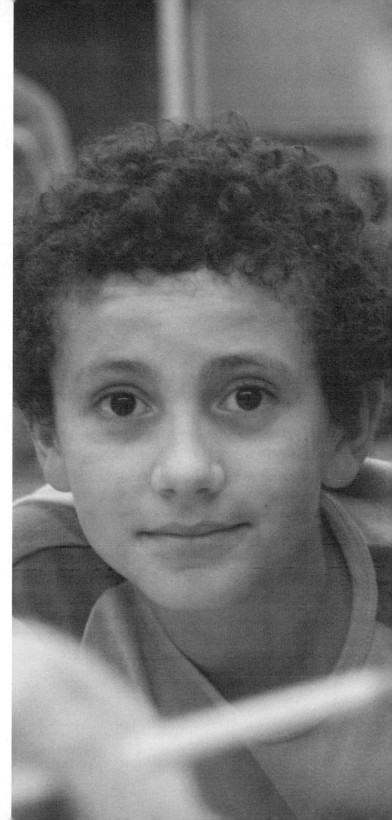

MINILESSON

Qualities of Good Writing: Focus, Detail, and Structure

CONNECTION

Celebrate that your children are using the strategies you've taught in order to write stories that matter. Do this in such a manner that you help writers recall these strategies.

"Writers, can I have your eyes and your attention? You have been coming up with people, places, and objects that matter to you, and I am so glad you realize your lives are worth writing about!"

"When you think of a topic and then list specific instances, sometimes those specific instances are still too big. After you jot down a place that matters—say the beach—your list may contain items like 'my summer at the beach.' You won't yet have come upon a small moment. So, here's some advice I can give you that will help your writing get better."

Name the teaching point. In this case, tell children that writers focus.

"Today I want to teach you that in addition to strategies for generating writing, writers keep in mind qualities of good writing that help us shape our ideas. Specifically, writers know that to write a story that draws readers close to listen, it helps to write about a small episode, something that happened in twenty minutes, or even in just three minutes! It is important to zoom in on one small story and to tell the parts of the story that matter, leaving out sections that don't matter. Writers retell the sequence of events in our stories, writing with details, telling the story in a step-by-step way."

"I wrote these qualities of good writing on a chart to help you remember that as writers, we think about not only *what* we're going to write about but also *how* we'll write our stories so they really affect our readers. The chart will be called Qualities of Good Personal Narrative Writing and we will continue to add to it as we learn other qualities of good writing that writers use when they write."

COACHING

Notice that I've not only reminded writers of the previous teaching points, I've also tried to consolidate the strategies I've taught to make them easier to remember. We hope our teaching gives students ready access to a handful of tools.

It is typical that a unit of study will begin with the teacher equipping children with a small repertoire of strategies for generating that particular kind of writing. The strategies will be a bit different depending on the genre or structure of writing under consideration, and embedded in the strategies will be some information about the genre or structure. I think it is important to limit the number of days you spend introducing strategies so that by the third or fourth day of a unit, you encourage children to draw from their repertoire of strategies, self-selecting one, while you shine a spotlight on qualities of writing that also merit attention.

Qualities of Good Personal Narrative Writing

- Write a little seed story; don't write all about a giant watermelon topic.
- Zoom in so you tell the most important parts of the story.

TEACHING
Highlight what you hope children will do. Contrast a less-than-ideal topic with a better writing choice.

"Let's examine the first quality of good writing on the chart: 'Write a little seed story; don't write all about a giant watermelon topic.' Usually, after we think of a place, for example, what comes to mind first are great big *watermelon* topics like 'My summer at the beach' or even 'My day at the beach.' But to get a really good story, it helps to select a particular, smaller subject, to tell not a watermelon story but a little seed story, like the story of one time at the beach when I made a sailboat out of some driftwood and a shirt."

"The other day, I was going to write about playing with my cousin," I said, spreading my arms wide. "But then I realized, 'Wait, that is a great big watermelon topic,' so I decided instead to write about how my cousin and I made a fort out of blankets." I held my thumb and forefinger a tiny bit apart. We draped the blankets between the sofa and the chairs."

ACTIVE ENGAGEMENT
Set children up to practice distinguishing between big topics and focused stories.

"Just before you write a personal narrative, a true story, pause to ask yourself, 'Is this a big watermelon idea, or is it a little seed story?'"

"Let's practice asking that question and discerning the difference between big watermelon ideas and little seed stories. Signal with your hand to show me whether I'm about to write a big watermelon topic or a little seed story." First I held my arms apart then I held my finger and thumb near one another.

"Let's see, I *could* write about the time when I was your age and I snuck away from the playground during recess to buy candy. I was waiting in line at the store, my hands loaded with candy, when my mother walked in and saw me there. Is that a big watermelon topic or a little seed story?" The children signaled by holding their fingers together, as if to hold a tiny seed, that this was a seed story. "What if I planned to write about my trip to Disney

In the series Units of Study for Primary Writing, I used the metaphor of "big watermelon topics" and "little seed stories" to distinguish unfocused stories from focused stories. Writers of every age need reminders to focus. In life, of course, there must be a place for stories that encompass more than twenty minutes of time. But one of the fastest ways to improve the quality of your children's writing is to help them focus, and the easiest way to focus a narrative is to write about a smaller chunk of time. Eventually, we will help children write with a thematic focus where they will create effective stories that span larger chunks of time. In the examples I provide here, notice that the unfocused and focused versions of a story match in every aspect but focus. Whenever I contrast two examples, I try to be sure that the only difference between them is the quality I'm highlighting.

In minilessons specifically and the writing workshop in general, we are teaching children to use knowledge on the run about writing. This means that when we teach children qualities of good writing, we attach these qualities to strategies and procedures. I don't want to tell children about a quality of good writing without showing them how they can put their knowledge into action. In the Active Engagement section, I essentially set children up to join me in reading over a list of topics. I know that in life, writers aren't given generic lists of topics and told to decide whether or not those topics are focused. So I try to engineer this active engagement in such a way that I show how and when I, as a writer, actually might pause for a second and think, "Wait, would that be a focused topic?"

World? I could tell all the stuff I did." The children used outstretched arms to try to encircle this gigantic watermelon topic.

"Now, what if I planned to tell the story of how I stood next to the sign that tells if you're tall enough to go on the roller coaster, and this year I was tall enough?" They signaled that this was a seed idea. "How about these?"

- "Fun times I have with my dog?" [watermelon]
- "When I first saw my dog in the cage at the SPCA and knew he was the one for me?" [seed]
- "When the person who is now my best friend first arrived in our classroom and we met each other?" [seed]
- "My best friend?" [watermelon]
- "The year I was on the soccer team and we won six games and lost two?" [watermelon]
- "I broke my leg and went to the hospital and had to use crutches for a month?" [watermelon]
- "The time I was playing with Susan Downer at recess and she and I found a quarter frozen in the ice so we chipped it out of the ice?" [seed]

"Would you and your partner look over the entries in your notebooks, the stories that you've written. At the start of each story, write 'watermelon story' or 'seed story.'" The room filled with chatter, and I listened to conversations.

Share the good work of one partnership in a way that allows you to explain that watermelon topics have many seed story ideas in them.

"Writers, I was listening in on Paul and Abraham, and they realized that Paul had written a great big watermelon story about his old school. But then Paul realized that *inside* that one watermelon, there are a lot of seed stories! He doesn't have to throw the watermelon topic out—instead, he can reread his entry and at the bottom of the page, make a list of all the little seed stories he could get from that one topic. The rest of you may want to try the same smart work."

LINK
Remind children that whenever they use qualities of good writing to think of a true story, they can pause to consider whether their story idea is focused.

"So writers, whenever you start writing a personal narrative story, pause for a second to ask yourself, 'Is this a little seed story?'"

This can progress really quickly, and needs to do so. Of course the list will work best if it's created out of your life together.

You can't make writers perfect overnight. Allow some kids to get by with drafts that are not totally focused and with narratives that sound rather like summaries. Remember, your primary goal for this first unit is not phenomenal writing. Instead, your goal is for kids to be engaged with writing for an increasing length of time, for them to begin to grasp some concepts of good writing and of the writing process, and for kids to work with some independence. If a child initially writes all about a vacation and then checks herself, zooming in to write all about one brimful day, note to yourself that the child will need further coaching. But for now, celebrate that the child independently drew on a concept she'd learned. Each month you will have more time to strengthen the lessons on good writing you have taught in your minilessons.

WRITING AND CONFERRING

Teaching Writers to Draw on All the Strategies They've Learned

I have sometimes compared a writing workshop teacher to the acrobat in the circus who gets plates spinning on the ends of sticks. The acrobat gets four plates spinning, then six. The first plate begins to wobble and with a touch, he helps that plate regain momentum. From across the room, he sees another plate wobble dangerously and rushes over to prevent its fall. You probably resemble this circus performer as you rush about, trying to keep your writers writing!

As you confer with one child and then another, remember that your conferences, table compliments, and small-group strategy lessons should reflect the cumulative content of your teaching. So today, for example, guard against the temptation to go from table to table, child to child, working only to help kids zoom in on smaller topics. Instead, you will help some kids generate ideas for personal narratives, you'll help others set volume goals for themselves and write toward those goals, and you'll remind some children that when writers are done, they've just begun. Of course, you will also see that some children have great big watermelon topics, and you'll help them focus on little seed stories, reminding them if their initial entry was all about a topic, they'll need to begin an entirely new and focused story.

Keep your priorities clear. You want every child to believe that he or she is able to generate topics, writing chronological and true entries; you want every child to work through a process that involves choosing a topic and perhaps rehearsing for the story by sketching or saying it. But you need to expect that some of your instruction will fall on rocky soil and that, until you intervene, some kids will continue to write unfocused and chaotically organized entries. It is more important for you to keep your plates spinning (and your writers engaged) than to fuss over whether each child is doing exactly what you had in mind.

Today you will especially want to confer with kids who haven't yet written any entries that seem to be in

---

MID-WORKSHOP TEACHING POINT *Telling a Story Instead of Writing All About a Topic* "Writers, can I have your eyes and your attention?" I paused until the room grew absolutely silent. "I want to teach you a smart thing Brooke did. She began writing an entry that went like this." *[Fig. III-1]*

> My family and friend
> Jamie is one of my best friends! I knew her for almost all my life.
> My mom is thirty years old, and has brownish gold hair. And works.

"Then she paused and said to herself, 'Wait a minute! I'm writing all about two people (my mom and my friend). If I want to write a story, I gotta choose one. I'm going to try to list stuff my mom and I have done together.' So she stopped right smack in the middle of writing her entry and wrote a list about her mom that went like this."

> Kissing me good bye before school
> Putting green ribbons in my hair

continued on next page

My Family and frend
Jamie is one of my Best! frends. I new her for almost all my live. My mom is thirty years old, and has brownish gold hair. and works

Fig. III-1 Brooke's initial unfocused entry

the ballpark. Within a few days, you'll be asking students to reread all their entries and to select one to work on for the next week, and it'd be great if every student could go into that endeavor with some strong entries from which to choose. To help your students write strong entries, help them select focused topics in which they tell a story they care about, and help them to tell the story in a sequential and detailed fashion. If you've heard some children telling lively stories to their friends during snack time, by all means help them put those same stories onto the page.

Pay attention to the volume of writing your children do. If they're not producing much text, you'll probably want to lead a second mid-workshop teaching point, this one reminding them that writers are like runners: we push ourselves toward goals that we set. You may resort to making smiley faces in the margins of writer's notebooks as a way to signify, "I love to see that you are writing more!"

continued from previous page

"Brooke picked the goodbye moment. She tried to remember it—not the whole before-school time, but just the things that happened right before and after her mom kissed her goodbye. This time, Brooke made a movie in her mind of exactly what happened and wrote what she remembered. Listen." *[Fig. III-2]*

> Mom's kiss goodbye
>
> One lovely day, on the first day of school, I told my mom to hurry up and get my backpack full of things like my lunch, my snack, my special pencils and pen, my very special, powerful writing notebook, and my glue stick. And so I zipped my back-pack and I walked outside, and the bus was already there and mom gave me a kiss, and ever since that day, I can still feel that exact same wonderful lovely kiss!

"Can you hear what a good start Brooke got when she zoomed in? So remember, if your writing feels like it's about a lot of things, you can stop, make a list like Brooke did, and zoom in! Okay, back to writing!"

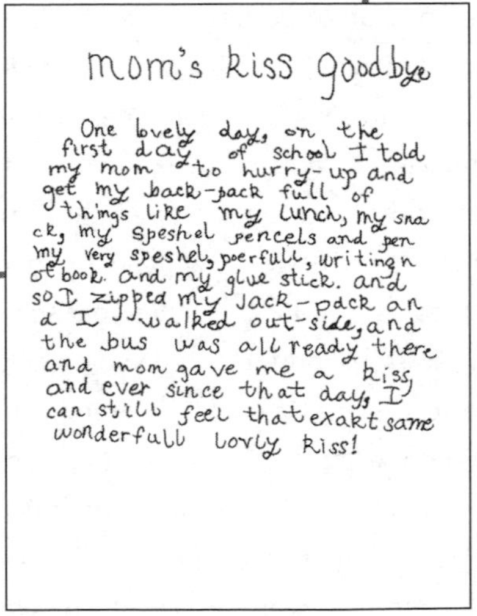
mom's kiss goodbye

One lovely day, on the first day of school I told my mom to hurry-up and get my back-pack full of things like my lunch, my sna ck, my speshel pencels and pen my very speshel, poerfull, writing n ot book. and my glue stick. and so I zipped my jack-pack an d I walked out-side, and the bus was all ready there and mom gave me a kiss, and ever since that day, I can still feel that exakt same wonderfull lovly kiss!

Fig. III-2 Brooke's later, more focused entry

SHARE

Writing with Specific Details

Convene children. Find an example of a child who has used a strategy you want more children to try. Tell what one child did in such a way that others could follow a similar procedure in their own writing.

"Writers, can I have your eyes and your attention, please? When I gesture toward your table, come find your spot on the rug."

"Your writing is giving me goose bumps. You are getting so good at writing Small Moment entries! I want to show you something Lizzie did that you can try also, a strategy that will make your writing even better. Lizzie did a *smart* thing in her writing. She didn't just write 'I got in the car'—a short, general sentence—and then stop. Instead, she added on, writing with specifics. Listen." *[Fig. III-3]*

> I got into the car with my feet scrunched up so I wouldn't smash the plants.
>
> My mom and I were decorating her classroom for the new school year. There were calendars, posters, plants, and supplies. We carried them in, up the stairs, and into room 205. I set up a magnetic calendar, did a puzzle of the USA, stuck short biographies on the walls, and hung my Mom's tacks up high so she could hang up high things . . .

"Lizzie didn't just say, 'I got in the car' and then stop her sentence, did she? Instead she said more. She said, 'I got in the car *with my feet scrunched up so I wouldn't smash the plants.*' She didn't just say, 'I set up the classroom' and then stop, did she? Instead she kept going, telling how she set up the classroom."

Fig. III-3 Lizzie

In this Share, I act as if I want to celebrate Lizzie's success. But actually, I chose Lizzie not only because she merits praise but also because lots and lots of kids were writing short sentences lacking detail, and I wanted them to recognize this and be able to self-correct. I use the positive example of Lizzie to get the point across. If the class had had different needs—say, a bunch of children staring at blank pages—then I would have had a different share.

"Another thing I love—Lizzie told us *exact* details. She could have written, 'I helped my mother unpack *a lot of things*.' If she'd said that, we wouldn't really be able to picture precisely what Lizzie did. Because she instead wrote, 'I set up *a magnetic calendar, did a puzzle of the USA, stuck short biographies on the walls . . . ,*' we can picture how she helped her mother unpack. I'm hoping some of you can learn from Lizzie's smart decision to write with precise details, even if it took extending her sentences."

Ask children to work with their partners to check for places in their own writing where they could apply this technique.

"Now let's help each other find places where each one of us could try saying more and writing with exact details. Will partner 1 from each partnership raise a thumb so we know who you are? Partner 1, will you read one of your entries? Then partner 2 (show me which of you is partner 2), see if there is a place for saying more and saying exact details. Your job is to listen and then point out specific places in the text where the writer could try this."

"If there are short sentences like 'I got in the car,' you and your partner may want to add to them, saying more. 'I got into my car with my feet scrunched up so I wouldn't smash the plants.' You can use a caret," I wrote one on the board, "and then add the details above your writing, or you can use the caret to point to a star and then, at another place on your page, write another star and write out the specifics you'd like to insert into your entry." I gave them time to do this.

Remind writers that they can use this technique in their own writing every day from now on.

"From this day forward, try to remember that specifics like 'I set up a magnetic calendar and did a puzzle of the USA' are more powerful than generalizations like 'I unpacked a lot of things.' To help you remember these qualities of strong narratives, you can refer to our chart." I pointed to the chart onto which I'd added a line about details.

> ### Qualities of Good Personal Narrative Writing
>
> - Write a little seed story; don't write all about a giant watermelon topic.
> - Zoom in so you tell the most important parts of the story.
> - Include true, exact details from the movie you have in your mind.

Here I do something we often do in Share sessions: I took one student's work and thought, "What actions has this writer taken that others could emulate?"

I don't really know how Lizzie went about writing, but I notice that, whereas many children write in simple sentences (the subject did [the verb] to an object), Lizzie extended her sentences by providing more details. She made a similar gesture to tell more when she told an action and then added a few sentences that elaborated on it with more details.

I always try to teach both a quality of good writing (writing with details) and also a procedure for achieving this quality in writing. That way, I hope, the writer can achieve this quality later, in her own writing. I teach the goal and the step-by-step procedure for achieving the goal.

HOMEWORK *Living Like Writers, Noticing Details* Today we talked about the importance of *writing* with details, but I want to remind you that we can't record details unless we first see details! Tonight, instead of writing with details, *live* with details. Watch your dog slide between you and the newspaper you're trying to read, as if she's saying, "Read to me!" Notice that the tower of books beside your bed shows how your reading tastes have changed over the last few weeks. Pay attention to the fact that in your household, there is only one person who can find the heads to Lego-people. Does your little sister have a stash of heads hidden away so that she can save the day? Most people wouldn't wonder about this. Most people walk right past details. But writers are people who pause and say, "Hmm . . . this is interesting!" The poet Naomi Nye says it this way: "Truly, I feel irresponsible when I don't notice things well enough, when I slide or slip through a day. . . . I want to hear the cat down the street turning the block."

TAILORING YOUR TEACHING

If your students need more support with zooming in on small moments in their stories . . . you might design a minilesson like this: "Writers, we're going to write in our notebooks today, choosing our own topics from our lives. Before you get started, I want to share with you something that I learned from my husband, who's a photographer. When he takes pictures, he doesn't swing the camera like this," I indicate a 180° panorama, "but instead he zooms in by focusing the camera on one small frame at a time. He usually doesn't take a picture of a whole meadow, but of three daisies. He usually doesn't take a picture of the whole city, but of a pigeon roosting on the arm of a statue in the park. Writers are like photographers. We focus when we write personal narratives; we focus on tiny incidents from our lives. Today I'm going to teach you how to focus, or how to zoom in on small moments from your lives."

Then, for the teaching component of the minilesson, you might demonstrate focusing. You could say, "Sometimes when I sit down to write, what comes to my mind first are the things I've been doing. The events of my life. But here's a secret. When one of these events comes to mind, I don't start writing. Instead I say to myself, 'Wait, I need to zoom in on a small portion of this event.'"

Notice that these early homeworks don't spell out how much actual writing you expect. In fact, they ask writers to live writerly lives but don't ask them to produce entries. This will change soon, but for now I'm aware that it may still be too early in the year to pull off assigning a significant amount of writing at home. These assignments, then, channel children to live as writers, coming to school prepared to write. You could tweak them and specify writing in either a portable take-home notepad or a writer's notebook, if you can shepherd children to do the writing you assign.

If you step back and look over this entire series of books, you'll see that there is never a time when I shift away from a focus on detail. Youngsters so often think that they write with words, and especially as they become more facile with language, they throw a lot of words around fast and loose. We write with information, with specifics, with facts. Our readers want information. They want specifics.

So begin now to encourage children to collect exactly, precisely true information. If they mention that their refrigerator door is covered with papers fastened with magnets, encourage them to describe the magnets. Are they china pigs and cows? Advertisements from local shops masquerading as magnets? Of course, once you encourage writers to write with detail, you'll need to go a step further and celebrate emblematic or revealing details.

COLLABORATING WITH COLLEAGUES

In the schools in which my colleagues and I work closely, the decision to support children's growth as writers is a whole-school decision, and every teacher devotes time each day to a writing workshop. Those writing workshops are structured similarly, so that children grow up expecting that they'll be explicitly taught skills and strategies of effective writing, and so they know that every day they'll have time to draw on all they've learned as they pursue their own important projects.

In these schools, teachers find it incredibly helpful to follow a shared curricular calendar so that at any one time, children across a grade level are delving into a shared unit of study. This means that teachers needn't invent our teaching alone, in isolation, but can instead teach alongside each other.

If you or your colleagues have decided to support each other through shared units of study, I can't emphasize strongly enough the enormous benefits you receive from using some of your grade-level meetings as opportunities to write alongside each other. If you live through a unit of study first as writers and only then as teachers, you'll be able to bring your own drafts and those of your colleagues into your

minilessons, and there is nothing that could make a bigger difference than this! Of course, the fact that you've tried the strategies I suggest will also give you an insider's appreciation for the challenges they pose, the detours to avoid, the tips that can make a big difference.

Joyce Chapnick is in a writing group, and I'm sharing the narrative she wrote and shared with her students to give you a glimpse into what you might decide to do as a writer. Remember, however, that Joyce's narrative evolved slowly, across a month of work.

Narrative: First Day of Third Grade with Reflection

It was September 1983, my family moved to a new house within the same town, but I had to start at a new school. I hated new. As a child I loved structure and routine.

My mom pulled through the circular driveway of my new school. The car halted. She said, "Good-bye, have a great first day," and she waited for me to get out. I couldn't move. It wasn't even like I was trying to move. I didn't want to move. No part of me wanted to leave the safety and comfort of my Chevy station wagon.

I looked up at my mom and did everything in my power not to cry. I tried to talk, but nothing. Finally, I heard myself say with a quiver in my voice, "Aren't you going to take me in?" She knew that if she didn't act fast the tears would flow.

As I walked into Fox Meadow Elementary School gripping my mom's hand all of the children looked like they belonged; some were carrying backpacks, chatting with friends; one was me, frightened and nervous, the new girl at school.

I held my mom's hand tightly as we moved down the hallway from left to right dodging and avoiding all of the children and backpacks. Every time we had to wait for someone to move I breathed a sigh of relief because it delayed the inevitable for at least one more minute. The door to my new classroom became visible. I grabbed my mom's hand tighter hoping that the sweat would bond us like glue. My knees felt weak and my heart beat quickened.

My mom looked down at me with her warm eyes, "Joyce, you will be fine." Why couldn't she just stop, turn us around, and take me home? The classroom door was open. I saw so many children, talking and laughing. They all knew each other, and I knew no one. With that first glance, I felt it, first in my toes, then in my knees, then in my stomach. I was totally overwhelmed. "Oh no," I thought,

"Please don't cry." But it was too late the tears were on in full force. It was like someone unscrewed the cap on a fire hydrant.

Just as the geyser blew I felt a hand on my shoulder. I looked up and through the glaze of my tears I saw a woman. She had curly dark hair and was wearing a blouse and long skirt. "You must be Joyce," I heard her say; "we have been expecting you." How did she know my name? "I am Miss Vopicelli." She reached down and took my hand. I looked up at my mom pleadingly. She smiled and whispered in my ear, "You are in good hands. Have a great day. I love you." And with those words she was gone. I had no choice but to follow the woman with the pretty voice who knew my name.

I learned that day that my mom couldn't always hold my hand and that change is not easy; especially change you don't choose. Right after I entered the classroom with Miss Vopicelli she introduced me to another little girl. At recess the girls asked me to play with them. I don't remember most of the details of the rest of that day, but I will always remember Miss Vopicelli. Ten years after that frightful September day in 1983 I reentered Miss Vopicelli's (changed to Mrs. Banks) classroom...this time by choice. Today, I teach third grade and every September I am reminded of her when I welcome my new students. As each child enters the classroom, somewhere in the back of my head I hear her saying, "we have been expecting you."

Fig. III-4 Joyce

IN THIS SESSION, YOU'LL
INTRODUCE CHILDREN TO THE
STRUCTURE OF A WRITING
CONFERENCE AND TEACH THEM
SOME WAYS WRITERS TALK ABOUT
THEIR WRITING.

GETTING READY

- Instructions on chalkboard telling children to bring their writer's notebooks (pens tucked inside) and sit with their partners in the meeting area

- List of questions asked during a conference (see a sample in the Connection section)

- Short transcript of two conferences (effective/ineffective)

- Strategies for Generating Personal Narrative Writing chart

- Qualities of Good Personal Narrative Writing chart

- See CD-ROM for resources

THE WRITER'S JOB IN A CONFERENCE

The writing process approach to teaching writing is sometimes referred to as the conference approach. This title is an apt one because writing conferences are not only occasions for teaching children, they are also occasions for us to be taught. In a conference, a young writer teaches us how we can teach. The writer teaches us what she has been trying to do, has already done, hopes to do next. Children as well as teachers need to be let in on the plan for writing conferences. If children aren't told otherwise, they sometimes see the initial phase of a conference as merely a time for pleasantries, before the teacher lays out the directives.

In this session, then, you will teach children that in a conference, they become the teacher. Specifically, you help children know that when you ask, "What are you working on as a writer?" you do not want to learn simply the topic ("I'm writing about my dog running away") or even just the topic and the genre ("I'm writing a personal narrative about the time my dog ran away"). You also need to know what it is the child is trying to do as a writer ("I'm trying to show, not tell, that I was worried"). After you ask, "What are you working on as a writer?" you will have to show some children the sort of answer you have in mind. Look over the child's entry and then answer the question yourself, saying, for example, "It looks like you have been experimenting with different leads—some include dialogue, and some include setting. Is that right?"

Once you and the child have established whatever it is that the child has been trying to do, you might say, "Can you show me where you tried that?" Then compliment. Try to compliment something that you hope writers will do another day in another piece. "I love the way you told where you were when you were bowling," I said to one writer. "Always remember that it can be smart to bring out the setting." Then you can teach them a strategy to help them reach their writing goal today and forever more.

MINILESSON

The Writer's Job in a Conference

CONNECTION

Tell children that, just as they can expect a daily minilesson, they can count on frequent writing conferences.

"Writers, we've been working together in a writing workshop for almost a week, and I think you've come to understand that you can count on every writing workshop beginning with a minilesson where I teach you a strategy that writers use. You can count on having lots of time to write and a chance to write on topics that are important to you using all the strategies you've learned. You can also count on the fact that often, I'll pull up a chair alongside you to confer with you about your writing. Many people believe that writing conferences are at the heart of a strong writing workshop."

Name the teaching point. In this case, tell children that writing conferences have a reliable structure. The child's job in the conference is to talk to us about her thinking.

"Today I want to teach you that you can also count on how a writing conference will tend to go. This can help you do your part of the writing conference well."

"When a writing teacher confers with you, the teacher will want to know what you are trying to do as a writer, what you've done so far, and what you are planning to do next. So the writing teacher will start by interviewing you, asking questions about your writing (not your topic). The writing teacher will tend to ask questions like these:"

- What are you working on as a writer?
- What kind of writing are you making?
- What are you doing to make this piece of writing work?
- What do you think of what you've done so far?
- What will you do next?
- How will you go about doing that?

"A teacher's job at the start of the conference is to study the writer in order to figure out how to help—and a writer's job is to teach the teacher. You are teaching us not about your subject, but about the ways you've figured out to write. That way, we can be helpful."

COACHING

It's a good sign when your children have enough momentum and direction as writers that they don't rely on the daily minilesson as their source of direction. If children know how to carry on as writers and have a small repertoire of strategies to draw from, then our teaching can focus on the finer points of their work, as this minilesson does. Minilessons aren't designed to set children up for what they'll do on any one day; instead, they are always designed to lift the level of what children are doing in general.

It's not important that children learn the exact questions writing teachers tend to open conferences with—this is not a chart. This list is intended to help children understand the kinds of topics writing teachers want to learn more about from them. Meanwhile, however, you will definitely want to take note of these questions!

TEACHING

Contrast a writing conference in which a child talks about his thinking with one in which he talks about his topic.

"Listen to this conference with a child who hadn't yet learned how to do his job well, and then listen how it changed after he learned to do his job well." I signaled to my young volunteer, who held a copy of the transcript and played the part of the student before and after. "In this first conference, you'll see that the writer doesn't yet know his job in a conference."

Teacher: What are you working on as a writer?

Child A: Writing about the baseball game.

Teacher: What are you trying to do as a writer?

Child A: Writing about winning the game.

Teacher: What will you do today in your writing?

Child A: Write about how I hit the ball.

"Now compare that exchange with this one. You'll see that by now, the writer has learned his job in a conference, and does it well."

Teacher: What are you working on as a writer?

Child B: I'm writing a personal narrative about baseball and I've zoomed in on the last time I was up at bat.

Teacher: What are you trying to do as a writer?

Child B: I want to really write with details, but I'm not sure I remember them.

Teacher: What will you do today in your writing?

Child B: I was going to sketch the scene to see if that gets me remembering details I've left out.

Debrief. Point out that in a good conference, the writer articulates what he is trying to do.

"Did you see the difference? During this early part of both conferences, the teacher asked the same questions: What are you working on as a writer? What are you trying to do as a writer? What will you do today in your writing? The difference was that in the second conference, the writer knew that he needed to teach the teacher the specific goals that were important to him and the strategies he used to reach those goals." I gestured to the Qualities of Good Personal Narrative Writing and the Strategies for Generating Personal Narrative Writing charts.

In this teaching component, I set up two contrasting examples: the first is a don't-do-this example; the next is a do-this example. To highlight what I hope writers will do, I often contrast my hopes with what I don't want to see. The trick is that in order to highlight one feature, the two versions need to be identical in all ways but the one feature I'm trying to showcase.

Notice that in the first conference, the child talks about his topic only. In the second conference, the child talks about his writing goals, strategies, and challenges.

If we want children to rely upon the charts of our teaching points, then it is important for us to demonstrate times when a writer might reference a chart. This is one such time.

ACTIVE ENGAGEMENT
Set children up to practice their role in a writing conference. Specifically, ask the questions you are apt to ask during a conference, and give them time to prepare responses.

"So I'd like you to practice the part of a conference that is your job. Right now, I'm going to ask you the same questions I asked our writer. Think about your answer, and if you aren't sure what to say, try looking at one of our charts. For now, no one will talk—just think—and when you have an answer in mind, give me a thumbs up."

"First, what are you working on today as a writer?" I gave them thirty seconds of silence in which to silently answer this question and then I said, "Remember, you can say your topic, but a good answer reveals more specifics about your writing goals than that. The chart might help. Here's a further question: What are you trying to do as a writer?" I waited, and when most children gave a thumbs up, I signaled, "Tell your partner what you are thinking."

The room broke into a hubbub of talk. "Here is one last question for you to answer first, silently, in your mind: What will you do today in your writing?" Again, I paused until most gave a thumbs-up signal. "Remember our example. The writer didn't just say, 'Write about my dog' or 'Write.' He said, 'I'm going to sketch to see if sketching it will get me remembering details I've left out.' Try to be as purposeful and planful as a writer. The answer to this question is what you need to do now, so go ahead and start writing."

LINK
Reiterate the active role children will be expected to play in writing conferences.

"So writers, from this day forward when I confer with you, remember that you have a job to do in conferences. I'll be coaching you not only on your writing but also on your conferring!"

Don't underestimate the importance of silence. When I ask the question, "What are you working on today as a writer?" it is critical that I actually sit there and wait for a length of time that communicates to the children that it's their job to fill the silence with real thinking. Only then, after time for thinking, do I say, "Tell your partner . . . ."

If your children don't seem to know yet how to answer these kinds of questions, you might try modeling a writing conference with one child in front of the whole group. Figure out as a class ways the writer might respond to each question, or process together the answers she gives. If this too seems a stretch, you could ask another adult to role-play being a student writer and hold your conference with this colleague in front of your students. This modeling offers the students language to use in describing their own situations.

WRITING AND CONFERRING

Teaching Children the Basics of Conferring

Let's work on the basics of your conferring. First, make your body language convey that a conference is a respectful conversation, not a lecture or an assignment. Sit alongside the writer, and let the writer literally maintain control of the paper by being the one to hold the text. Then say something like, "Hi, Amanda, what are you working on as a writer today?" Today your children will be ready for that question, but even so the child is apt to answer by telling you her topic, not telling about what she is working on as a writer. If the child says, "I'm writing about playing Capture the Flag," you want to convey interest in the topic, but don't linger in a conversation about it. Say, "Oh! Great! I love that game." Then restate your question about the child's intentions. "And what, exactly, are you working on, are you trying to do, as a writer?" The child may look at you blankly, because she is still not sure the sort of answer you expect, or she might shrug and say, "I'm just writing." Ask to see her paper. Look to see if you can glean from the text itself some sense for what she has been trying to do as a writer. Could she have been trying to do one of the things you have taught the class? Name what you see or almost see. "Oh! I see. So you've written an entry about a time you remember. It looks to me like you tried to make your characters talk; you've recorded their exact words. Is that one thing you were working on?" The writer will probably nod. "Am I right that you were rereading it just now? Were you thinking about whether you'd zoomed in enough?"

The writer will probably go along with whatever you see in the entry. If she nods to indicate that yes, she had just been about to reread the entry and to think whether it was a focused story, you can say, "So why don't you do that while I watch."

MID-WORKSHOP TEACHING POINT — *Writing Stories Step-by-Step* "Writers, can I have your eyes and your attention? I want to show you the smart work that Amanda just did. I came over to her and asked (as I often ask), 'What are you working on as a writer?' She answered that she was rereading her entry, trying to decide if she'd talked all about an event or told it like a story. Listen to her entry and ask yourself the same question. Is this a summary or is it a story?" I read it.

> I was 4 and my brother wanted to play capture the flag with me. It took about 20 minutes to finally understand how. He got frustrated from all my questions and threw a snowball at my face.

"Amanda decided she'd written a summary," I said, tweaking the truth a bit so as to make Amanda look like she'd been in the driver's seat more than was accurate. "So Amanda made a movie in her mind of exactly what happened on one day and then asked herself, 'What happened first? Where was I?' This is her next draft.

continued on next page

In this instance, Amanda's entry went like this:

> I was 4 and my brother wanted to play capture the flag with me. It took me about 20 minutes to finally understand how. He got frustrated from all my questions and threw a snowball at my face.

Before you proceed to teach, find something to compliment as well as something to teach. "You didn't just *tell* the reader that your brother was frustrated. You thought about what he did to show his frustration, and you added a tiny detail. That detail brings your brother to life on the page."

Then I said, "Can I teach you one thing?" and proceeded to tell her that she'd actually written a summary, not a story, of the event. So I helped her to tell this episode as a story. To do so, I gave her prompts that I use countless times over the first few weeks of a narrative unit of study. "Amanda, can you remember exactly how this started? Where were you at the beginning? Then what happened? Exactly what did he say? Can you say what he did, exactly? What did you do then?"

Once Amanda began telling this like a story, I repeated back what she said. Then I got Amanda to write the words.

---

continued from previous page

Listen and give me a thumbs up if you think this version sounds like the start of a story."

> I was at the kitchen table eating macaroni. My big brother, Chris, came in and said, "You gotta play capture the flag with me and Nate. You are on my team." I followed him out to the front lawn...."

The children signaled that this was indeed a story. "You are right! What a difference. Listen again." I reread the two versions again, emphasizing the differences with my voice— reading the summary in a monotone and the story with a "once-upon-a-time" lilt.

"So writers, right now would you get with your partner and read one of your entries aloud, and decide together whether you have written a story, telling it step-by-step, or a summary. If your entry is not yet a story, try to start it over, telling exactly what happened first and then next."

SHARE

Naming Exactly What Works Well in Writing

Convene writers. Ask them to study their partner's writing and name what is working well in it.

"Writers, can I have your eyes and your attention, please? Now let's share with our partners a little bit of what we've written. Partner 1, will you read what you wrote today to your partner? Then partner 2, please talk about your classmate's writing. Instead of just saying, 'It's nice,' name some specific technique the writer used that really worked. If the writer helped you get a movie in your mind, point to the part of the writer's story you can really envision. If the writer wisely zoomed in and told a whole lot about one tiny time, tell that to the writer. Perhaps the writer wrote what happened first, then next, in a step-by-step way. Or perhaps the writer included true, exact details of what happened. Your job is to listen and then to name exactly what the writer did that worked well. Then point out specific places in the text where the writer did this."

Remind writers to use the Qualities of Good Personal Narrative Writing chart as they write.

"The chart we created earlier can help you remember qualities of good writing that are worth celebrating. When you look at your partner's writing, I'm sure you'll find examples of those qualities."

Qualities of Good Personal Narrative Writing

- Write a little seed story; don't write all about a giant watermelon topic.
- Zoom in so you tell the most important parts of the story.
- Include true, exact details from the movie you have in your mind.

You should be finding that the format and methods of minilessons are beginning to feel familiar to you. Usually in a Share, we celebrate what a few children have done in a manner that allows us to reiterate what we hope all children are doing. The teacher needs to name what one child has done in such a way that the one instance of good work is transferable to other days and other children. Then children often get an opportunity to work in pairs, seeing if they've already done similar work or planning how they, too, could do that work.

You may decide to make copies of this chart so that each child can hold onto his or her own copy. See the CD-ROM for a master copy. You may go a step further and turn this chart into a self-assessment checklist.

I listened while Raymond read his entry to Christina: *[Fig. IV-1]*

> When I was in the train to Canal Street I was fooling around with my sister. I keep on tickling my baby sister and my baby sister was tickling me. Then we stop and I was bothering her and when she looks at me, I say, "I did not do nothing." And my baby sister did the same thing I did. We both laughed and so did my Mom and we did not notice that everybody was staring at us. I laughed a little.

Christina said, "You told about one time on the train."

I added, "That was smart of you to notice that he zoomed in on one time. Let's listen again and Christina, can you try to give more specific compliments? Try to name exactly what Raymond did that works."

Raymond again read the entry. This time, Christina said, "I could picture that 'cause the same thing happens with my brother!"

"Can you point to where Raymond wrote that one part you especially liked?" I asked, and Christina did.

Addressing the whole class, I said, "Writers, I've heard some *amazing* conversations just now. Many of you referenced the chart, which was a brilliant thing to do. Remember that when you write, you can look up at our charts to remind yourself of goals that can lead you to write really well."

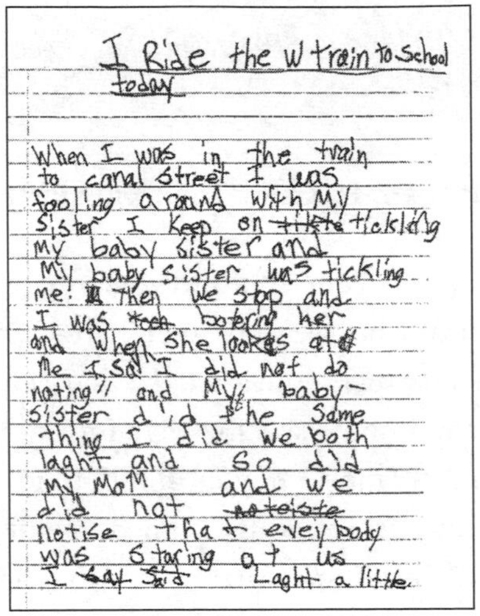
I Ride the W train to School today

When I was in the train to canal Street I was fooling around with My Sister I Keep on tickling My baby sister and My baby sister was tickling me! Then we stop and I was botering her and When She looks at Me I Sa I did not do noting" and My baby sister did the Same thing I did We both laght and So did My MoM and we did not notise that every body was staring at us I Laght a little.

Fig. IV-1 Raymond

HOMEWORK **The Writer's Job in a Conference** Today you learned about your job in a writing conference. For homework, you'll rehearse for that job. Tonight imagine that a teacher pulls up a chair next to you. Think about your writing so you'll be ready to talk about it with the teacher. Remember, teachers tend to ask questions like the ones below in conferences, so be ready to answer them:

- What are you working on as a writer?
- What are you trying to do as a writer?
- What will you do today in your writing?

I'll be looking forward to talking with you and teaching you based on what you say!

TAILORING YOUR TEACHING During the first few weeks of this unit, you will need to teach children self-management skills. For example, you will need to teach children what writers can do when they are stuck, or how they can get help if the teacher is busy, or how to talk more quietly.

If your students need strategies for working independently through difficulties . . . you might teach a minilesson that begins like this: "Writers, something happened to me last night when I was writing, and I know that the same thing happens to you. Last night, right before bed, I was trying to write about this memory I had of chipping a precious dish when I was little, and I got stuck. I know that sometimes happens to you, too. You get stuck. Well, in my case, I forgot exactly what my mom had said when she found out I broke the dish. I could have called my mom to ask her to help, but it was too late at night. I didn't have anyone around to help me, so I had to help myself. Let me tell you how I helped myself— because you may want to try the same technique. I thought about what she probably would have said if I'd gone to her for help. I helped myself without asking anyone else! That way, I kept on writing without needing to wait for help. So one way we can help ourselves as writers," you might say, "is to ask ourselves the question instead of taking it to someone else. Usually we can answer our own questions; usually we don't have to wait for help!"

If your students wait for help with the same predictable questions . . . you might show a list on chart paper of some questions students have asked you over the past week. "Let's take a look at this first question that was asked of me this week. When you think you have an answer, thumbs up." Give them a moment to think. "Wow, a lot of you answered that question quickly. Let's try the next question on the list." After one or two more, underscore how quickly and easily they were able to answer these questions when they took the time to ask themselves. "From now on, whenever you have a question, remember, the first person to ask is yourself. If necessary, you can also ask one of your fellow writers. Maybe they have had this problem before and you two can work it out together."

ASSESSMENT

If several people read and comment on the same piece of children's writing, the variety of their responses will be startling. The reason for this diversity is that what we see in our students' writing comes as much from us as it does from the children. The good news is that we can look at our students' work through lenses we've deliberately chosen, and not be limited by our instincts and habits. At this point in the year, I strongly urge you to look at your children's writing to see if and how your instruction has influenced it. As you do this, you are, of course, learning as much about your own teaching as you are learning about your children's work.

Ask yourself:

- "How many of my children have learned to write about small moments, about events that begin and end within a short span of time?" Jot lists of the children who have and who haven't yet learned this.
- Or ask, "How many of my children write a sequence of events, telling one after another?"

Don't ask yourself whether your children do any of this well yet—only ask if they've written a sequence of events.

I encourage you to make a pile of notebooks that don't contain much evidence that your instruction has made a dent. The authors of those notebooks need more of your attention. Assume for now that you, not the child, have some catching up to do and set out with great resolve, planning to do more to connect with the child who doesn't seem to be grasping what you are trying to teach. These children need to become your teachers, teaching you how to make a more significant difference in their lives. Study their written work and observe them during class time in order to untangle the puzzle. Give each of these children your best attention and gather data

that can inform you. Realize that you may need to recruit a colleague to join you in puzzling through the mysteries of these children.

As you study these strugglers, consider whether your teaching perhaps asked them to take a step that was too giant, all at once. For example, you've asked these children to write about *small* stories that are nevertheless significant to them. The paradox involved in that charge may have been confusing, and perhaps for now you'll decide to forgo the emphasis on writing about significant stories, and to focus only on writing about tightly focused events. Although you may not have emphasized writing conventionally correct entries, some of these children may be obsessed with a concern for correctness and may, therefore, have little brain space to devote to envisioning precise details. If these children seem to you to be struggling because you or they have taken on a challenge which is too demanding for them at this time, then be sure to talk with the child about the goals that really matter right now, and those that can wait for a later time. Then be vigilant in watching for signs of progress toward the newly clarified goals. Keep in mind that a child may still be doing lots of things that are less than ideal . . . Yet if you see palpable progress toward a goal, this merits a celebration.

Meanwhile, think also about the whole class again. Look at their written texts as windows onto their growth processes. You've taught stamina; look to see if their notebooks suggest they've developed more stamina. Which children show that they can finish one entry and begin the next without needing your help?

If your instruction is making an impact, you'll want to celebrate this even if the resulting pieces are still laden with other problems, problems you have yet to address. As you look at what children *are* doing, you'll see next steps.

GETTING READY

- Instructions on chalkboard telling children to bring their writer's notebooks (pens tucked inside) and sit with their partners in the meeting area
- Two versions of a story to tell: one a summary, one a sequential unfolding narrative
- Chart paper and markers
- Idea for a shared class event the children can retell orally, step-by-step
- See CD-ROM for resources

BUILDING STORIES STEP-BY-STEP

Since the start of this unit, your children have spent their writing time collecting one entry after another. In the next session, they will select one of these entries to develop, revise, craft, and edit toward publication.

The writing process is cyclical. This means that the phase you and your children have just experienced is not over. Each time your children write, they'll begin their work by watching the world, living like writers, and then collecting entries that could eventually grow into the kind of texts they're aiming to write.

You will want to be keenly aware of what you and your children have and haven't accomplished thus far. Look back at your goals for this unit and notice which you've met. Hopefully by now, most of your children have come to realize that their lives are full of stories to tell, topics to write. Hopefully most children live with a writer's consciousness, noticing funny predicaments or poignant moments and saying, "That'd make a great story!" Hopefully they've grasped the concept that during this writing workshop, they can draw on strategies they learned before. If any of these lessons have been learned, this is cause for great celebration.

Today's session is crucial. We need to move heaven and earth to be sure children have made the gigantic leap from summarizing to storytelling. When children summarize, they will probably be the first to feel that their writing is not very effective. That feeling will quickly lower their enthusiasm and lessen their investment in writing. Just as troubling, when children summarize instead of storytelling, it probably means that they have not yet realized that writing is a process of making choices about what to say and how to say it. Once children begin telling their story moment by moment, however, a world of writing choices opens up for them. Writers begin to sense all the possible ways to tell a story when they realize there are endless possibilities even for leads. "It was a damp day and my shirt was sticking to me" or "My little brother looked up at me and asked, 'Are you happy?'" Storylike openings imply choices and reasons not implied in summaries.

In this session you'll help children see their own writing as a crafted story, not just a recounting of thoughts as they occurred to the writer. In this session you'll help children feel their power as creators.

MINILESSON

Building Stories Step-by-Step

CONNECTION

Celebrate that your students are writing with some focus.

"Writers, I took your stories home last night and, reading them over, it was clear to me that most of you remembered to write not about a big watermelon idea but about a tiny, tiny seed story. Instead of writing about your visit to your grandmother's and telling the whole day, you zoomed in and wrote focused stories—writing, for example, a story about planting hyacinth bulbs with your grandma. That is so smart."

"But there is one thing I noticed in your writing that I want to talk about with you. Sometimes, after you get a small story in mind, like the story of planting bulbs with your grandmother, you aren't writing the story in a step-by-step way, telling *a story* of what happened. Instead you are making comments about the gardening (or whatever the episode is that you are capturing). For example, instead of writing what you did first and then next like this:"

> I knelt down under the tree with my grandma. "Is this a good place for one of the flowers?" I asked.

"you instead *talk about* (or comment on) the gardening."

> I did some gardening with my grandma. It was fun. We planted about five bulbs. She showed me how to plant bulbs so a deer can't dig them up.

Name the teaching point. In this case, tell children you want to teach them that personal narratives are often organized chronologically, told as a sequence of events.

"Now, writers *do* sometimes write all about a topic. But for now, in this class, we are writing true stories, or personal narratives. And today what I want to teach you is that stories, or narratives, are almost always organized to tell what happened first and then next and then next. One writer's strategy we can use to help us write true stories is to start by thinking back to the very start of the memory; then we make a movie in our mind of what happened first, then next, and next."

COACHING

You'll notice this minilesson opens the way so many of our writing conferences with children open: with a compliment. In every case, we strive to make the compliment focus on something that a writer has done that is worth emulating often. The trick is that we can't say to children, "From this day on, write about planting hyacinth bulbs with your grandma." We need to determine what it is that the child has done that is replicable, and name the action in ways that can guide not only today but also tomorrow.

This is a great time for hand gestures. You'll find that often this year, you'll need to highlight the difference between commenting on a subject (imagine a gesture that suggests the writer swipes this way and that over the subject) and writing a sequentially structured narrative (imagine a gesture that suggests a horizontal timeline).

It is important to me to give kids precise, clear instructions, which means that sometimes I oversimplify things to make a point. But I try to maintain intellectual honesty. So in an instance like this, instead of saying, "Writers do not talk about an event; we instead retell the story of the event," I acknowledge that writers do sometimes write all about a topic, but then I go on to explain that in this class right now, we are writing narratives. It is important to me that I acknowledge that it is entirely possible to write an effective all-about piece; on the other hand, I want to make it clear that for now, I am asking the class to generate narratives. All-about (informational or expository) writing involves quite a different skill set, and I'll help children do that kind of writing during other units of study.

TEACHING

Demonstrate that you resist talking all about an event and instead storytell the event.

"Let me show you what I mean. I'm going to write about the first time I saw Dad cry (remember that was one story I thought of when I used the strategy of thinking of a person and then listing small moments the person and I shared). I could just talk about that time, commenting on it."

> I remember when my dad's brother died and my dad cried. I never saw my dad cry before and I didn't know what to do. I was worried. My dad isn't the sort who cries often.

"But I'm trying to write a story, and to do so, I want to tell what happened first and then next and then next. So watch and notice how I go to the start of the memory, then make a movie in my mind of what happened first, then next, and next."

"Before I get started, I need to remember to ask myself, 'What am I trying to show in this story?' In this story, I want to show that it was really surprising to me when my big, tough dad cried."

"Now I'll remember that episode, getting the memory in my head. Then I think, 'What happened first? What did I do or see or hear first?'"

"So let's see. I'm remembering Dad crying. What did I do, see, or hear first? Oh yes. I heard dad talking on the phone." I touched my thumb as I recalled this, wordlessly demonstrating how I use one finger and then the next to scaffold the chronological progression. "He said, 'Oh no,' and 'How bad is it?' and 'He's gone?' I didn't know what he was talking about. Then he hung up the phone," I touched a second finger, in a way that suggested this was the second event in the story, "and he sat down on the chair like this." I reenacted my dad plopping himself down and sitting heavily, like the weight of the world was upon him. "He looked awful, and I knew something bad had happened. 'Grove died,' he told me. I sat beside my dad." I touched a third finger. "I looked at Dad and said, 'He was your big brother.' Dad nodded. I saw tears filling in his eyes, real tears. They started to stream down his face. I didn't know what to do or to say." I touched a fourth finger. "Then I hugged him." I touched the final finger.

Often when I am trying to teach children how to do something, I first dramatize the option I don't want them to do. By showing that I could have written all about the time my dad cried but rejected this in favor of writing a sequential story, I hope to draw attention to the point I am trying to make. I don't think my teaching would be explicit enough if I simply wrote a story about one time my dad cried, and assumed kids would attend to the chronological structure of the text.

In the teaching component of most minilessons we are giving writers a set of how-to directions. Part of the challenge in designing minilessons is that often we are teaching a strategy that is second nature to us. In order to make it accessible to kids for whom it is not second nature, we need to become conscious of the work that we do instantly and effortlessly, so that we can teach this to kids. The trick is to be explicit and clear. In an effort to teach the separate steps of a strategy, we can inadvertently describe the strategy in a way that doesn't ring true, and that is something to check for and avoid.

In the series for K–2 writers, teachers and children "told stories across their fingers," but did so with one sentence for each finger. As children get older, one important development will be that they write not in sentences-of-thought but in paragraphs-of-thought. It was intentional that each new finger (or dot) in my story sequence represents several sentences.

Debrief. Emphasize that instead of discussing the event, you retold it as a story.

"Writers, do you see how I didn't just talk about when Dad cried?" Sweeping my hand to illustrate that I could have commented this way and that way about the subject, I said, "I also didn't just say, 'I remember when Dad cried. It was really sad. He cried because his brother died.' Instead I thought about that time as a movie, almost, and thought, 'What happened first? If this was a movie, what would I see first?' I made the movie in my mind and told it, scene by scene."

"Now I'm ready to start writing." Touching my first finger, I repeated the start of the story: "I heard Dad talking on the phone. He said, 'Oh no. . . .'" I pointed to the piece of chart paper, to signal that I'd write those words.

ACTIVE ENGAGEMENT
Set children up to practice what you've demonstrated, using a whole-class topic.

"So let's try it together. Remember yesterday when we had a fire drill? We could talk all about the fire drill, saying, 'We had a hard time at the fire drill because the first graders slowed us down and because it rained and we had to stand far from the building.' But today, we are writing stories. To tell the story of the fire drill, we need to recall what happened first. Scroll back in your minds and think, 'What happened first?' I'll start you off and then you can try telling the story to a neighbor. 'Our teacher told us to copy the math problems and so I got out some paper and started copying numbers from the board. (Do you have the movie in your mind?) Just then I heard . . . . ' Keep going. Tell your neighbor what happened, step by step, bit by bit. If you want, tell it across your fingers."

Debrief. Highlight what students just did that you hope they use another time, with another text.

"Writers, can I have your eyes and your attention? I loved hearing how you retold the story of the fire drill. I was really able to make a movie in my mind as I listened to you tell this story across your fingers. You didn't just say, 'Tuesday we had a fire drill. The bell rang while we were copying a math problem and we all had to go outside and we got in trouble because we followed the first graders down the stairs and they were so slow they made us late.' No."

Don't write the story! It is tempting to progress from one part of the writing process to another and another in the teaching component of a minilesson. Such a demonstration would no longer illustrate the targeted teaching point! Become accustomed to fragmenting your writing process so that you show kids only what they need in order to see that day's teaching point put into action. In this instance, the point was that writers need to guard against writing all about an episode and instead tell the episode as a story. You can demonstrate this without doing any writing at all. If you want to write something, write only the first sentence or two. In general, it is wise to constrain yourself so that you write three to five lines at the most during a minilesson.

In this Active Engagement section of the minilesson, I made the choice to have all writers practice the strategy while working with what I call an exercise text. I deliberately rallied the group around the story of the fire drill because it is certainly a sequential narrative with an obvious beginning (the blast of the fire drill), middle, and end. Then, too, I knew this particular class was in an uproar already over what they regarded as unfair treatment during the fire drill, so I knew they'd have a great time reliving the event. I was trying to recruit their enthusiasm for writing and, more specifically, for storytelling. However, if I was teaching a class of struggling and reluctant writers, I might have asked each child to think about what he or she would write that day, then to storytell it and even write the first sentence while the children sat together in the meeting area.

In the series Units of Study in Primary Writing, *we also used a fire drill story to introduce kindergartners and first graders to the idea of writing focused chronological stories (the introduction of Small Moment stories). There is nothing magical about fire drills, of course, but it might be interesting for you to look at the instruction involving the fire drill story in* Small Moments *and to notice ways in which instruction in writing is similar and different depending on children's grade levels.*

"Listen to Takeshi's retelling of the fire drill and notice how he tells it, like this is an amazing story that could be in our libraries. While you listen, see if you can get the movie in your mind of what happened, because great authors write so that readers can feel like they are there, in the story."

> Just then I heard the fire alarm. Everyone stopped writing and looked around. I counted each dong: one, two, three. After a pause, the alarm began again. I jumped up and headed toward the door because I was the line leader. I walked quickly to the stairs. We hurried down the stairs. We got to the second floor at the same time as the first graders. We had to let them go first. Man, were they slow."

"Did you see how Takeshi took a tiny event that happened to him (to all of us) and he thought about that time as a movie? He thought, 'What happened first?' He made the movie in his mind and told the story, step by step. We could really picture the whole story, couldn't we!"

LINK

Tell the children that you expect all of them to write their stories in a sequential, blow-by-blow fashion from now on.

"From now on, whenever you are writing a story, don't just talk all about what happened; instead say exactly what happened first, then next, and next. Retell the story just like Takeshi did in a step-by-step fashion. This strategy will help you anytime you want to write stories. Let's start today by rereading our stories from yesterday and making sure we have told them as stories."

You'll notice that usually after children turn and talk in their Active Engagement section, I only cite one child's work as a model. I'm always aware that other children did good work too, but I'd rather develop the one example in some detail than rush to convey several good examples. Always, my decisions are influenced by a sense that time is limited. Above all, children need to be writing.

Remember to use the gesture for swiping this way and that way past a subject, juxtaposing that gesture with the one you use to represent the process of writing a sequentially organized narrative.

WRITING AND CONFERRING

Addressing a Host of Writing Situations

Sometimes, we need to stop teaching, step back, and take a bit of time to watch children as they work, trying to ascertain patterns that merit attention.

You may see that a bunch of children leave the minilesson and then simply sit until you arrive to give them a personalized jump-start. If you've got this group, resist the temptation to deliver each child his own personalized pep talk. Instead, gather these kids together, tell them what you've noticed, and help them think of a strategy or two for getting started on their own. Then watch them use one of these strategies to do just that.

You might find that another cluster of children writes incredibly slowly, producing only half a page or so in a day. Gather these youngsters together and tell them that you're going to help them double the amount of writing they can do in a day. First, these writers need to be clear about what they intend to write. So set them up, making sure each child has a story to tell and is proceeding chronologically through that story. Don't worry about the quality of writing just now—to focus on fluency and speed, these children need permission to lower their standards (temporarily). Now help children to dictate a full sentence to themselves and write that whole sentence without pausing. These children are apt to pause at the ends of words or phrases—that won't do! Then help children dictate the next sentence to themselves and write it quickly, too, without rereading in the midst of writing.

In general, cluster children into smaller groups based on your diagnosis of what they need. Every child's writing will have a host of issues. Try to prioritize. You can't repair everything at once, so ask yourself, "What are the really fundamental issues?"

> **MID-WORKSHOP TEACHING POINT** *Spelling High-Frequency Words with Automaticity* "Writers, can I have your eyes and your attention? You are remembering to do so many things. Instead of writing about big huge watermelon ideas, you are writing tiny seed stories. Instead of telling all about an event, you are reliving the event in a step-by-step fashion. You are using strategies that grown-up professional writers use. What I want to remind you now is that when you are writing for readers, it is important to spell common words as correctly as you can. That way, everyone can understand you easily."
>
> "So when you are writing, take a second to spell the words on our word wall (and other words you know) correctly. Right now, would you reread what you've written so far, and if you find a word wall word that is misspelled, would you fix it? If you aren't sure how to spell it, look at the word wall. But instead of copying the word letter for
>
> *continued on next page*

You will eventually find that a small group of children need more help shifting from summarizing and commenting on one episode toward storytelling that episode. That is, some children will write like this: "My sister and I played at the beach. We made castles and buried ourselves in the sand. It was fun but it was hot. I had a good time with my sister. She is nice." In an instance like this, recognize that the writer summarized the story, commenting on several main things that she did. She probably then realized her story was too short, leading her to add some sweeping comments to the end. This is a very common thing for writers to do. We can give a child a predictable sequence of prompts to help that youngster loosen her hold on summarizing and begin to storytell. Try something like this:

"You've written about lots of moments! Do you want to tell about the time when you [possible topic for this child]? Or maybe the time when you [alternative topic]?"

"Oh! Great choice! I'm dying to picture how that really happened. So how did it start? What exactly did you do first? What did you say?"

Then you could retell what the child says in story form, and press for more story from the child. "So one morning you [did a specific action] and then you thought [a specific thought]. Then what did you do?"

"What a story!" Then, you would retell it. "Write this down." Finally, dictate the start of the story as the child records her own words.

> continued from previous page
>
> letter, when you look at the word wall, go through all the steps we go through when we are learning new words. Look at the word. Think about what you notice about it. Now try to imprint the word on your mind. Close your eyes and try to see the letters in your imagination. Say the letters aloud. Now open your eyes and check to see if you were right. When you have the correct spelling fixed in your brain, write it. Check that you were right."
>
> "And after this, for the rest of this year and for the whole of your life, remember that it's important to get into the habit of correctly spelling the words you use a lot. If you are writing a word and you think, 'This is on our word wall' and you aren't quite sure how to spell it, take an extra fifteen seconds to try to spell (and write) like a pro!"

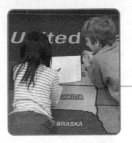

SHARE

Appreciating Children's Writing

Convene writers. Use one child's story to demonstrate how a good story allows readers to live alongside the narrator.

"Writers, when I read the stories you are writing, it is almost like I am with you at your kitchen table, on the subway, in the park. Listen to Song Moo's story of an adventure he had in the park last Saturday, and see if you don't agree that a good story allows readers to live in it. Listen." *[Fig. V-1 and V-2]*

> On Tuesday I wanted to go to the park, so I asked my father to go to park with me. At the park, I saw Ttomy waving at me and saying "Hi Song Moo!" Then I say back to Ttomy, "Hi Ttomy!"
>
> While we were walking, Ttomy saw a worm wiggling in the dirt so Ttomy said to me, "Look, there is a worm." And then he pointed at it and then I said, "Oh, it's a worm." And then Ttomy said, "So let's cut the worm. It will be fun!"
>
> Next to the worm we saw a piece of glass so Ttomy picked up the piece of glass and he cut the worm into 1/2 but the worm didn't died so Ttomy cut the worm into 1/4, but the worm didn't died so I said, "This is interesting" and Ttomy said, "Yes, this is interesting." But we had a trouble to know which side was head and which side was tail so we decide to cut both sides but the worm was still wiggling in 6 little pieces so I said, "Let's just wait until the worm died because it will not died even if we cut the worm into 1/10." So we wait and wait and finally the two pieces of worm died but the other pieces of worm didn't died so we wait another while. After a while the wiggly worm died so I said, "Finally the wiggly worm died."

When you select writing to read aloud, be sure that you don't find yourself drawing on the same six or eight children day after day. A child once showed me that in the back of his writer's notebook he'd collected a list of every child that his teacher mentioned by name in minilessons and Shares. Looking at that list, I was reminded of the agony I felt in gym class when team captains took turns choosing children to be on their teams. As teachers, we have more power than we realize. With a single gesture or word, we can raise or dash a child's hopes.

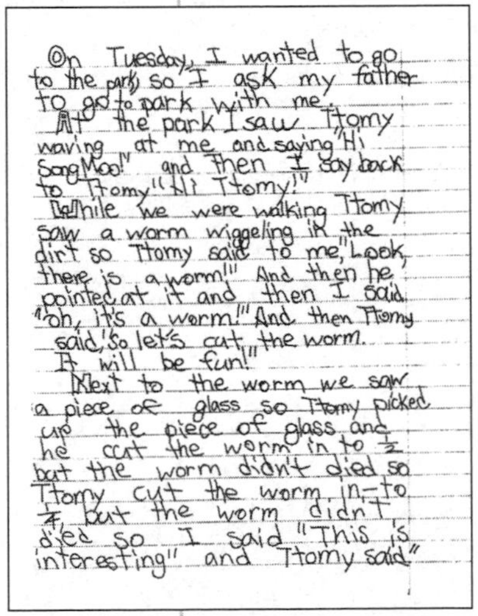

On Tuesday, I wanted to go to the park, so I ask my father to go to park with me.
At the park I saw Ttomy waving at me and saying "Hi SongMoo!" and then I say back to Ttomy "Hi Ttomy!"
While we were walking Ttomy saw a worm wiggeling in the dirt so Ttomy said to me, "Look, there is a worm!" And then he pointed at it and then I said "oh, it's a worm!" And then Ttomy said, "So let's cut the worm. It will be fun!"
Next to the worm we saw a piece of glass so Ttomy picked up the piece of glass and he cut the worm in to 1/2 but the worm didn't died so Ttomy cut the worm in-to 1/4, but the worm didn't died so I said "This is interesting" and Ttomy said"

Fig. V-1 Song Moo

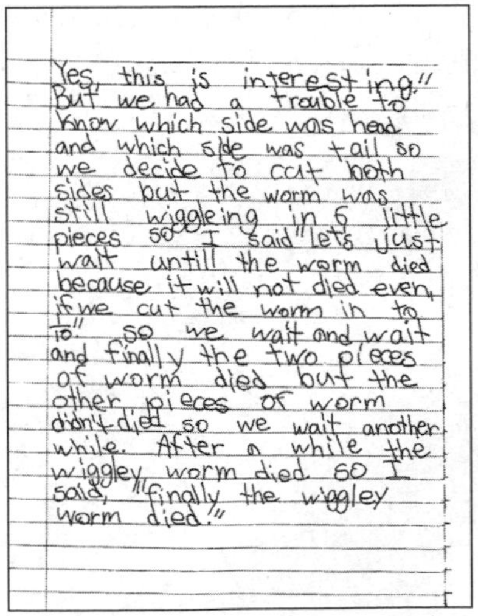

Yes, this is interesting." But we had a trouble to know which side was head and which side was tail so we decide to cut both sides but the worm was still wiggleing in 6 little pieces so I said "let's just wait untill the worm died because it will not died even, if we cut the worm in to 1/10." so we wait and wait and finally the two pieces of worm died but the other pieces of worm didn't died so we wait another while. After a while the wiggley worm died so I said, "finally the wiggley worm died."

Fig. V-2 Song Moo

Ask children to share their story with a new partner.

"I can't wait to read all of your stories! Right now, would you get with someone who has not yet heard your story, and read what you've written aloud to that person? When you finish reading, storytell the part you haven't written. Remember to storytell it in a way that gives your listener goose bumps."

HOMEWORK *Practicing Spelling* There are many things you may know by heart: addition facts, your phone number, the lineup and batting averages for the New York Yankees, the order of the planets, your best friend's e-mail address, and so on. Of course, there are lots of words we can spell by heart, too. The great thing is that this list of words we can spell by heart just keeps growing!

Even so, brave writers still use words in their writing that they may not be quite sure how to spell. We give these words our best try, but then we move on in our piece, even if we aren't quite sure of the spelling. Fortunately, writers reread their work often, and when we reread, one of the things we can do is take another try at spelling these tricky or unfamiliar words.

Your job tonight as a writer is to go back at least three entries and circle words that you think you have misspelled. Ask yourself, "What seems right here? What seems wrong here?" Next, you'll find space in the margins of the page to give the spelling a couple more tries. You can then pick the try that seems to be most correct and change the spelling in your piece.

Here are some things to remember to do:

- Reread a piece and when you get to a word that you think is spelled incorrectly, circle it.
- Think about what is right with the word and what is wrong with the word you spelled.
- Try to spell it a few different ways by asking yourself, "Are there other words I know that can help me with this word?"
- After you've spelled it a few different ways, decide which try looks the best. Change the word in your piece to match your best try.
- Do this spelling check in your last three entries. You can do it in more entries if you want!

It's not likely, of course, that you'll actually read Song Moo's story aloud. Instead, you choose an entry that one of your children has written. When you read the text aloud, read it as well as you can. Focus through the words to whatever the writer is saying. When I read the section where Song Moo wrote, "And then he pointed to the worm," I see that worm, squiggling in the ground. When I read how he and Ttomy studied the worm, trying to decide which end was the head, I picture the two friends squatting close to the writhing worm. This matters. If we read aloud well, seeing not just the words on the page but the life drama, then listeners, too, can see through the words to the drama.

Here's an example of what you'll be doing, right on your notebook pages:

Example sentence: I got chills when I heard the aplaws. (Note: aplaws needs a circle around it.)

Then try using what you already know about other words. For example:

applaws (change the beginning to look like *apply* or *appear,* but the *w* looks strange)

applaus (change *aw* like *law* to *au* like *auto,* but it still looks weird)

applause (change the end of the word to look like *cause*)

TAILORING YOUR TEACHING

If you have students who struggle with oral storytelling or with sequencing events . . . you could offer them the option of creating a storyboard to help them move through their narrative bit by bit. Create a storyboard template with squares for quick sketches and lines beneath them for jotting quick notes, four per page, like this:

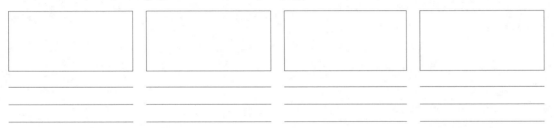

It's important to consider which students will benefit from working from a storyboard. For some students, doing so will only delay their drafts; for others, the necessity of doing so will support their drafts.

If you notice students getting into a writing rut, always writing one page a day or always starting a new entry each day . . . break the rut. You may decide to change the structure of your writing workshop, for example, by having writers start each day with some time devoted to rereading what they worked on the day (or night) before. Writers often begin any writing session looking for places to add on to, places to fix, places to elaborate upon, etc. They may also reread to make sure their pieces sound the way they want them to, so they might decide to make different word choices, to restructure sentences, to fix parts that don't make sense.

If you notice your students growing careless with their writer's notebooks . . . you might spend a minilesson or a share session teaching your students how you expect them to take care of their writer's notebooks. "Writers, yesterday at lunch time I was reading through your writer's notebooks. I can't think of a better way to spend my lunch hour than reading your stories. I loved them! But you know what? I want to talk about something that seems to be a growing problem. As I looked through your notebooks, I saw that many of them are beginning to look messy. There were pages with missing dates, some pages were skipped, some notebooks even had pages that were ripped out or crumpled up! I was so surprised, because a writing notebook is a very important tool for writers and it's so important to take care of the tools that help you do your work."

"So today, I want to spend a bit of time talking about how to take care of your notebook. We treat it like a book from the library as we handle it and turn the pages. Then when we write in it, we should respect it, because it's holding the stories of our lives. We can show respect by writing as neatly as we can, by going page by page, and by not using it for scratch paper. Watch me as I pretend I'm a student during writing time. Notice whether or not I'm taking care of my notebook, and then think of suggestions that would help me become more careful with it."

If you notice lots of abandoned entries in the notebooks or lots of similar entries about recurrent subjects, such as particular birthday parties or first days of school, for example . . . you may decide you need to help children get more invested in their writing. Over and over again, writing workshop teachers see that if writers do not take seriously the job of choosing a subject, then they will not be emotionally invested enough in their story to continue writing it until it is finished. You may want to teach a minilesson where you model the thought process behind topic choice. Teach your writers that if a story is important, you should be able to talk for a few minutes about it—even on a first telling. Demonstrate picking one story that is a thirty-second tell and another story that is a two-minute tell.

MECHANICS

It is important for you and your grade-level colleagues to spend some time reflecting on what you notice about your children's control of written conventions and devising a plan for how you will support this aspect of their writing development. You'll probably find that it is challenging to decide on strategies for spelling and punctuating that will be applicable to all children. That is, whether a child is spelling with just initial and final consonants or spelling perfectly, that child can still benefit from learning to tighten her narrative to tell a focused story with detail. But a child who is spelling with just initial and final consonants won't benefit from studying why writers do or do not double a final consonant before adding an ending. Instruction in conventions must be tailored to the individual child more than other kinds of instruction. Use your judgment before transferring what I teach about the conventions of written language into your classroom!

When you and your colleagues think together about written conventions, you will probably choose to talk about spelling because it will be the elephant in the room. I suggest you devise an approach to spelling that you can discuss with parents, and that you do so right away. Send a letter home to parents in which you let them know that, across the year, you will definitely be helping children become more conventional as spellers. You'll want to write your own letter but this one may give you some ideas.

In general, there are principles that can guide you as you and your colleagues devise an approach to spelling. First, you need to convey to the parents of your children that you recognize that spelling matters. This is important for your students, but it is especially important right now for the parents of your students. Research has shown that when parents are becoming acquainted with you as a teacher, one of their biggest concerns is your approach to spelling. If you show parents that you value their child's progress in spelling, they will be more apt to trust you. Since you certainly do care about the children's progress in spelling, among other areas of writing, your letter to parents should convey this.

Second, it should be a priority to help children spell high-frequency words with ease and automaticity. Fifty percent of the words children write come from a list of thirty-six most common words, so helping children master those words has great payoff.

Finally, it is important to teach children strategies for tackling tough words so they aren't hesitant or ill-equipped to do so. That is, the job is not only to teach lists of words; the job is also to teach tools and strategies for spelling. One strategy that you'll teach is that you'll help children know they can approximate a spelling and return to it later to problem-solve. If a child believes she has misspelled a word, suggest she look at what she's written and think, "What part of this seems right? What part seems wrong?" This is helpful because it gives the child a sense of control. The child who is writing "international" may believe she's spelled "inter" and "na" correctly. So now she's working only on one or two problematic syllables. Next, suggest that writers think: "What other words do I know how to spell that can help me spell the hard parts of this word?"

Dear Parents,

As we start this year together, I want to take a moment to convey to you some of my plans for helping your children grow in their abilities to spell conventionally. I have been assessing your children's spelling during these first few days of school, and I've come to believe that some children in the class are choosing only "easy" words to write because they are worried over whether they can spell the more precise words correctly. My first goal, then, will be to make sure that every child is a fearless and inventive writer, and that every child is willing to write "enormous" rather than sticking with "big" even if that child cannot spell "enormous" conventionally. You will see that I do not expect perfect spelling in children's first-draft writing.

The second thing I have noticed is that many children in this class haven't yet learned to spell some of the most important high-frequency words—words like *because, said, although*—correctly. So, each week, I will directly and explicitly teach children a list of high-frequency words. Children will bring that list home on Mondays, they will be quizzed on those words on Fridays, and more important, they will be expected to incorporate those spellings into their writing whenever they write. I'll help them do this!

Meanwhile, there are a few children who will need extra help with spelling. We all know that many great writers and thinkers struggle with spelling. I'll be meeting with a few children to let them know that they will need to put extra time and receive extra help in spelling, and that together, we can make huge progress. Meanwhile, these children need to be reminded that although their progress in spelling matters and merits attention, they meanwhile need to also work towards other goals as well. Like all children, I'll encourage these youngsters to write a lot, and to write with voice and detail. I look forward to supporting and studying your children's progress towards writing more correct and more effective pieces of writing.

GETTING READY

- Instructions on chalkboard telling children to bring their writer's notebooks (pens tucked inside) and sit with their partners in the meeting area
- Your own filled writer's notebook
- Selected books with great leads (*Salt Hands, The Paper Boy, Shortcut* to read aloud; varied collection of books for a reading table)
- Paper clips
- Blank booklets with four or five pages, one for each child
- Writing folders, one for each child, to hold the booklets and future loose-leaf work
- See CD-ROM for resources

CHOOSING A SEED IDEA

Jerome Bruner, the great American cognitive psychologist, once said that the ideas that are essential to any discipline "are as simple as they are powerful." Children at any age level can experience the essentials of a discipline, "learning to use them in progressively more complex forms" (1960, 1977, pp. 12–13). This understanding of discipline-based knowledge underlies a writing process approach to composition. The approach is based on the belief that even very young children can experience a version of the professional writer's process.

In this curriculum, we invite children to experience the writing process. So far, we've helped children live like writers, seeing the fine fiber of their ordinary lives as worth recording. Today, we show children that writers return to their writer's notebooks, rereading them and asking, "Of all that's here, is there one story that says the most about me or my life, or one story that I especially want to share with readers? Which one story will I choose to develop and publish?"

Today, then, you are inviting children into revision, which means quite literally re-vision, to see again. You will help children discover that because they've put their life stories onto the page, they can now hold their lives in their hands, rereading those lives. And in doing so, they can take the rush of life, and slow it down in order to re-experience it, this time seeing the colors, feeling the wind, hearing the words all the more intensely. They can take one of the ever-so-fleeting episodes of their lives and pause long enough to see it, to frame it, to share it.

When we write the stories of our lives, we reread them and select one to linger with and to develop. It is as if we press the pause button of time. Pause. Rewind. Replay. This is what you will teach your children to do today. It's exquisitely important work.

MINILESSON

Choosing a Seed Idea

CONNECTION

Solidify what children already know by summarizing the early parts of the writing process they've learned so far.

"Writers, so far in this class, you've lived like real writers, learning that you can think of people, places, and things, and these can jog your minds to recall particular small moments, and you can write those into detailed entries. You've also learned some essential qualities of good writing, and these help you shape your entries into ones readers will draw close to hear."

Name the teaching point. In this case, tell children you'll teach them to choose one entry to develop into a publishable piece.

"Today I want to teach you that writers don't just write one entry and then write another and another as we have been doing. As writers, after we collect entries and ideas for a while, we reread and we find one story, one entry, that especially matters to us, and we make a commitment to that one entry. We decide to work on it so that it becomes our very best writing ever."

TEACHING

Show children that writing allows us to slow down and find treasure among the everyday events of our lives.

"I love the picture book *Roxaboxen*, by Alice McLerran. In it, some children are playing on a desert hill. There's not much there: just sand, some cacti, a broken crate. But then Marian finds a rusty tin box, and the children circle around her, declaring it to be treasure. And it is. Inside the box are smooth black stones. The children lay them out on the sand to make roads, and soon they've created the pretend kingdom of Roxaboxen. And it all started with Marian finding a rusty tin box and the children declaring it to be treasure."

Notice that in some teaching sections, I rely on my writing. In some, I rely on a child's writing. In this minilesson, I refer to a published picture book. Variety adds interest.

"I write because writing allows me to take the stuff that is all around me in my life—the little stories, the everyday events—and hold one small piece of life in my hands, declaring it to be a treasure, declaring it something worth thinking about. Our new white sneakers get grass stains during recess. Our hamster circles round and round before curling up into a golden pom-pom. A best friend shares a secret at lunch. Writing gives me a way to declare one of these events to be a treasure. It gives me a way to pause."

"When I write, I reread my notebook (and rewind my life). I find one entry that for some reason sort of matters, and I say, 'This is the one that I'm going to linger with, and make into a publishable book.'"

Ask children to notice exactly what you do as you demonstrate choosing an idea from your notebook to develop into a finished piece.

"Watch me while I reread my notebook, thinking about whether one of my entries might be worth developing into a story that I'd like to publish. Later I'm going to ask you to tell each other what exactly I did, as a writer, in order to choose one story, one entry, to turn into my best writing."

"Hmm . . . I'm reading this entry about seeing a homeless man without shoes. That doesn't really say that much about me. Here is an entry about how I longed for a crow as a pet, and had a crow cage ready in case I caught one. I'll star that as a possibility because I bet I could explore that one and find some interesting stuff there. Here is that list of small moments about my father. I like that one about the first time I saw him cry . . . . Now I'm reading the entry about the first time I saw my dad cry. That's a possibility because it really mattered to me, and I have a lot more I could say about it. I will star that one and keep on reading. After I read all these entries, I'll decide between the entries I've starred."

During these early days of getting the writing workshop up and going, I have choices to make and priorities to set that will ultimately affect the tone and the energy that will drive the workshop forward throughout the year. If children think their stories are irrelevant or insignificant, they will not be able to sustain the energy necessary to be writers. I want each child to declare his story to be a treasure.

Notice that before I slip into the role of writer and demonstrate, I usually frame the demonstration with remarks meant to orient children so they know what they are watching, and what they're expected to do with what they see.

When you demonstrate, as in this instance, be sure your intonation and gestures suggest you are mulling over, thinking aloud. You aren't talking to the children. Your eyes aren't on them. Instead you are poring over your notebook, thinking aloud as you do, letting children eavesdrop on your thinking. But don't look at the children or direct these remarks to them.

You may notice that after the demonstration, I didn't debrief as usual. That's because I'm going to incorporate debriefing into today's active engagement.

ACTIVE ENGAGEMENT
Give children a chance to think through the process you've demonstrated.

"Writers, you've probably already noticed lots of strategies that I used in order to choose an entry that matters to me. Would you turn and tell your partner three specific things you saw me doing that you could try?" The children talked, and I listened to several pairs.

Voice the observations children make in a way that allows you to review the process you demonstrated.

"I heard some of you say that I carefully reread my entries. You noticed that I didn't just flip, flip, flip through the pages of my notebook when it was time for me to choose an entry. I took my time and reread thoughtfully."

"And you realized that when I reread, I thought about whether the episode matters to me, and whether it says something true about me. I thought about whether I had more to say on the entry. Some of you noticed that I starred some entries as possibilities and kept on reading, planning to come back when I'd read through them all so I could choose one. You can do all these things as well when you reread your writing today, deciding which entries you'll star, which entry you'll declare to be treasure."

LINK
Remind children that after they start collecting entries like writers do, they'll want to choose an idea to develop into a publishable piece.

"Today, and whenever it is time for you to stop collecting entries and begin working on one writing project, remember that you—like writers everywhere—can reread your entries and think, 'Which of these especially matters?' Look for entries that draw you in, that seem to be saying, 'Pick me!' Off you go."

Your intonation will change at this point, and now instead of thinking aloud, you are talking directly to children.

This is not a usual Active Engagement. When possible, we try to give children a chance to actually do what it is we have talked about and demonstrated. In this Active Engagement, children instead talk about what they have heard and seen; they do not actually use the strategy themselves. I think their talk gains energy when I give the specific instruction to list three things I did.

I know to tell children that I don't just flip, flip, flip through my notebook only because I've taught this minilesson before and been dismayed to see kids choose seed ideas by racing through their notebooks saying, "Nope, nope, nope!" Every time you give a minilesson and children's work doesn't proceed the way you hoped, take note and amend your minilesson for the next time!

Years ago, I suggested kids "nurture" their seed ideas in their notebooks for several weeks before beginning a draft. I have come to believe, however, that until youngsters have had a lot of experience with the writing process, they can be swamped if they collect too much loosely related material. I don't want children to lose hold of their organizational structure or their focused message. So during the first units of study, I keep this "nurturing one's seed idea" phase streamlined. It will become longer and more elaborate in later units in this series.

WRITING AND CONFERRING

Learning to Be Best Listeners

In any unit of study, my favorite day for conferring is always this one: the day when children reread all their entries in order to select just one to nurture, revise, and develop. Usually I find children are tentative about their choices. "This one?" they say, looking for confirmation.

"It's a hugely important one, isn't it?" I respond, and I say this acting on faith, whether or not the evidence is there yet on the page. After all, out of all the child's life, he has already made the decision to record this story in an entry, and now, out of all the entries, the child has chosen this one. The significance is not always apparent to me, but I find that if I confirm the entry's importance and then lean in to listen, saying, "Tell me all about it. How, exactly, did it start?" I can help children tell the story with engagement.

The challenge of this day is that every child will want this intense attention, and we can't listen respectfully and offer generous amounts of time and focus to every single child! On this day, especially, I try to make appointments to confer at lunch or recess, but I also set children up to listen well to each other. "Now that you have your seed idea chosen," I'll say to one writer, "will you listen to Robbie like I listened to you? Get him to tell you the whole story and to tell it with detail. Help him tell it in a way that gives you goose bumps."

For some children, today's work will require all of thirty seconds. Some children will know exactly which entry they want to develop, and you may find yourself in an awkward situation because you won't yet have had a chance to teach the class ways to develop their seed ideas. My suggestion, in this instance, is to either confer with those children or interrupt the class to offer a mid-workshop teaching point to solve this problem.

MID-WORKSHOP TEACHING POINT · *Rehearsing for Writing by Storytelling* "Writers, can I have your eyes and your attention? Thumbs up if you've chosen one entry that matters to you, an entry that you think you could work on more. Great. I'm going to pass out paper clips. Mark your entry with a paper clip—we'll call it your 'seed idea' because we are going to grow the entry, like one grows a seed, into something wonderful! Before you write the story of that entry, please turn to the person next to you, and partner 2, *tell the story* of your seed idea. Tell it long. Tell it in ways that gives your listener goose bumps."

After just a couple of minutes, I intervened. "Writers, let me stop you. I'm not surprised you selected these particular stories from your notebooks. They are incredible! I loved hearing that the stories grew as you told them; you seemed to remember more things right in the middle of the stories! That's exactly why we often storytell before we write. But let me tell you something else. Writers don't just tell our stories once before we write them—we tell and retell them. Robert Munsch, author of *Thomas' Snowsuit*, says that he never writes a story until he has told it at least a hundred times!"

"When you go back to your writing, would you tell your story again to yourself, not to your partner. I'm going to give you blank booklets and I'd like you to *storytell to yourself* across the pages." I showed children what I meant by this. Holding a blank book, I storytold the first bit of my father-crying story, then turned the next page and storytold the next bit. Then I sent children off to storytell . . . and to write.

SHARE

Immersing Ourselves in the Kinds of Texts We Plan to Write

Convene children. Suggest that they immerse themselves in the kind of text they plan to write. Read some texts aloud.

"Writers, can I have your eyes and your attention? You are on the brink of beginning your first draft. Now that you've found your seed idea, try doing what writers the world over do: read. Read books and stories that remind you of what you want to write. I've put a collection of books and short texts out on this table—ones that remind me of what we are writing. Most of them you know, which is the way it should be."

"With your seed idea in mind, take some time to read one of those books. Read it and reread it 'til you get the sound in your bones. A man named Hirsch wrote, 'I feel words creating a rhythm, a music, a spell, a mood, a shape, a form.' You'll want to feel that, so that you can create it with the entry you've chosen."

"To get you started, I want to read aloud the beginnings of some published stories so that you get the music and rhythm and lilt of a storyteller's voice into you. After I read, I'm going to ask partner 2 to tell your stories again, this time as if your stories are books on library shelves." I read aloud the leads to Jane Chelsea Aragon's *Salt Hands*, Dav Pilkney's *The Paper Boy*, and Donald Crews' *Shortcut*. After both members of each pair told their stories, I asked for everyone's attention again.

Suggest that children ask themselves, "What do I want my listeners to feel?"

"Writers, your stories are sounding like literature. What a difference this makes! I want to suggest one more thing that'll make a world of difference. Before you continue your story, ask yourself this: 'What am I trying to make my listeners *feel*?' It might be that you are trying to convey one feeling at the start of the story and another feeling later, in the middle of the story. Tell the story so that your listeners *feel* what you want them to feel. Embellish it a bit, build up certain parts, get through to your listeners."

Hand out folders where kids can store their booklets and other related papers to keep with their notebooks.

"Now that you are about to write drafts, you need a new kind of paper and a place to store it, so it's always easy for you to find. Here are some folders you can keep with your notebooks to hold your drafting booklets and eventually all your final pieces."

As writers progress from writing entries toward writing a publishable piece, it is especially important that their writing takes on the cadence of literate language. The music and voice of stories are important. Mem Fox has said that for her, the ability to write well "came from the constant good fortune of hearing great literature beautifully delivered into my ear, and from there into my heart, and from my heart into my bones." The "rhythms," she said, "remain in the marrow of my memory" (1993, pp. 113, 116). In this Share, I'm trying to get the lilt of story into the marrow of children's memory. I'm urging children to say their stories aloud, and to tell their stories in ways that give listeners goose bumps in hopes that "I went rollerblading in the park" shifts to "One morning last summer, before anyone was up, I put on my skates and headed to the park."

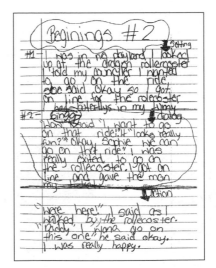

Fig. VI-1 Sophie experiments with leads

HOMEWORK   ***Storytelling, Over and Over***   This afternoon on your way home from school or at home, retell your story again to yourself. Tell it to your mom or to your friend. And think about your story too. Stories get much better if we play them over in our minds, trying to tell them in ways that really affect listeners and readers. Do you want to make people shiver with worry, laugh aloud, gasp, wince? Try telling your story so that you make listeners feel whatever it is you want them to feel.

TAILORING YOUR TEACHING   You may not want to devote more than one minilesson to helping your children choose a seed idea. There is plenty to teach at this juncture, but your children probably can't keep themselves productively busy for days of work on this. If your children are revisiting this minilesson in their second year in writing workshop, you'll want to remind them of what they already know and teach something new.

If your students are skilled at thoughtfully choosing a seed idea . . . they may need help in reflecting on the significance of their chosen seed idea. You may decide to use your own writing. "Watch how I think and write about why I have chosen this entry about seeing my dad cry for the first time." Then I thought aloud about the hidden meaning in the entry, writing as I did so, "Hmm, I picked this entry because I had never seen my dad cry before. But why is that such a big deal? What does this say about me?" I tucked in a comment to the children, "Do you see how I am asking myself questions? Then I write a bit: 'Seeing my dad cry still surprises me to this day. I felt so surprised and worried at this one moment and all I wanted to do was help my dad feel better.'" I paused, and then I asked the children to turn to their seed ideas. "Writers, always reread seed ideas, thinking about why it matters. Writers ask, 'What does it say about me?' Writers, whenever you are choosing a seed idea from your notebook, it is important to ask yourself questions about it to make sure it will be an idea worth developing."

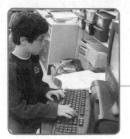

Assessment

Because this lesson marks the end of collecting entries and the start of developing one entry, today marks a bend in the road. You'll probably want to look over your children's writing and notice ways in which they've changed as writers. What seems to be getting better? What hasn't changed?

Try reading this small collection of one child's work. Simeon goes to school at a public school in Harlem and the work you see comes from his first year—in fact, his first few weeks—in a writing workshop. Try reading this work looking for his strengths, assessing his growth, and thinking about future instruction for him. *[Figs. VI-2, VI-3, VI-4, and VI-5]*

The first thing I notice is that this boy has the soul of a writer. He's a dreamer; I love the image of this child, living among the huge buildings in Harlem, thinking about how he'd climb to the rooftop in Trinidad, lie in a hammock under the stars, looking up into the sky and thinking about a lot of stuff. My heart went out to him when I read in the fourth entry about him wearing a pink tuxedo because he was to be the ring bearer in his cousin's wedding, then falling in the mud and feeling so messed up that, as he put it, "I felt to hit somebody."

Next I notice the dazzling, dramatic growth toward understanding the genre of narrative writing. In the fourth entry, Simeon is writing with setting and dialogue. His story focuses on a dramatic event and is even structured like a traditional story with a problem, rising action, and solution.

1. This is my house when I was in Trinidad. It has a lot of memories the motorcycle that I use to ride and I was good at riding it. I also had a nice ladder I use to climb on the roof. I had hammock and up into the sky and think about a lot of stuff up there and I like to in Trinidad because it had a pool in the back yard and I all ways went swimming.

2. My dog Brownie
It saved me
The day my dog died
First day with my dog
One day when I was in Trinidad for summer vacation I was sleep and I heard somebody footsteps my dog Brownie was there with me and the bandit walked to the living room. I was scared so I got up to see who it was I went to get my dad but he was in the bathroom. When I caught my step mother I said look somebody is in our house.

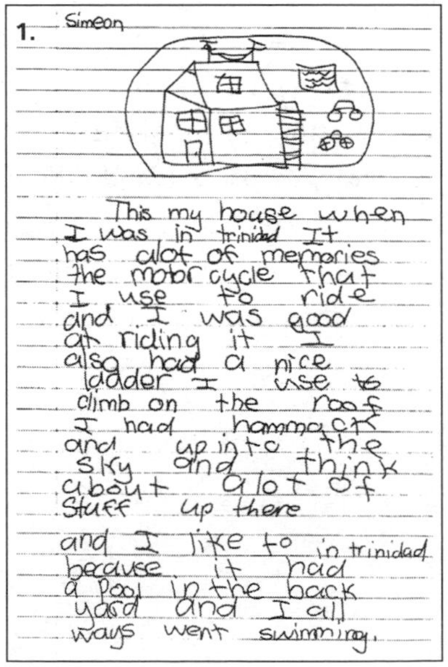

1. Simeon

This my house when I was in trinidad It has alot of memories the motr cycle that I use to ride and I was good at riding it I also had a nice ladder I use to climb on the roof I had hammack and up into the sky and think about alot of Stuff up there and I like to in trinidad because it had a Pool in the back yard and I all ways went swimming.

Fig. VI-2 Simeon

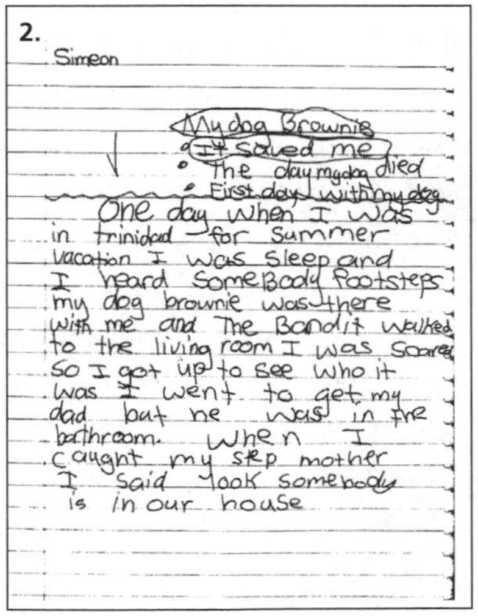

2. Simeon

My dog Brownie
It saved me
The day my dog died
First day with my dog
One day when I was in trinidad for summer vacation I was sleep and I heard SomeBody footsteps my dog brownie was there with me and The Bandit walked to the living room I was Scared So I got up to see who it was I went to get my dad but he was in the bathroom. When I caught my step mother I said look somebody is in our house

Fig. VI-3 Simeon

3. My dad came over and said "What happen with Brownie" I said "I don't know." So we took it to the veterinarian. And he said the dog is getting old When we got home it was useless and I went to sleep and when I got up and looked outside it was dead and I cried a lot so we buried it.

4. One day it was a rainy day and I had on a pink tuxedo and it was my cousins wedding so I was so excited I ran to her. I was like "Are you excited" I said. "Yeah" she said. So I ran to my dad and then I fell in the mud and I was messed up so I got so mad that I felt to hit somebody.

Simeon's syntax suggests he hasn't done a lot of writing. His sentences are composed of a long chain of very simple, short independent clauses (they could be short sentences) chained together with either *and* or *so*.

> <u>So</u> we took it to the veterinarian
> <u>And</u> he said the dog is getting old
> When we got home it was useless <u>and</u>
> I went to sleep <u>and</u> when I got up
> <u>and</u> looked outside it was dead <u>and</u> I
> cried a lot <u>so</u> we buried it.

Simeon would profit from being encouraged to write with end punctuation, trusting that readers will read on to the next sentence without the overuse of connectors. His teacher may want to say "Think one thought, write that thought and then put a period. Think your next thought, write it out and then put the next period." Once he is writing sentences that do not run-on, he could be taught how to include subordinate clauses. Another possibility is to teach him to use alternative connector words so that instead of relying exclusively on *and* or *so* he begins to also use connectors such as *because* or *while*.

Simeon could also be explicitly taught to be more specific in his use of references. When looking at his second entry, for example, I might ask who or what he meant by the word *it*. Simeon would probably answer, "That's my dog, Brownie. He died and we had to bury him." It would help Simeon if his teacher encouraged him to reread, checking to be sure that readers would always know who or what he referred to in his sentences.

By explicitly teaching Simeon something about referents and alternative connectors, his writing can become more cohesive and elaborate. But meanwhile, if Simeon continues to write and read a lot, if he is encouraged to use end punctuation, to convey feelings, and to include dialogue, all of this work will lead him toward more mature syntax.

Fig. VI-4 Simeon

Fig. VI-5 Simeon

REVISING LEADS:
LEARNING FROM PUBLISHED WRITING

*In some ways, using the word **lead*** *to describe that first sentence or first paragraph of a piece of writing is so misleading! A better word might be grab, pull, or yank. Writers of every genre know that the first bit of text on a page must cajole, beg, or even jerk the reader into the text so that she will invest the time and attention it takes to finish, to appreciate, the story.*

Inexperienced writers often become paralyzed when writing the first words or sentences of a story because the words represent a huge mental decision: Out of all the information that I have swimming about in my head, where do I start? I tell students that it's like standing on a high diving board, looking down that scary distance to the water. It seems impossible to step off, yet once we do it, we realize it's not that hard; in fact it's a blast, and we can't wait to climb up the ladder to dive again!

In this session, I help students gather their courage and take the plunge; I try to make it less frightening to get started on a draft by encouraging children to expect revision. They don't pick up the pen and write the lead. Instead, they write several possible leads, then choose one.

By looking closely at several leads in published texts, I help students notice and name some techniques authors use to craft some good leads. I then teach students how to apply one or two of those techniques immediately to improve their own leads. Children's lead sentences are utterly and easily revisable, and when we help them start a story with specific action, dialogue, setting, and so forth, we lead children to write stories that sound like literature. At the same time, we can tuck into this lesson a reminder that writing is pliable, claylike.

IN THIS SESSION, YOU'LL TEACH STUDENTS THAT WRITERS CRAFT THEIR LEADS. YOU'LL SHOW CHILDREN HOW WRITERS CAN LEARN TECHNIQUES TO TRY IN THEIR OWN WORK BY STUDYING PUBLISHED WRITING.

GETTING READY

- Instructions on chalkboard telling children to bring their folders holding their notebooks and drafting booklets and sit with their partners in the meeting area
- Examples of children's leads that show improvement
- *Peter's Chair* (Ezra Jack Keats), *Whistling* (Elizabeth Partridge), *Fireflies* (Julie Brinckloe), *The Witch of Blackbird Pond* (Elizabeth Speare), *Because of Winn-Dixie* (Kate DiCamillo), or any familiar books with great leads
- Example leads on chart paper
- Chart paper and markers
- Two different leads in mind for your story from previous session
- Qualities of Good Personal Narrative Writing chart
- Plan for how you will tell your story using the pages of a drafting booklet

See CD-ROM for resources

MINILESSON

Revising Leads: Learning from Published Writing

CONNECTION

Celebrate that your children's stories sound like literature.

"Writers, something magical happened in this classroom yesterday. You told your stories, and then I read aloud the leads that Mem Fox and Dav Pilkney and Donald Crews wrote to their picture books. And you told your stories again—only this time, the stories sounded like literature!"

"Lizzie's first version of her story about reading with her reading buddy began like this."

> My buddy is absent. She's sick so Mrs. B found another k
> student for me.

"Listen to the miraculous changes that happened after Lizzie heard other authors! She wrote several new drafts of leads, and each one sounds like it could be the start to a picture book on our library shelves! Listen."

> On a warm September afternoon, we strolled outside to
> find our buddies.

> I scan the playground, in search of my kindergarten
> buddy. "Why don't I look from someplace high I think like
> the slides! I sprint across the playground and using my
> legs and arms, I climb up the tan colored slide. This I
> think should give me a good view! I check again. She's
> nowhere in sight. Puzzled, I go down the spiral slide,
> without a clue about my buddy. Wth my head down,
> I begin walking slowly toward the steps, where the
> kindergarteners poured onto the jungle gym.

Name the teaching point. In this case, tell children that writers improve leads by studying the work of authors and then applying their techniques.

"Today I want to teach you that the lead in a story matters. It matters tremendously because a great lead sets us up to write a great story."

COACHING

Learning to read as a writer is not a small undertaking. Not so long ago, we were coaxing these same children to learn to see right through the words on the page, into the story. Now, in this session, we are asking them to do the opposite, to step back from the story and to think about the words themselves and how they are put together to make the story. It is easier for children to do this when the examples we use are ones they've already read. They have already thought about the story, and now they can think about how the story is told.

"More specifically, I want to teach you that we don't just improve our leads by trying and trying to make them better on our own, or by simply reading beautiful leads written by other authors. We improve our leads by closely examining work we admire, asking, 'What exactly has this author done that I could try?'"

TEACHING
Demonstrate how to study the work of mentor authors. Show children that setting, tone, and action in leads can create mood.

"Watch how I study the lead of Ezra Jack Keats' story *Peter's Chair*." I turned to chart paper on which I'd written the lead and reread it aloud to myself. I read it once, then reread it. "Do you see that I read and then reread it, and I read it quietly but aloud to myself? I'm trying to get the feeling for the lead."

> Peter stretched as high as he could.
> There! His tall building was finished. CRASH!
> Down it came.
> "Shhhh," called his mother. "You'll have
> to play more quietly. Remember we have a
> new baby in the house."

Again I read the text. "I'm thinking, 'What has Ezra Jack Keats done that I could do?'" I muttered to myself.

"The first thing I'm noticing is that Ezra Jack Keats has Peter doing a small action in the very first line—if this were a play, as soon as the curtain opened, the main character would be up on stage doing something. He is putting the last brick on the top of his building. In a second, the building will collapse and we'll imagine Peter's feeling of disappointment. I also notice dialogue—Peter's mother's words are here." I reread the starting lines again and said, "Right from the start, Keats has the main character doing something very specific, very particular. If this were a movie, I know what I'd see on the screen—and it'd be the main character doing a small action. I'd know he would first do something and then he would think something. Then his mother would speak. In this lead, the author includes these elements:"

- the main character doing a specific action
- the main character saying or thinking something
- another character doing an action

It's not necessary for you to use these exact pieces of literature. Refer to children's books you and your class love. You may need to practice putting into words what you see the lead achieving and how it achieves it. It's not easy to explain the work a given sentence does in a way that helps young writers try the same thing!

Notice that this story begins with an action, then there's dialogue. Eventually I'll teach children that stories are often built from a tapestry of actions, dialogue, and thoughts.

You may find that at first, some children interpret "the main character doing a specific action" very generally, and in that form, it won't help their writing much. They might start their writing with a line like, "We drove to the airport to pick up my mother." It is important for you to notice that the child who starts a narrative in such a way is attempting to start the story with the character doing something. The action is still general and therefore it won't be an especially effective lead. Still, celebrate the child's approximation, and help her understand that starting with a small action might, instead, mean starting, "I walked through the big doors and into the airport."

You could easily pull different replicable qualities from Keats' lead. Perhaps your list would include:
- *one character acting and another responding.*
- *actions that reveal a character's wants and struggles.*
Guard against telling children too many characteristics of a strong lead all at once—the real work of the session is to write differently, not just to talk differently about writing!

Demonstrate taking what we've learned from the published writing and using it to improve our own writing.

"So let me think how I can use those same techniques in my story about my dad crying. I want to try a lead that starts with me doing an action, or maybe with me talking. Um . . . I don't *really* remember exactly what I did, but I'll write what I probably did."

> I held the phone receiver against my chest.
> "Dad, it's for you," I said. "I think it's your sister."

"Did you see how I tried to follow part of the pattern that Ezra Jack Keats set? That's one way the lead to my story could go." Then I said, "Let's look at the lead another author has written. Let's look at Elizabeth Partridge's *Whistling*."

> "Jake," Daddy whispers. "It's almost time." I poke my head out of
> my warm sleeping bag. The air is tingly and cold.

"Partridge also uses action and, this time, the lead also establishes the setting," I said. "And again she incorporates the character's exact words. I will try the same thing in another draft of a lead."

> I held the phone receiver against my chest.
> "Dad, it's for you," I said. "I think it's your sister."
> "At this hour?" Dad said, his face clouded with worry as
> he took the phone from me.

"See how I put in the time to add some more setting? I chose to put in that part about it being very early so my reader might know why my dad and I were already worried the instant the phone rang."

ACTIVE ENGAGEMENT

Share a lead written by one student. Ask children to revise the lead out loud with their partners by using an action or a setting.

"Writers, listen to the work Milan has done. He's writing about a Tae Kwon Do meet. In his first lead, he begins with dialogue—the words the announcer says. That's one way the authors we studied started their stories. Listen." *[Fig. VII-1]*

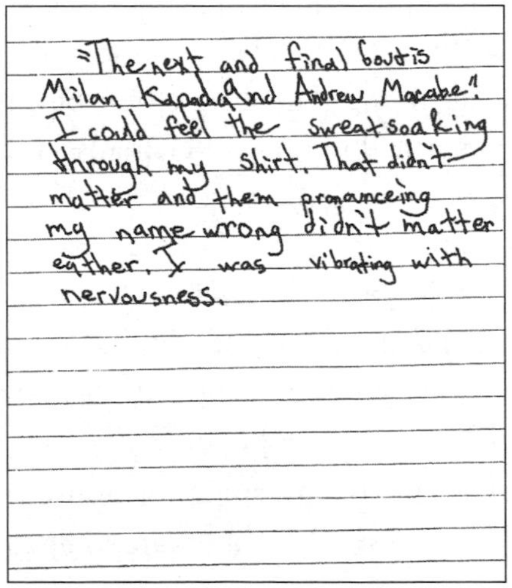

> "The next and final bout is Milan Kapada and Andrew
> Macabe." I could feel the sweat soaking through my shirt.
> That didn't matter and them pronouncing my name wrong
> didn't matter either. I was vibrating with nervousness.

If the goal of the session is to teach children that writers draft and revise lead sentences, and to show children some of the qualities of an effective lead, then it is much more helpful to examine the leads to several texts rather than to read one lead . . . and then continue reading that entire text. When we incorporate texts that we and the children already know well into our minilessons, it is reasonable to examine just one aspect of one text, then of another text.

Fig. VII-1 Milan

"Did you hear the exact words of the announcer start us off? Now, let's pretend to be Milan for a minute and see what other leads we can try for this story. He might end up sticking with this one, but let's just experiment for a moment. With your partner, try writing another lead for this same story, this time starting not with dialogue but with an action or with the setting. You won't know the real story since you aren't Milan, but that's okay, just imagine what it might have been like." I paused while partners worked together to draft a lead for Milan's story.

"Those are some great leads you are making! Before Milan rewrote his lead, he studied *Fireflies!* by Julie Brinckloe."

On a summer evening
I looked up from dinner,
through the open window to the backyard.
It was growing dark.
My treehouse was a black shape in the tree
and I wouldn't go up there now.
But something flickered there, a moment.
I looked, and it was gone.

"He noticed that she began by showing the setting in a way that created a mood, so he made a lead patterned after hers." *[Fig. VII-2]*

The stadium dark with one single light.
The spotlight shining on my face, the stadium quiet as the forest in winter.
I could feel the sweat soak through my shirt, I was vibrating with nervousness all around me. I see the referee standing there in the light waiting for me.

"Wow, that's quite a lead, right? Do you see how he added to the setting in a way that created a mood just like Brinckloe did?"

As you listen to the children tell their revised leads to their partners, you will soon see how well your minilesson is taking hold. If it doesn't seem that the kids yet understand how to examine a lead, see what it does, and try doing the same thing, you could extend this minilesson by repeating the process again for them with another mentor text's lead.

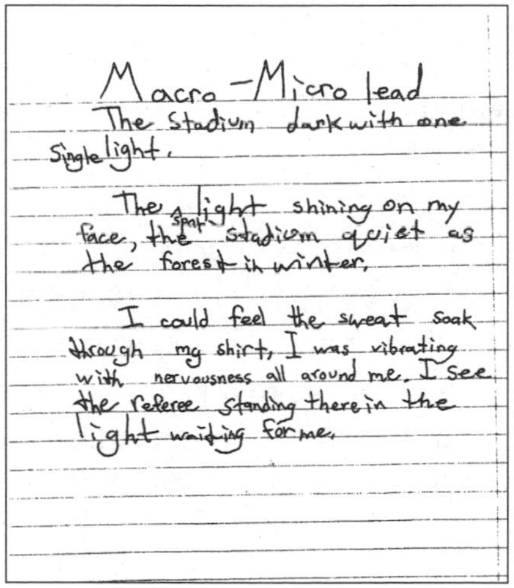
Macro-Micro lead
The Stadium dark with one Single light.
The spot light shining on my face, the stadium quiet as the forest in winter.
I could feel the sweat soak through my shirt, I was vibrating with nervousness all around me. I see the referee standing there in the light waiting for me.

Fig. VII-2 Milan

Restate your teaching point. Send children off to write new leads, using the techniques they've learned from mentor authors.

"If we want our stories to continue sounding like literature, we need to closely examine the work of other authors, asking, 'What has this author done that I could do?' Today we did that with leads. You noticed that some authors begin their stories by telling us actions, and some start with dialogue, or with setting. I'm going to add that to our Qualities of Good Personal Narrative Writing chart."

I believe that children are well served by working on their leads early in their writing process. The leads can bring life and possibility to their writing—they can lift the level of the whole piece of writing to follow. Leads can also point out new directions stories can take, and it's much easier to explore those directions before the whole draft is written than it is afterwards.

Qualities of Good Personal Narrative Writing

- Write a little seed story; don't write all about a giant watermelon topic.
- Zoom in so you tell the most important parts of the story.
- Include true, exact details from the movie you have in your mind.
- Begin with a strong lead—maybe action, setting, dialogue, or a combination which creates a mood.

"When you go back to your tables to write, think about what you have learned about writing leads and then try out three or four different leads in your notebook. Try starting with the setting, or actions, or dialogue, or a combination of these. If you'd like, study the leads other authors have written, to expand your repertoire of options. And from this day on, for the rest of your life, always remember that your lead matters—it merits attention."

WRITING AND CONFERRING

Teaching Writers to Talk Well about Their Writing

I often remind children that on any given day, their work during the writing workshop should draw not just upon that day's minilesson, but on all the strategies they've learned. Similarly, your teaching needs to draw upon all the strategies you've taught. Today, however, is a bit of an exception because everyone will be doing the same work—studying and drafting leads. The one prior lesson you can draw upon, though, is the one helping children consider their role in a conference.

Children will be able to assume their roles only if you set them up to do so. Try starting your conferences by asking children to teach you what they've been working on as writers. "How's it going?" you might ask. "What are you trying to do with the lead you are writing?"

If a child doesn't respond to your questions by teaching you what he or she is trying to do, give the writer some feedback. "When I ask, 'What are you trying to do as a writer?' I'm expecting you to tell me not so much what your story is about, but the decisions you are making over how to write the story well. What did you notice another author doing that you are trying to do? How's it going?" In this instance, it should be relatively easy for a child to tell you, "I'm trying to begin with an action." Prepare to extend that. "How'd you decide on this particular action? What other ones did you consider?" You may end up teaching some children that it helps to start with actions that are close to the main event of the story, or that it helps to select actions that reveal what the character cares about and that set us up to understand the character's main struggles. Of course, *Peter's Chair* can help you make that point!

You can enter today anticipating that some children will pop out a lead and want to call it a day. Be ready to help those children embrace revision, perhaps by shuttling between reading and writing leads. If your own memories of revising writing are such that you cringe at the prospect of revision, try to put your

> MID-WORKSHOP
> TEACHING POINT   *Using Quotation Marks* "Writers, can I have your eyes and your attention? I love that you are trying out different leads for your story. That's amazing. Now I want to teach you a rule for using quotation marks, because many of you are trying leads that begin with people talking. You need quotation marks; otherwise the sections where you have people talking will be confusing."
>
> "Quotation marks signal the exact words a person has said. They let the reader know that someone is talking. Let's look at the lead from Elizabeth Partridge's *Whistling* (2003) looking closely at where she places her quotation marks."
>
> > "Jake," Daddy whispers. "It's almost time." I poke my head out of my warm sleeping bag. The air is tingly and cold.
>
> "Notice that she surrounds the daddy's exact words in quotation marks. The quoted section begins with a capital and ends with punctuation. It's usually a comma or a period. And the quotation marks have surrounded it all."
>
> *continued on next page*

distaste for revision out of your mind and role-play the part of being a writer who loves revision. Like most other writers, I love tinkering with sentences until they are just right. I listen to the sounds of the words, fiddling with the punctuation, syntax, and word choice until the sentence sounds pleasing. I say my sentences aloud, testing them for sound just like I say proposed names for a newborn baby aloud. I mimic the sentences of writers I admire. Act as if you can't possibly imagine how it could be that a child doesn't love this work as you do.

continued from previous page

"Let's try this together right now. I am going to talk. As I begin, capture the beginning of my talk by hooking your two fingers on your left hand. When I finish talking, catch my last words with two fingers on your right hand." I did this, and they made quotation marks in the air. "You can do the same thing in writing by using quotation marks. Look over your story right now and check to see if you have included talk. If you have, make sure your quotation marks surround the exact words being said, and that what is said includes its punctuation."

I moved among the class, coaching children to help each other punctuate the dialogue they'd already written. This seemingly straightforwad lesson was not at all straightforward when children tried to apply it to their drafts. Some, like Takeshi [*Fig. VII-3*], had sections of text in which one character and then another talked back and forth, interjecting brief comments. When the text didn't name the speaker or include any actions, it was often difficult to discern when one voice ended and another began. Then, too, some writers summarized conversations rather than quoting verbatim.

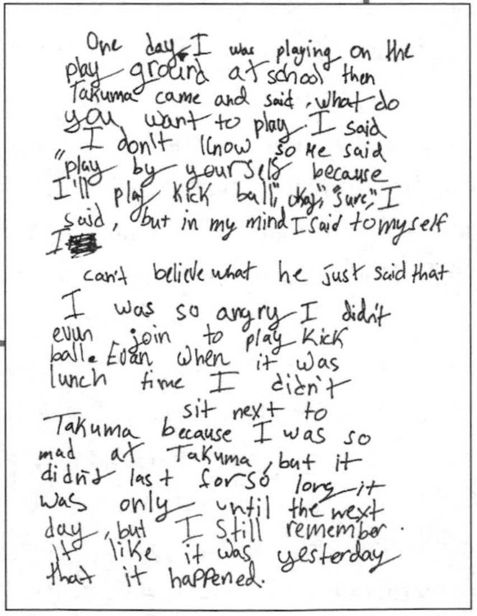

One day I was playing on the playground at school then Takuma came and said, what do you want to play. I said I don't know so he said "play by yourself because I'll play kickball." "Okay." "Sure," I said, but in my mind I said to myself I can't believe that he just said that.

Fig. VII-3 Takeshi's first entry, with beginning attempts to mark the dialogue using quotation marks

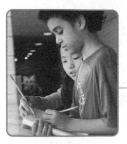

SHARE

Listening to Leads

Convene children on the rug. Ask writers to share their best work of the day—in this case, a favorite lead.

"Milan's whole story will be different because he's taken the time to try different leads, and modeled his leads after those he admires in books. I know many of you did similar work. Would you share your leads with your partner? Talk over the techniques you tried to use."

I listened as Rebecca read her favorite lead to Sofiya, and Sofiya in turn shared her choices. *[Figs. VII-4 and VII-5]*

Rebecca Leads:

I peered into my bag. Nothing. No gym tights, no leotard. I felt tears welling up in my eyes. I thought back: yes, no, yes. I hadn't putten my leotard back in the bag. I jerked down my head and pulled my tee shirt over my school tights.

Sofiya Leads:

"I like snakes, don't you, Sofiya?"
She's got to be joking.
"No I don't!"
I don't know since when, but I dont like snakes.

I was sitting in the circle waiting. What kind of animal was the lady about to bring out? A bird, a parrot, a spider or two, maybe a fish in a bowl of water? A snake!

I listen in as children share with one another to show my interest in hearing what they have to say. Listening also gives me important insights into the children's understandings and interpretations of what I have asked them to do.

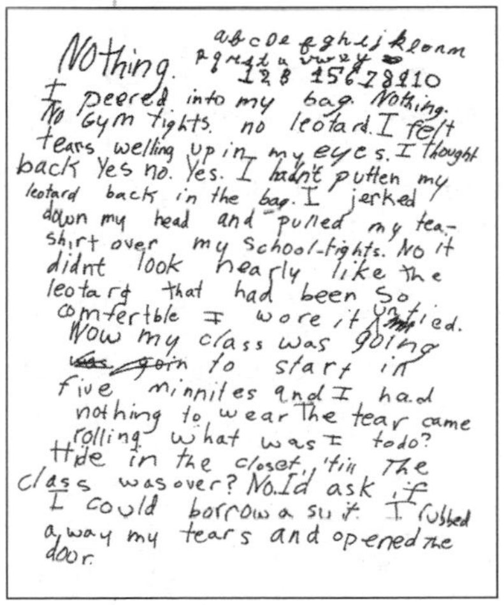
Nothing. abcdefghijklmn opqrstuvwxyz 123 45678910
I peered into my bag. Nothing. No Gym tights. no leotard. I felt tears welling up in my eyes. I thought back Yes no. Yes. I hadn't putten my leotard back in the bag. I jerked down my head and pulled my tea-shirt over my school-tights. No it didnt look nearly like the leotard that had been so comfertble I wore it untied. Now my class was going to start in five minnites and I had nothing to wear The tear came rolling what was I todo? Hide in the closet, 'till The class was over? No. Id ask if I could borrow a suit. I rubbed away my tears and opened the door.

Fig. VII-4 Rebecca

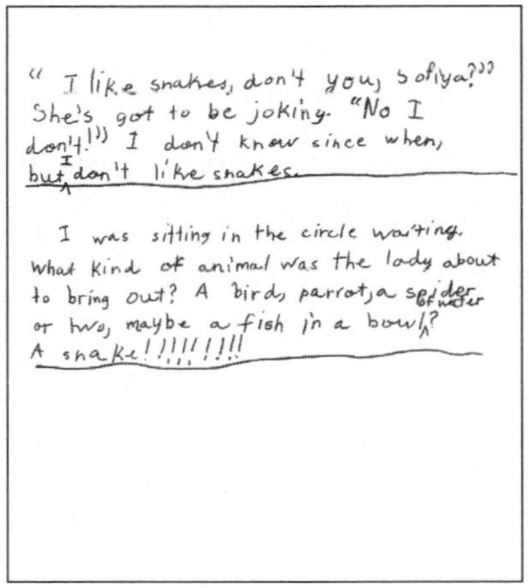
"I like snakes, don't you, Sofiya?" She's got to be joking. "No I don't!" I don't know since when, but I don't like snakes.

I was sitting in the circle waiting. What kind of animal was the lady about to bring out? A bird, parrot, a spider or two, maybe a fish in a bowl of water? A snake!!!!!!!!!

Fig. VII-5 Sofiya

Show children the next steps. Introduce drafting booklets.

"I want to show you what I mean about how your story will flow from your lead. Right now, take out the blank booklets you were storytelling into yesterday. Those booklets are what writers call *drafting booklets*. This is where you'll write your rough draft story. Right now, copy the version of your lead which you've selected onto the first page of this booklet, and then try telling your story across the pages of the booklet. Watch how I repeat the lead I chose and then storytell, touching each page as I say the next bit of my story."

> "Dad," I said. "The phone's for you." Dad arched his eyebrows as if to say, "For me? So early?" All of us kids looked up from our sections of the <u>Sunday Times</u>. We listened while Dad said into the phone, "Hello?" The silence was deadening as we waited.

I turned the page.

> "Oh no," we heard Dad say. "When did it happen?" My mind raced through catastrophes. Who'd died? Who was hurt?

Again I turned the page. "Do you see how I turn the page when I shift to the next part?" Then said, as if dictating:

> A few minutes later . . .

Pausing, I said, "Try telling your story across the pages of your booklet!"

In this Share session, my reference to drafting booklets sets children up for the next day's lesson. By having each child copy his lead onto his first page, a lot of the preparation work for tomorrow's workshop is done ahead of time. This will allow me to get right to the point of what I want to teach in the next session—how to write a draft.

I find that if I want children to tell or to write a story with a clear plot, with one event leading to the next, it helps for them to write across a sequence of pages. If your classroom has a shortage of paper, a single piece of notebook paper can be folded in half to create a booklet with four pages.

HOMEWORK **Studying Leads** When a chef goes out to dinner, he pays attention to the sauces and the spices he admires, thinking, "How was this made?" Similarly, you will want to find sections of the books you've read that you admire and pause, asking, "How was this made?"

Cynthia Rylant once said, "I learned how to write from writers. I didn't know any personally. But I read." She is not alone. The writers we love will all agree that they learned to write from authors. So tonight, would each of you spend some time reading like a writer, noticing not only what authors say, but also how they say it. Bookmark places in beloved books where an author has used a technique you'd like to try.

Especially notice leads. Come to school ready to talk about what you learned by studying the work of a pro. For example, last night I noticed that books often begin with a paragraph that establishes a big context, then zooms in to a small action. Sometimes these leads seem shaped like a funnel. For example, *The Witch of Blackbird Pond* begins:

> On a morning in mid-April, 1687, the brigantine *Dolphin* left the open sea, sailed briskly across the sound to the wide mouth of the Connecticut River and into Saybrook Harbor. Kit Tyler had been on the forecastle deck since daybreak, standing close to the rail, staring hungrily at the first sight of land for five weeks. "There's Connecticut Colony," a voice spoke in her ear. (Speare, 1958, p. 1)

Because of Winn-Dixie also begins by establishing context, but when I compared this lead with the lead to *Witch of Blackbird Pond*, it seems to me that in *Because of Winn-Dixie* it is the narrator and main character, Opal, who creates the context:

> My name is India Opal Buloni, and last summer my daddy, the preacher, sent me to the store for a box of macaroni-and-cheese, some white rice, and two tomatoes and I came back with a dog. This is what happened: I walked into the produce section of the Winn-Dixie grocery store to pick out my two tomatoes. (DiCamillo, 2000, p. 7)

So tonight do similar research. Come to your own conclusions about techniques authors use that you could emulate.

TAILORING YOUR TEACHING

If your students each write only one kind of lead over and over again . . . you might introduce them to a variety of leads, each other's leads, as inspiration. One way to do that is to ask every student to star a lead he's written in his writer's notebook and then leave the notebook open at his writing spot in the room. Then, ask everyone to walk around the room, reading and researching the types of leads on display. Then, gather writers together, and ask them to discuss their findings. After you have charted the types of leads they've discovered, suggest they try making their own leads in these new ways—first aloud with their partners and later independently in their writer's notebooks.

If many children in the room have all written the same kind of lead, this sort of museum walk won't be inspirational to writers. In that case, you will want to find leads from published writing and make those leads available to students to study and discuss and imitate.

Another way to approach this problem, as any problem, is to simply point out to the students the patterns you notice in their work, and why the pattern isn't one to settle into. Then ask children to brainstorm with you possible solutions to the problem. Then, you can chart these suggestions and send children off to try them, taking note of which invented strategies help and which ones don't, revising them along the way.

If your students don't seem excited by spending time revising leads . . . bring excitement to the topic by making a big deal out of leads you notice throughout the day. Show children your collection of "favorite leads" that you've accumulated over the years (or maybe over the last few days) and ask their opinions of them. Make a fuss when chapters start with great leads in your read-aloud book. Bring in leads you find in magazine articles that are either horrid or wonderful, and ask children to join you in thinking about them and collecting others. Start a bulletin board of great leads from the students' notebooks; ask students to keep an eye out for leads in their own and others' notebooks to join the display. Reiterate overheard comments that could make great leads, "Did you all hear what Paul said just now when he was talking about how things used to be arranged on that back shelf? He said 'Back when the daisies were alive . . .'. That could make a great lead to a narrative if you were looking for that particular ominous tone, don't you think?"

COLLABORATING WITH COLLEAGUES

It may appear as if your instruction in this session has put a spotlight on the characteristics of an effective lead, but really your teaching in this session, as is usual within this unit, has focused above all on ways children can improve the quality of their personal narrative writing.

If your education in the qualities of good writing was anything like mine, you'll probably find that you are learning about narrative writing right alongside your children. Know, first of all, that you are not alone.

When I was in school, I was taught to write with my five senses, to use adjectives and adverbs, and to include similes and alliteration. But I was not taught anything else about narrative writing until I was out of graduate school and teaching third graders. I wanted to write an article about my students and therefore got hold of Donald Murray's *A Writer Teaches Writing*, and the rest is history.

I strongly advise you to read some books on good writing as you teach this unit and the one that follows it. I also suggest you talk with colleagues about this professional reading, working together to use what you learn in your own writing and teaching. Start with chapters 4 and 5 of Katherine Bomer's *Writing a Life*. Then try Ralph Fletcher's *What a Writer Needs* or the

book that started me on my journey, Murray's *A Writer Teaches Writing*. Or William Zinsser's *On Writing Well* if you want to teach toward clear, simple prose. Or Barry Lane's *After THE END*.

But you needn't learn qualities of good writing only by reading professional books. Good writing itself will teach you. Open any great narrative text and put to words what the author has done. Try examining the first chapter of Kate DiCamillo's *Because of Winn-Dixie* (mentioned in the Homework section). Try any page of Patricia MacLachlan's *Journey*. Find "Mr. Entwhistle" in Jean Little's *Hey World, Here I Am*. It's two pages long and my colleagues and I spent hours poring over it. If you hear yourself describing these texts by relying on clichés, saying, "The author paints a picture," force yourself to go past those words to be more precise, exact, replicable. What exactly has the author done that you could try?

Once you name the technique, what's there to stop you from trying it yourself? Pull out the entry you began earlier and see how your sentences turn out, rewritten under the influence of Julie Brinckloe, Jane Yolen, or Alma Flor Ada.

WRITING DISCOVERY DRAFTS

The world is bursting with options, *but a writer and a teacher both must reach into the hurly-burly of life and select just one word, then the next—just one teaching point, then the next.*

I've helped thousands of teachers launch writing workshops, and there is a dazzling array of options for how one might proceed into drafting. Do we begin by teaching children to make a timeline of the event, then tell the story following that timeline? Do we begin by studying a touchstone text closely, then encouraging children to write in the same fashion or with the same structure? Do we start the year with an emphasis on content only? "Teach your readers what you know," we could say, postponing discussion about structure until later.

Out of all the options, I've chosen to channel children toward writing well-structured, chronological, focused narratives because I've come to believe that structure is absolutely fundamental to good writing, and that children—and teachers, too—care more about writing when it turns out well.

I've decided to put forth the concept of a discovery draft because I want children to understand that drafting is an exploratory process that resembles shaping in clay more than inscribing in marble. I want children to write fast and long so they feel that a first draft is tentative and improvable. Then, too, I've chosen to emphasize writing discovery drafts because I find that sometimes when children are fast-writing, those who have regarded themselves as struggling writers find an internal source of power and surprise themselves (and us too) by writing with a passion and freshness that takes our breath away.

IN THIS SESSION, YOU WILL SHOW CHILDREN THAT ONE WAY WRITERS DRAFT IS BY WRITING FAST AND LONG IN ORDER TO GET A WHOLE STORY DOWN ON PAPER AS IT COMES TO MIND.

GETTING READY

- Instructions on chalkboard telling children to bring their folders with drafting booklets to the meeting area
- Piece of writing, preferably a child's discovery draft, copied onto a transparency
- Overhead projector
- Chart paper and markers
- See CD-ROM for resources

MINILESSON

Writing Discovery Drafts

CONNECTION

Remind children of the work they've done so far in the process of drafting, and tell them they are ready to go one step farther.

"So far, you've rehearsed for your writing by storytelling and by thinking of leads. Now is the time to write a draft!"

"There is no one right way to go about writing a draft. This year, I'll teach you a variety of strategies that writers use to draft, and I'll ask you to try them on for size. You know how we try shirts on for size, saying, 'This one is too bulky for me,' or 'This one's arms are too short for me,' and 'This one is just right.' In a similar fashion, writers try writing processes on for size. Some writers find one method of proceeding fits best; others prefer another. But no matter which strategy, all writers rehearse for writing, and all writers write a rough draft. And when we are done with our rough drafts, all writers reread and revise what we've written, just like we will do."

Name the teaching point. In this case, teach children that some writers fast-write discovery drafts to get their story out on paper.

"Today I'm going to suggest that you all try writing a discovery draft. Writers sometimes decide that after carefully crafting each word of a lead, it's a good next step to do the opposite kind of thing and just fix our eyes on our subject, writing our story fast and long, without stopping."

TEACHING

Use a metaphor to tell children that writers sometimes fast-write a discovery draft. Tell how this is done and show an example.

"A friend of mine is studying to be an artist, and in her class on painting portraits, her professor has taught her that one way to get unbelievable power into her drawing is to look at her subject, to gaze deeply and totally at the person she is portraying, and to sketch what she sees without even looking down at her paper. She keeps her eyes on the person, and sketches with the goal of putting down the truth of what she sees—all of it—onto the page."

COACHING

Notice that whenever I summarize the work children have done to date, I try to name parts of the writing process I hope they will cycle through again and again. I know that when children first progress through the writing process, they sometimes proceed with tunnel vision, seeing only the next step. In the movie Platoon, *a character says that war means putting one foot in front of the other, trying to see three inches in front of us. I know that by retelling the broad vista of the writing process, I help children gain a greater sense of control.*

Once a thoughtful lead has pointed a way through the story, the draft can follow more easily.

The friend I am referring to here is the writer Georgia Heard. She writes about this technique in her book Writing Toward Home. *(1995, p.121)*

"Writers do something similar. We fill ourselves with the true thing that happened to us. We remember the very start of the episode and storytell what happened first (only we scrawl the story onto the paper rather than tell it) and then, without worrying much about perfect spelling or word choice or anything, we keep our minds fixed on everything that happened and write fast and long without stopping."

"Let me show you Felix's discovery draft. I'm going to show it using the overhead projector so you can see that it doesn't need to be well spelled—listen to the power of this fast-write." [Fig. VIII-1]

"Felix, wake up, we have to go to the church." We went to the church. I started seeing all my family members. I did not know what was happening. Then I saw a big box coming out of the church. My grandma laied her head against the big brown box and stared crying. I tugged on her shirt, "Grandma grandma what's in there?"

"Just look."

I stared through the screen. It was my grandfather. He was as pale as glue. "Grandfather get out of there, come and help me make the paper airplanes you make! Don't go. Don't! I am sorry about what I said to you." I knocked on the screen. It did not help. He would not wake up. "I want to see my grandfather now." I knew now what was going on. My grandfather had just died. I did not know what to say to myself. I felt scared. What was I going to do without my grandpa?

No no no. There's no paper airplanes that he's going to make me. Who is going to say the funny stories everyday? Whose going to put a smile on me everyday? I stop. A tear runs through my face. I stomp over to my grandfather but my uncle holds me back. I see his white face. His hard boney hands on his sides.

"Grandpa, let's go to the window and throw the paper airplanes." I see him coming, his pale white face grinning at me. He slowly starts walking with a long brown stick, his weak hands holding on the stick.

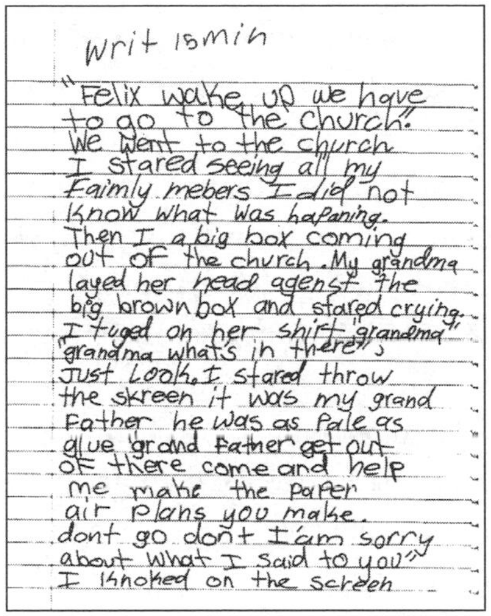

Fig. VIII-1 The first page of Felix's draft.

Felix has gone through school with the reputation of being a struggling writer. Like some other children with this reputation, Felix is in fact a very powerful writer—but one who struggles with the conventions of written language. He needs explicit instruction in these conventions, but more important, he needs a teacher who can see the power of his work. This piece reveals his difficulties with the surface mechanics of language, yet it also reveals his willingness to write honestly, with deep emotion, and his enviable gift for simile: "pale as glue." I want children to see Felix's handwriting and spelling errors because I want every child in the classroom to realize that powerful, honest writing is within grasp. Spelling well does not necessarily correlate with writing well. Both are important. Children who care about writing and believe they have something to say will be much more willing to do the work of becoming more effective spellers.

ACTIVE ENGAGEMENT

Recruit children to be willing to write discovery drafts and channel them towards being ready to start this work.

"A famous writer named Faulkner once said, 'There are some kinds of writing that you have to do very fast, like riding a bicycle on a tightrope' (Murray 1990, p. 143). To stay up on bikes, we need to pedal fast and go full speed ahead! Many writers find that in order to make listeners feel what they want them to feel, it helps to write fast and long. Today we'll do that, writing the same stories (only better) that we told each other yesterday."

"To get started, reread the lead you already copied onto page one of your drafting booklet, and then just touch each page of the booklet and say the story you'll write on that page. Do this for the whole story, spreading it out across pages, and then go back to page one. Reread your lead and remember the beginning of the event. Pretend you are storytelling the story to listeners. Make them feel whatever you want them to feel. Start writing and write fast, keeping your eyes on the true story. Then I said to children, "Get started while you are here on the carpet, and once you feel like you are ready to keep going, go to your seat."

LINK

Remind writers of what you've taught today, and tell them they can use this new strategy for the rest of their lives.

"So writers, you know that we sometimes storytell a story to ourselves or aloud before we write it, as a way to take a story idea and stretch it into a wonderful, long story, the kind of story that can give people goose bumps. Today, you learned that writers often write discovery drafts, writing fast and long in order to get your story down on the page. Try on this way of drafting just like you might try on a shirt. See if it fits!"

If this is the first time you have asked your students to write while sitting together in a clump of bodies in the meeting area, you may run into predictable problems with kids finding it difficult to sit still, to concentrate, and to get words flowing onto the paper. Don't despair! Every aspect of writing workshop requires practicing over and over until it becomes routine. Throughout the units in this curriculum, there will be opportunities for children to practice and get better at both "writing in the air" and literally writing while sitting in the meeting area. Also, as your students become more independent and begin to draw from your instruction to help themselves get better at writing, they will welcome any and all variations on the usual procedures as a new way to stretch themselves!

The poet and novelist Naomi Shihab Nye says it this way: "Write luxuriously, abundantly, fill whole pages, making little notes to yourself in the margins. Don't worry about saying it perfectly." (Flynn and McPhillips 2000, p. 46)

WRITING AND CONFERRING

Supporting Writing Fluency

When the children in your room are writing discovery drafts, trying to write quickly and for a long time, your conferring will probably be a little different than usual. Most of the time when you confer, you won't hesitate to interrupt children at work since you know that your interruption—your conference—will provide a strategy to help them strengthen their work. The nature of conferring is that you engage with children in the midst of writing, teaching them about their work as they are doing it. If the conference is not an interruption, it's probably not your strongest conference.

Today's situation is a bit different, however. Today, many of the children are pushing themselves specifically to write without interruption—to write fast and long. Interrupting them to determine if there is a way to help them write without interruption might seem like a contradiction. On the other hand, if you can tell without much research that some children could be writing faster and longer and stronger, you should go ahead and interrupt them to confer.

> **MID-WORKSHOP TEACHING POINT** — ***Rereading to Build Writing Stamina*** "Writers, can I have your eyes and your attention? When I feel myself lagging in energy, I reread my writing. But I reread in a special way. I reread it to myself as if the story is an utter masterpiece."
>
> "I don't fuss over the details; if a word is awry I mentally fix it, and keep going because I want to read with a rapt focus on my content, filling myself with the story so it wells up in me. When I come to the last word I've written, I just pick up my pen and write for dear life, scrawling down the page."
>
> "So writers, if you are lagging in energy and want to give yourself a second wind, pause and reread. Reread your own writing as if it is a masterpiece, and let your rereading give you a boost for more writing."

- If a child is tapping the page and staring into space instead of writing, you might teach the child that he can get a running start into writing by going to the first page of the booklet and storytelling the parts that belong on each page.

- If a child is using the word wall to help her spell a word exactly right and that process is more than a slight diversion from getting the story down, you might teach the child that she can write the word as best she can, circle it so as to keep writing and then come back to it later to rethink the troublesome spelling.

- If a child is stopping to erase, you might teach the child to put a light line through the part of the writing that is leading him astray and simply keep writing.

- If a child is thinking and rethinking how any given part of the draft goes, teach that child to make marginal notes about alternatives to how she's written the draft and just keep going.

- If a child is judging every sentence, encourage the child to think, "Oh well, I'll just do the best I can and keep going."

SHARE

Savoring Favorite Parts

Remind writers of the strategies they already know for giving themselves more writing stamina. Lay out a new one.

"Writers, in our share session today, I want to teach you another strategy that writers use to give themselves that 'second wind'—one in addition to rereading our writing like it is a masterpiece. Sometimes we take time to reread parts of our writing that we know just sing, parts that we are proud of because we have found the right words to express what we want to say. When I do this in my writing room at home, I pretend I'm on a stage, reading that particular part of my writing out loud to an audience. I use my best reading voice; I even give the characters different voices. I slow way down when I come to the dramatic parts; I speed my voice up when I come to exciting parts. Sometimes I ask people in my family to listen to the small part of my writing that I think I've written well."

Ask students to try this strategy by reading favorite parts to the whole class.

"So take a moment to reread what you wrote today. Choose a phrase or sentence you particularly love, either because of the way it sounds or because you think it is exactly true. When you have found a section you like, show me with a thumbs up." I waited until most thumbs went up. "Let's read these parts to everyone, into the circle. Read your line whenever you are ready, whenever there is a space for you to speak. Let's begin now."

I gestured towards Ahra. She read, "The trees were swaying back and forth like they were dancing." My eyes caught Tasnim's. She whispered, "My bravery was blowing away with the wind." I smiled and nodded towards Genesis. She read, "The cake was mush as if I was holding oatmeal." Joseph followed with, "The icicles pointed north." Soon the room was filled with powerful phrases and favorite lines.

Voice your appreciation for the writing the children have read aloud. Remind children to use this strategy when they need writing energy.

"Wow, what exquisitely chosen words you've read! Can you feel all the writing energy in the room right now? I bet you can hardly wait for the next opportunity to write! Remember, you can always do something like this when you need writing energy!"

Notice that this is a new way of conducting the Share session for this unit, but it's one that you will see my colleagues and me use often, with variations, throughout the school year. We love this one because it reminds us to celebrate the power and beauty of writing. We forget sometimes, in keeping our noses to the grindstone, to appreciate where we are and how far we have come.

Even though there might not be a formal teaching point in this type of Share, the lessons learned carry more weight than you might imagine. Children learn, for instance, that their words have the power to move others to laugh, to frown, or simply to think about something. They learn that everyone in the community has written something beautiful or amazing, and not just the "good writers." This Share also spurs revision because sometimes after a writer reads out loud, he hears parts that need to be changed.

Some people refer to the previous Share as a "Quaker Share" because children can just begin to read when they feel ready, rather than going around the circle round-robin style. Keep in mind that the first few times you try a Quaker Share, the silences between each reading might feel awkward. Children are accustomed to being called on when it is their turn to speak, so asking them to "speak when the spirit moves you" might cause some fidgeting. With repetition, however, students learn how to enter their voices into the stream of sound, and the results are always beautiful! Use this format to share small bits of writing, such as leads, titles, and favorite lines, perhaps once each week. This offers the opportunity for everyone's words to be heard and celebrated in a quick and joyful manner.

Finding a Favorite Writing Place Writers, we will begin writing at home pretty soon, in addition to the writing we do in school. And writers need a place to write, a place they can call their own. So tonight, look around your home for a place you might be able to make into a writing place. It doesn't have to be big or even your own space. It can be a corner of a room or a table that travels. Find a spot where you can think and write without being easily distracted. Try out a few different spots, then pick the one you like the best and think of ways you might make it your own. One way writers try to create a special writing place is by surrounding ourselves with objects that mean something special to us. Writers often gather our favorite books, photographs, objects, inspirational quotes, poems, artwork, music; anything that makes us feel comfortable. You will also need to gather the tools you will need to write. Ralph Fletcher in his book _How Writers Work_ (2000) recommends this:

> Make sure you have what you need to start writing. These may seem like small details, but I have found they matter a great deal. Just as a carpenter has tools particular to his or her trade, so does a writer—pens, a notebook, paper. If you have these tools in your writing place, you won't have to go rummaging around when it's time to write. Everything you need will be right where you want it (p 10)

Draw a picture of your special writing place. Label the picture showing the things that will make it a good place to write. Remember, it may be the kitchen table or a favorite chair or your bed. Your objects and tools may be on a shelf or in a basket or a bag. There is no one kind of place writers find to write. The important thing is that it is a place you can go to anytime you want or need to write.

You will continue to find ways to help students develop identities as writers. Writers love to gather objects and tools that might stimulate writing. Carving out a place at home will also encourage both the children and their caregivers to provide a time and a place and the tools required for homework.

TAILORING YOUR TEACHING

If you notice that students' writing fluency is hampered by their worries about accurate spelling . . . you may want to show them a strategy for getting their words down the best they can so they can keep going. From spelling expert Sandra Wilde, I learned that it can be helpful to teach children the concept of placeholder spelling. In order to do this, I said, "Writers, yesterday I taught you one method for drafting: writing long and fast. Some of you were slowed down by trying to spell hard words exactly right. Today I am going to teach you a strategy for getting words down the best you can by using placeholder spelling."

"Watch how I use placeholder spelling to help me get my tricky words down quickly enough that I can focus on what I want to say." Using chart paper, I wrote, "I stood by the lake watching the sun . . ." I paused, and then said the next word to myself several times. ". . . shimmering, shimmering, shim-mer-ing." Turning away from the chart paper, I explained, "I am saying the word a few times, then once slowly, so I can hear all the sounds. Then I will write the word the best I can, underline it so I know to check it later with a dictionary or a friend, and keep writing. This is a great strategy for when you need to write a word you are not sure how to spell, because it doesn't slow you down."

I then set the class up for guided practice by preparing a practice sentence that contained a couple of words that I knew would stump the class. I reminded children, "When you get to a hard word, say the word out loud, out loud again, then slowly, listening for all the sounds. Okay, get the word down the best you can, underline it, and let's keep going."

If you notice that your students simply copy their writer's notebook entries into their drafting booklets . . . explicitly teach them that when writers turn a notebook entry into a draft, we usually enlarge and elaborate on the entry. You may want to use an entry from your writer's notebook that is familiar to your students. "Writers, when I move this entry to my drafting notebook, I'm not going to just copy it in word for word. Instead, I'm going to use the entry and build on it. The entry is almost like an architect's blueprint for a house. The blueprint gives an idea of what the building will be like, where the rooms are, how long the hallways are, but when it's actually being built, you can begin to see all the details, like the color of the paint, the view from the windows, the noise the floor makes when it's stepped on. That's what happens when you move from your entry to your drafting booklet. You add more and sort of build upon the entry. Watch me as I do this." Think aloud as you write in your drafting booklet, showing students how writers might add details that are not in the entry, elaborating on certain parts of the entry.

MECHANICS

Earlier, I suggested that you and your colleagues gather your children's writing and look at their control of conventions in order to devise a plan for supporting this aspect of their writing development. Some of the overarching questions to ask yourself are these: Are my children generally on track in their spelling development? In their control of punctuation? In their use of standard English syntax and grammar? In their sentence complexity? In their vocabulary development?

To answer that, you need general guidelines. Here are some of my recommendations for finding or setting them:

- Pat Cunningham has provided a recommended list of high-frequency words that she suggests teaching at each elementary grade level. For example, the second-grade list contains words such as *about, before, didn't, into, many, other, then, were*. The fourth-grade list, on the other hand, contains words such as *because, become, guide, journey, laugh, straight, through, question*. It's worth obtaining her list of high-frequency words that she believes are appropriate for each grade level, and determining which grade-level list is aligned to most of your children. Ask yourself, "Do 80% of my fourth graders spell the second-grade words correctly when they write?" If the answer is no, then it is fair to say that your kids are definitely not on course as spellers! Ask yourself whether the majority of your fourth graders are able to spell the words on her fourth-grade suggested list. This will give you one indication of how you can assess your children's spelling . . . and will meanwhile suggest starting points for their continued growth.

- Then, too, by the time children are in third grade, they should be able to tackle a word they do not know how to spell—say, *subordination*—and their spellings should reflect that they have broken the word into syllables and used a knowledge of how those syllables are usually spelled in order to produce an approximation that is at least as informed as these: *subordenasion, subordanation,* or perhaps *subordenaysen*.

- Sandra Wilde, author of many books on spelling, once gave me this as a rule of thumb. She said, "By the time children are in fifth grade, 90% of the words on their rough drafts should be spelled correctly, and children should also have the skills necessary to find correct spellings for many of the misspelled words."

If your kids need some extra help with their control of conventions, then chances are great that your children also need extra help with their writing. Please don't let a focus on mechanics overrun your writing workshop. Instead, provide a separate time in your day for mechanics, spelling, and vocabulary, while still weaving this work into the writing workshop. During the writing workshop, you can show children how to incorporate what they've learned during mechanics time into their ongoing writing.

GETTING READY

- Instructions on chalkboard telling children to bring their writer's notebooks (pens tucked inside) and sit with their partners in the meeting area
- Ending of *Fireflies!* by Julie Brinckloe, or another strong ending that kids know well, written onto a transparency
- Mental notes about what makes that ending strong that kids can try
- Overhead projector and marker
- Qualities of Good Personal Narrative Writing chart
- See CD-ROM for resources

REVISING ENDINGS:
LEARNING FROM PUBLISHED WRITING

Narrative stories have a plot and also a resolution. *A good story needs a good ending. Many writers I know say that the endings of their stories and poems and essays are their favorite parts. Some even say that they know their endings before they know anything else about their piece! The writer Katherine Anne Porter claimed, "I always write my last line, my last paragraph, my last page, first." Our students may not feel that their endings are their favorite parts, but endings are crucial. For if leads have to do the work of inviting, even begging readers to spend time with the story that follows, the endings are what stay in readers' minds the longest. Endings can cause readers to sob, to applaud, even to get up and vow to change themselves or the world. Writers know this, so we spend extra time on the last paragraphs and last sentences of our stories. Long before you teach this lesson, you can convey the power of a good ending to your children during your read-aloud time. Let the pace and intonation of your voice showcase each story's final passages.*

As Frank Smith says in his groundbreaking book Joining the Literacy Club, *"Children must read like writers in order to learn how to write like writers. There is no other way in which the intricate complexity of a writer's knowledge can be acquired" (1988, p. 23).*

While teaching children to draft and revise endings, then, you'll also be teaching children that writers read the works of other authors as insiders, noticing not only the content but also the craftsmanship. You'll teach, also, that writers pull in to write, then pull back to look at what we've written, thinking, "What's good about this?" "What could be better?"

In Session VII, we learned how to craft powerful leads by studying the opening paragraphs of several mentor texts. In this session, we will do the same work with endings. After this session, we'll support those children who are ready to leave this first piece of writing and begin another.

MINILESSON

Revising Endings: Learning from Published Writing

CONNECTION

Remind children of the writing work they have been doing and prepare them for learning something new.

"I love the way you have been writing fast and long on your discovery drafts. I have something incredibly important to tell you today, now that you've done that! It's a kind of a secret that good writers know, but many beginning writers don't know. You will need to listen carefully."

"Remember when we worked really hard to get leads that would capture and hold the attention of a reader? Adam took his lead *[Fig. IX-1]*: 'Last night my dad, Harrison and I were in the car going to a restaurant.' and turned it into 'One warm evening last spring, Harrison, my dad, and I climbed into our car and zoomed off toward the highway.' What a big difference just putting in a few words about the weather and using strong verbs like *climbed* and *zoomed* made! Adam's little changes set a mood for the story. I get a picture in my mind of a warm night, when you drive in your car with the windows rolled down, the wind blowing in your face—when you feel excited, like anything can happen."

Name the teaching point. In this case, teach children that authors craft not only beginnings, but also endings that have an effect on the reader.

"You've all discovered how we writers lead into stories, luring the readers to follow us with a special lead. But the secret that many beginning writers don't know is that writers work just as hard—well, maybe even *harder*—on our endings. Today I want to teach you some ways to do that using the ending of one of our mentor texts, *Fireflies!* by Julie Brinckloe."

TEACHING

Demonstrate using a mentor text to learn ways to make writing more powerful. Read the text aloud and explain your thinking.

"We have to be sure that we make something at the end that fits with the idea we're writing about, something that will stay with the reader. Let's look at the ending of *Fireflies!* I've projected it using the overhead projector so we can study Brinckloe's writing and learn ways to make our endings powerful. Watch while I reread and think about what Julie

> NHL Game 7.
>
> Last night my dad, Harrison and I were in the car going to a restaurant or where me and Harrison thought we were going. Then we got to the continental Airlines Arena we still thought we were going to a restaurant. Third we went in the Stadium and I got a little suspicous. After that we went to our seats. Finally we relized we were all going to a restaurant we were at the 12th game 7 in all of hockey history and the Devils won.

Fig. IX-1 Adam's first draft

Brinckloe did here to make her ending powerful." I read the following section aloud, marking the things I noticed on the transparency.

> I flung off the covers.
> I went to the window,
> opened the jar,
> and aimed at the stars.
> *"Fly!"*
> Then the jar began to glow,
> green,
> then gold,
> then white as the moon.
> And the fireflies poured out into the night.
> *Fireflies!*
> Blinking on, blinking off,
> dipping low, soaring high above my head,
> making circles around the moon
> like stars dancing.
> I held the jar, dark and empty,
> in my hands.
> The moonlight and the fireflies
> swam in my tears,
> but I could feel myself smiling.

As always, you needn't use the exact text I've chosen to demonstrate using a mentor text to learn about writing. As long as you choose a narrative text with which children are already familiar, one with an ending that is succinct and memorable and has moves in it children can see, then this minilesson will be strong.

"This is such an ending, isn't it?! Let's read it again, and this time, I'll think out loud while we read it. Look, the first thing in this ending is the boy flinging off his covers. Julie made it so the boy is doing something, right? But not just doing any old thing; he's not scratching his nose, he's flinging off his covers. I bet the author chose that action for him to do because it's just like he's flinging off the comforting idea that he can keep those fireflies forever in the jar. I think she put that action in the ending because it can give us more thoughts about the important parts of the story. I'm going to write 'important action' right here to remind me of something I can try in my endings." On the transparency, I wrote a marginal note and continued reading the ending. "Yes, these are all important actions, right? I'm really getting the idea I can put important actions in my ending."

"Now here it has exactly what the character says—one carefully chosen word! It says: *'Fly!'* That makes me realize I could try putting important dialogue, the exact important words people say, into my endings. I'll write that." I wrote "important dialogue" in the margin and read on.

Notice that when I read aloud the book's ending, I am not reading only the last sentence. Usually an author regards both the lead and the ending of a story as longer than a line or two.

Two decades ago Mem Fox, author of Koala Lou, *led a workshop on children's literature at the Teachers College Reading and Writing Project. I was a member of her class. She taught us many things that I'll never forget and one was this: When you read aloud and come to the end of a text, slow . . . your voice . . . down . . . to . . . a . . . stop.*

Notice the assumption that writers have characters doing actions for a reason. Brinckloe didn't need to tell that the boy flung off his covers, and does so for reasons that are not accidental.

"So much of the rest of this ending is helping us understand what the moment looked like, isn't it? All those colors and comparisons help us picture how it went. Julie uses a lot of images. I could try that too." I wrote "images" in the margin and read the last sentences.

"This very last part—'I held the jar, dark and empty, in my hands. The moonlight and the fireflies swam in my tears, but I could feel myself smiling'—brings our attention back to the boy. It helps us see him, sad and happy at the same time. That sort of makes us remember the whole story—how he saw the fireflies and then, all excited, he caught them in the jar and loved them there and then he decided to set them free. Julie reminds us of all the things that happened and all the feelings the boy had in just one short bit of writing." I wrote "reminds us of whole story" in the margin.

"Maybe later you can find some other things that Julie did as a writer that make this a powerful ending for you. The things I notice she put in were important actions, important dialogue, images, and a short reminder of the whole story. We can try doing those things ourselves with our endings!"

Debrief. Name what you hope children learned from the demonstration. Add this lesson to the ongoing chart.

"Did you notice how I didn't just read the ending? I read it several times and studied it closely to see what the author did to make her ending powerful! Let's add what I noticed to our Qualities of Good Personal Narrative Writing chart." I wrote:

> Qualities of Good Personal Narrative Writing
>
> - Write a little seed story; don't write all about a giant watermelon topic.
> - Zoom in so you tell the most important parts of the story.
> - Include true, exact details from the movie you have in your mind.
> - Begin with a strong lead—maybe use setting, action, dialogue to create mood.
> - Make a strong ending—maybe use important actions, dialogue, images, and whole-story reminders that make a lasting impression.

You always need to decide whether your teaching aims to nudge children one small step along in their development, or whether it aims to immerse them in a world of literary language. So far, this unit has leaned towards giving simple, do-able guidance. Here—just for a patch of time—I break loose and immerse children in the heady world of literary language. There's no question that I'm teaching over their heads here— what else is a sky for?

Of course, you could decide to make a short-term chart titled, "Good Endings." The chart could list important actions, important dialogue, images, and reminders of the whole story.

Some teachers highlight that writers often try to make the reader feel like the character feels. Others highlight the technique of making an ending reminiscent of the story's beginning. Some teachers help children focus on choosing the emotion they want to convey at the end of their story. Choose only a few techniques to try—ones that are well illustrated in the mentor text, and that your children can have success with.

ACTIVE ENGAGEMENT

Remind children that writers work hard on endings. Writers study mentor endings, make plans for their endings, then write rough draft endings.

"Before today, you might have thought that writers write endings in a snap! I used to think that when it came time to end a story, I could just slap, 'And they lived happily ever after' onto my last line. But I think now you understand why some writers say that when we come to the last page of a story, we're halfway home!"

"While we're here in the meeting area, we can't each write an ending for our stories. That would take too much time. But we can begin to plan—to rehearse—for an ending. One way to do this is to reread our drafts, asking, 'What is the important message I've conveyed?' Would you reread your draft and mark the places in the text that seem to you to be especially important—your ending will want to somehow relate to these places."

After a few moments of silence, I said, "Will you reread your draft again and this time mark any important actions, words, images that could maybe be woven into your final scene, your final image?" Again I let children work quietly.

LINK

Rename your teaching point.

"Writers, today I'm not going to ask you to tell your partner your thoughts. I don't want to break the spell! Just slip back to your writing space, and start drafting an ending. Remember that now, if you've reached the final page, you're halfway home!"

If you and your class have also been working on a shared text, you could instead ask students in the Active Engagement to turn to their partners and talk about strong actions, images or important ideas that could come into the story's ending of that text. Another option is to reread the final page of a beloved novel—say, Where the Red Fern Grows—*and to invite children to talk with a partner about ways in which that ending illustrates the characteristics listed on the chart.*

WRITING AND CONFERRING

Grouping Writers for Conferences

You'll probably wish you could clone yourself so that you can be at every child's side today. You'll want to get this child back on track, and that one, and this one—so breathe. Realize that the agendas you've laid out for children represent the writing work of the year (or really, of a lifetime), not the work of a week. It's okay that the children who are trying to write focused narratives are still swamped with other problems (perhaps they are including mind-numbing detail, or perhaps they are writing with run-on sentences). It's okay if a large group of children still struggles to fully understand what it means to write a narrative. When we're teaching writing, we're teaching people entirely new habits, a whole new way of living and thinking. That cannot be easy!

But, having said that, yes indeed, you need to work hard at your conferring today. You will need to group children who currently need the same kind of support. Perhaps five children really need you to remind them about end punctuation. Another four need a push into focusing their narratives. These two write and write and write, but their stories are hard to follow. These three write with detail, and now need to learn to be selective in which details they include.

> **MID-WORKSHOP TEACHING POINT** **Checking for Sense** "Writers, can I have your eyes and your attention? I've noticed a bunch of you are having a problem that I have too, when I'm writing. When I write a true story, I already know how the story goes because I'm the one it happened to! Sometimes I forget that my readers weren't there. I'll say, 'Michelle got lost,' and my reader doesn't know if Michelle is a cat or a child! When I leave out important details, my story doesn't make sense!"
>
> "This is what I do to fix that problem: Now and then, I read my draft to a person who doesn't know the story. I ask 'Can I read this to you? Will you stop me if it's confusing?' Sometimes instead of reading to another person, I pretend to be a stranger and I read my draft through the stranger's eyes. As I read, I find places where it's confusing and then I fix those places."
>
> "Could everyone take a moment right now and read your draft through a stranger's eyes? If you find confusing places, stop and revise. You'll need to do this from time to time from now on."

After you've figured out a group of students to confer with, you can just stand up and announce, "Can I meet with . . . " and read your list. Once you've convened the group into a huddle, tell them, "I called you over because I've noticed you are ready to learn . . . " Then tell them, "What I do in this situation is I . . . " and show them how you punctuate as you write, or how you narrow your topic. You need to have examples at their writing level and you need to highlight the one thing you intend for them to learn how to do. Then say, "So work on that right here, right now." Be specific. Do you want them to reread and correct, to list, to start a new piece or page? Should they work alone or with a partner? Tell them you need to meet with another group but you'll be back in five minutes to see what they've done. Then call the next group. Don't limit yourself to working with only one group just because you perhaps haven't had a chance to plan a careful lesson for more than that one group. Wing it! These children need face-to-face talk, and they need to be noticed more than they need your teaching to be perfect.

SHARE

Appreciating Endings

Convene children. Share the work of one child who wrote several possible endings, trying to be sure they referred to important actions, dialogue, images from the story.

"Writers, can I have your eyes and your attention? I want to remind you that writers know our endings will be the last thing readers encounter, and so we usually write several drafts of them. Jill did some smart work today. She reread her narrative about waterskiing, deciding she wanted her ending to emphasize the pride she felt in herself afterwards because she'd circled half the lake. So she wrote three drafts of endings. She's planning to combine them into one best ending." [Fig. IX-2]

> "Wow" I thought. That was me. I went around half of the lake. I couldn't wait to rest my legs. I was ready to do it again.
>
> I walked off the boat with a smile on my face and excitement flowing through me. I couldn't wait to talk to my parents and tell them I got half way around the lake.
>
> "Bye" I said, "Thanks." I was so happy that I wanted to jump right back into the lake and do it again! I walked onto the dock and was ready to do it 50 more times.

Jill read aloud the entry she planned to stitch together:

> "Wow," I thought. "That was me. I skied half of the lake." I walked off the boat with a smile on my face and excitement flowing through me. I walked onto the dock and was ready to do it again.

Extract lessons from the one child's work.

"Writers, did you notice that Jill reread her whole narrative, paying attention to what it was she really wants to say in her ending? Then she drafted three versions of an ending. Next she plans to take the best of all three—but she could have selected one. At the end of today, she'll have produced four lines of text—but that'll be a good day's work."

> 3 posible endings
>
> "WOW" I thought. That was me. I went around half of the lake. I couldn't wait it to rest my legs. I was ready to do it again.
>
> I walked off the boat with a smile on and exciment flowing through me. I couldn't wait to talk to my parents and tell them I got half way around the lake.
>
> "BY" I said, thanks. I was so happy that I wanted to jump right back into the lake and do it again! I walked onto the dock and was ready to do it 50 more times.

Fig. IX-2 Jill

HOMEWORK   *Studying Endings*   Today, writers, we studied the endings in one or two picture books, noticing that the author wove together important actions, important dialogue, images, and short reminders of the whole story. Tonight, would you be investigators? Return to books you've loved, and especially to those whose endings have worked for you. Would you copy down two endings that you think merit more study. Choose endings in which the author does something you imagine that you, too, could do, and choose two endings that represent different kinds-of-endings. Tomorrow, we'll see if we can lay out some of the options, mapping the field of possibility. When you arrive in school tomorrow, let's use our empty bulletin board as a place to sort kinds of endings. You can post the ending you've brought in alongside others that are somehow similar, and write labels or diagrams to show how these endings are similar. Maybe in the end, we'll put the endings you write on the bulletin board, in the same categories we designed for Kevin Henkes' endings and Lucille Clifton's endings!

TAILORING YOUR TEACHING

If students tend to write flat endings such as, "After that we went home." Or "Then I had to go finish my homework." . . . you could teach your students that if the ending tells an action, that action needs to be closely related to the main event of the story.

You can share examples from the work of published authors, and highlight the choices the authors made by reminding children they could have chosen otherwise. For example, Jane Chelsea Aragon could have ended *Salt Hands* with, "Then I went back to bed." Instead she ended with a small action, one related to the heart of the story. The story is about a nighttime visit from a deer. It starts with the deer's arrival, and ends with his departure. Describing the giant deer, Aragon ends the story like this: "When he was finished, he raised his head and turned away slowly and walked off into the night." You could, in a similar fashion, help children notice Polacco's craftsmanship. What if she had ended *Thunder Cake*, her story of getting over her fear, "After we made the Thunder Cake, I had to wash all the dishes." Instead, Polacco's ending revisits the heart of her story. She writes, "We just smiled and ate our Thunder Cake. From that time on, I never feared the voice of thunder again." You could teach children that some writers do decide to write endings that involve an event that isn't closely related to the main event, but usually these contain reflections rather than actions. In *Bigmama's*, Donald Crews ends by saying, "Some nights even now, I think that I might wake up in the morning and be at Bigmama's with the whole summer ahead of me."

MECHANICS

As you read your students' writing, guard against the temptation to conclude that no one has ever taught them about periods, capitals, and other forms of punctuation. Chances are good that your students have heard lessons about punctuation marks since first grade!

But, as you may be seeing in their writing, it is not enough for us to simply teach rules for using conventional punctuation marks—we also have to help children apply this knowledge as they write. Do your children the favor of reminding them that writers always put end punctuation at the end of a sentence, and capitalize the start of the next sentence. Sometimes children believe because it isn't crucial that their rough drafts and their entries are totally correct, this means they are free to write for days on end without any end punctuation. They sometimes think that just prior to publication, they need to reread their drafts and insert periods and capitals.

Of course, there is a grain of truth to these perceptions. It is true that writers focus more on content and craft during early drafts, and don't obsess about every last mechanical detail until it's time to publish. But this certainly does not mean that children should postpone writing with end punctuation until just prior to publication!

Instead, they need to develop ease and automaticity with end punctuation. Therefore, children need to write with punctuation even when they are only writing entries in their notebooks. You may need to find times throughout the workshop to insert punctuation prompts. "Writers," you might say, "I'm finding that a few of you are so focused on what you are saying that you are forgetting to write with punctuation. Forgetting punctuation reminds me of a time when I drove to work and realized as I pulled into the parking garage in the middle of Manhattan that I'd forgotten my shoes! I had to walk in stocking feet on the sidewalk to my office, and I had to spend the whole day without shoes. I bet that anyone I spoke to that

day had a hard time listening to me because they probably kept thinking, 'How weird! She's in her stocking-feet!' Forgetting your punctuation is like forgetting your shoes. It's just not done! Go back over your writing in your notebook and make sure it's punctuated. Remember to punctuate as you go so that readers can listen to your message!"

If children use what they know about punctuation to punctuate, then you can see their developing understandings. If writing with punctuation (and I'm not saying with complex punctuation or even with correct punctuation, but with *some* punctuation) is a challenge for your children, you'll need to carve out a separate time in each day to teach mechanics. You might, for example, teach them to correctly punctuate quotations and ask them to reread their notebook looking for instances in which they could improve their punctuation of dialogue.

Errors in punctuation, for example, often begin to show when children attempt to write more complex sentences than they have in the past. Their mistakes may be signs that the children are pushing themselves beyond the syntactical structures they already know; they may be signs of learning and growth, not simply signs of ignorance about the rules governing comma or period use.

You might also remind them that a writer usually tries to write in a consistent tense. If we tell a story of an event that occurred in the past, we usually would use past tense. Some writers choose, however, to use present tense as a way to help readers feel in-the-moment. I find, however, that writing stories about past events and doing so in present tense often leads writers to either teeter between time frames or to be locked into a sportscaster-like, "I am running down the field. I am catching the ball. I am throwing the ball . . . " Again, writers can reread entries in their notebook, noticing their tenses and perhaps making New Year's resolutions.

GETTING READY

- Directions on chalkboard telling children to bring their folders and sit with their partners in the meeting area
- Strategies for Generating Personal Narrative Writing chart
- Monitoring My Writing Process checklist on chart paper
- Monitoring My Writing Process checklist in each child's folder
- Qualities of Good Personal Narrative Writing chart
- Writer's notepad for each child to take home
- See CD-ROM for resources

TAKING CHARGE OF OUR WRITING WORK:
STARTING A SECOND PIECE

When I help teachers design their own units of study, I tell them that although it's tempting to focus on the content of our minilessons, the truth is that the words that come out of our mouths are not as important as the work that our children do. When planning a unit, we're wise to think first about the nature of our children's work. Will children write one piece or two? Will all children progress in sync with each other? Will they write in booklets, stretching their stories across a sequence of pages, or on single sheets?

I decided in this unit of study that I would give children extensive opportunities to rehearse for writing, expect minimal revision for now, and support them in writing two narratives rather than just one. In this session, you'll see that after children write one narrative, instead of revising it immediately, I ask them to write a second piece, only then selecting just one of their two stories to revise and edit.

You could decide on a different course. There is not one answer to the question of how many stories you should expect children to write within a month-long unit. When deciding, keep in mind this general principle: The more skilled a writer is, the longer that writer can profitably sustain work on a single piece of writing. At the start of kindergarten, children are apt to write fifteen stories in a single month. Meanwhile, a professional writer will often work many years on a single story! Your third, fourth, or fifth graders will be somewhere in between.

The words of this minilesson emphasize independence, but in truth, it is a limited sort of independence. We're really saying, "Some of you will start your second story today; some need more time and will start the second one tomorrow." Your implicit message is that everyone will progress through the same sequence of writing work. You will support more diversity in writing work as the year progresses because in the end, our goal is to help children author rich writing lives for themselves.

MINILESSON

Taking Charge of Our Writing Work: Starting a Second Piece

CONNECTION

Celebrate your children's rough drafts.

"Writers, I have been reading your stories every chance I get. When you were at music earlier this morning, I didn't go to the faculty room. I just sat here with your stories. I read about how violins sound when you first try to play them, I laughed about the pigeon with the wink that Carl saw on the sidewalk, I tried to guess the ending of the mysterious disappearance in Christina's story . . . Then I looked up and saw I was out of time! I was so disappointed! When I had to stop reading, I felt like someone was taking a prize right out of my hands. You all are turning into such strong writers—congratulations!"

Name the teaching point. In this case, tell children that writers need to take charge of their writing, assigning themselves jobs.

"Some of you have reached the end of your drafts; others still have lots to write. Either way, what I want to teach you today is that you don't need to line up alongside me and ask, 'What should I do in writing time today?' You are in charge of your writing—writers make their own writing decisions."

TEACHING

Tell children the work you expect them to do next, explaining the options: continue drafting or begin a second story.

"A girl I knew once wrote, 'I am the mother of my story. No one else can tell me, "Do this with your story" or "Do that" because I am the mother of my story.' And it is true that you are the parent or the boss or the job captain of your own writing."

"You do not need to come to me and ask, 'Is my story done?' You can decide if you have reached the end. You do not need to come to me and ask, 'What should I do now?' You can decide whether you have more to write in your story, whether you want to revise your first story right now or whether you are ready to move to your second story. In the next week, all of us will write a second story; some will start it today, some will start it tonight, some will start it tomorrow or the next day. After we have written two stories, we will look back on them both and choose the one we like best to revise again, edit, and publish."

COACHING

Time and again you will notice that I try to convey general messages through details. Madeleine L'Engle, the great fiction writer, once told me "If you say, 'I once saw some flying elephants,' that isn't particularly believable. But it feels more believable if you say, 'Last Tuesday, when I walked from the school to my car, I saw something flying over the far parking lot. At first I thought it was a blimp but then I looked again and it was two pinkish purple elephants, with a baby elephant trailing behind them.' Because I want children to believe me when I say that I have really, truly enjoyed reading their writing, I don't rely on generalizations, saying only, "I have enjoyed reading your writing. The stories are really great." Instead I try to use details that will make my words more convincing.

The truth is that your children have probably not yet internalized the writing process enough to take over the task of being job captain. You are only making a first move toward handing over this responsibility. Although you tell them they're in charge, for now they are mostly in charge of the timing for when they progress to the next bit of work rather than the decision as to what that work will be.

"Of course, if you are going to start writing another story, you know what to do—start gathering some new entries in your notebook. You already know strategies you can use to generate personal narrative writing," I reminded them, gesturing toward the chart listing those strategies. "On the other hand, you may not need to gather entries—you may simply reread your notebook and say, 'Wait, I already have another seed story that I want to develop!' Either way, once you've chosen a seed idea, you already know that you can tell the story to yourself or write leads as ways to develop that seed idea. The important thing is that you can be your own job captain and tell yourself, 'The next thing I should do is to collect some new entries' or 'I think now I should write a few different leads.'"

Explain how you use a chart to keep tabs on your progress through the writing process, and give children a similar chart.

"When I'm organizing my writing life, I keep tabs on my progress. I know my writing process usually involves certain steps, so I have a list of them near me and a system for checking off when I have completed each step. That helps me know what to try next."

Monitoring My Writing Process	First Piece	Next Piece
Gather entries		
Select and develop one seed idea		
Storytell to rehearse for writing		
Read published writing that resembles what I want to write		
Draft leads—try action, dialogue, setting		
Choose paper, plan story across pages, copy lead		
Write draft with each part on a separate page		
Reread and revise for clarity		
Draft endings—try using important actions, dialogue, images, or reminders of the whole story		
Revise and edit more now or decide to wait until later, or not to revise		

So often in schools, we try to act as if everything children do is always new, new, new! Let me caution against this. Recall how important it is to you when the principal, at the start of the year, says, "This year we'll continue working with last year's initiative." We breathe a sigh of relief because this means we'll have a chance to revisit what we tried once, to gain some sense of mastery. Children, too, long to hear that they'll have a chance to return to work they've done before. Now is their chance!

It is very important to teach children the way in which a writing curriculum cumulates, leaving the writer with a repertoire of skills and strategies. Today gives you a chance to convey the cumulative nature of your teaching.

Make sure the language you use on your Monitoring My Writing Process chart matches the language you've used to explain each step in the unit so far. Repeating the same words is yet another way to help children recall the previous teaching and learn that each new lesson will be referred to again and again in future lessons, just as these past lessons are referred to here.

ACTIVE ENGAGEMENT
Set children up to use charts to track and plan their progress through the writing process.

"I think it will be helpful for you to have these steps laid out so that when you act as job captain for yourself, you can keep tabs on your progress and remember what you usually do next. Therefore I've put a checklist like this inside each of your writing folders."

"Right now, before we head off to work, will you think about your writing process? Look over the chart in your folder and ask yourself, 'Which of these steps have I already done for my first piece of writing?' Then think, 'What will I do today?' Ask yourself also, 'Does this chart contain all of the steps I've been taking as a writer lately?' As the year progresses, we will definitely learn other things writers do, and we'll add those to this checklist. For now, though, tell your partner which of these things you have done, and which of these represent work you will do today."

LINK
Remind children that they need to decide whether to continue working on their existing drafts or to shift to new stories. Tell them writers are always job captains for themselves.

"For now and for the rest of your life, keep in mind that we writers are job captains for our own writing. It is important to always keep one eye on our subject and another eye on our progress along a sequence of work. You can keep tabs on your progress by charting what you have already done as a writer."

"When you go off to work today, reread your draft and decide upon a plan of action. Since you are your own job captain, decide whether to add to or revise your existing draft, or whether you will start collecting new entries in your notebook and finding a new seed idea for a second story. You can use the chart to help you remember your options."

Some teachers keep a whole-class, wall-sized version of the chart, with each child moving his or her magnetic plaque along on a white-board chart. You'll need to decide whether this chart is an individual one kept in writing folders or a whole-class one, displayed on a wall, or both. If your school leader wants you to use charts and rubrics, then by all means turn this into a whole-class, white-board chart. It has more potential to function as a living representation, one that actually helps children, than do most charts and rubrics.

Later you'll find that I teach children they can write a planning box or a self-assignment box for themselves at the start of a day's work. If you prefer to teach that now, you could do so.

WRITING AND CONFERRING

Encouraging Independent Problem Solving

In your conferring today, try to teach independence. Invite children to identify and solve their own writing problems. As teachers, especially, we love to feel useful, and we love to feel as if we are teaching something, so we often rush to suggest solutions to every problem. It's wise to remember, however, that our job is to put ourselves out of a job. I sometimes enter a workshop planning to turn issues back to the child. So if a child says that he feels "done," I do not generate a list of five things the writer could do next. Instead, I say, "I know that feeling of being finished with something. But since I know (and you do too!) that when I'm done, I've just begun, I look back to find what else I can work on. You try that now. Figure out what else you can work on. I'll check with you at the end of writing time to see what you came up with!" When I expect the child to find his way out of a predicament, I find the child rises to the occasion.

So guard against being the problem solver. For today, anyhow, if the writer expresses a problem, try mulling the problem over aloud, as if you are thinking of a solution: "Hmm . . . I'm trying to think of what writers do when we encounter this problem. Hmm . . . ." The writer will probably supply a possible course of action. Go with it! "So are you suggesting . . . ?" you can say, and as you retell what the child has suggested, sneak in a few little tips of your own.

Keep a copy of the Monitoring My Writing Process checklist in hand as you confer. If a child isn't certain what he or she might do next, help the child use the checklist to find what she has done and might do next: "Where are you in the process and what on this list might you plan to do next?" Turn the question or problem back to the children, and soon enough, children will find their ways to independent solutions.

MID-WORKSHOP TEACHING POINT   *Solving Our Own Problems*   "Writers, can I have your eyes and your attention? Look what I have following me!" I gestured to the line of children trailing me. "Writers, listen while I talk with each of the writers who are in line for help. Listen closely, because this could be you, lined up for help."

Then I said to the first child, "What is it you are wanting?" The child explained that he was done and wasn't sure what to do next. I kindly but firmly asked if he thought he could figure that out, and he admitted that he probably could. "Okay, off you go then," I said.

The next child wanted to know if I liked his lead. "Hmm, is it vitally important to know whether *I* like your lead? Do *you* like it?" The writer confessed that he really wasn't that fond of it. "So I bet you can figure out what to do next, can't you?" and he, too, went on his way. After one more child went back to handle his own problem, I turned to the class. "Writers, do you get my point? You need to become your own job captains and make your own decisions. I can't be the person who decides what every one of you should be doing. From this day on, when you feel like coming to me for help, take a second to think, 'Do I really need help? Could I solve this on my own?'"

SHARE

Remembering Qualities of Good Writing

Convene children. Ask writers to examine their work for examples of some qualities of good writing from the class chart.

"Writers, I was really blown away today to see that so many of you could figure out what you needed to do and pleased that you were able to resume gathering narrative entries in your notebooks. You also wrote those entries much more quickly than you wrote them earlier this year. But what especially impressed me was that you kept in mind the qualities of good writing that we talked about earlier this month."

"I'm going to read a quality of good writing from our chart, and then I'd like you to look at what you've written so far in this unit and see if your writing illustrates that quality. If it does, give me a thumbs up."

Qualities of Good Personal Narrative Writing
- Write a little seed story; don't write all about a giant watermelon topic.
- Zoom in so you tell the most important parts of the story.
- Include true, exact details from the movie you have in your mind.
- Begin with a strong lead—maybe setting, action, dialogue, or a combination to create mood.
- Make a strong ending—maybe use important actions, dialogue, images, and whole-story reminders that make a lasting impression.

"So first of all, did you remember that when you are writing personal narratives, it's easier to write well if you don't write all about a giant watermelon topic, but instead tell a small seed story? Thumbs up if your writing today included a focused story."

"And would you look at the writing you did and think whether instead of writing all over the place, making comments about and chatting about your focused story, you instead told the story in a bit-by-bit fashion. Thumbs up if you focused and then let the story unfold bit by bit," I said. Then I added, "Writers, let's listen to Jake's story and see if we agree that he did these things." *[Figs. X-1 and X-2]*

> I sat behind the bleachers, waiting for my race to be called. "Second- and third-graders, please line up by the entrance," the announcer said.
>
> Just like last time, I thought. We always go there.
>
> Quickly, I jogged to the asphalt by the start point.
>
> When it was my turn, I leaned forward. I was ready for the gunshot.
>
> BANG! The gun went off, and I did too.
>
> For the first half second, I stayed in position by Daniel Fabrezio. This time I'm going to win, I know I will.
>
> Then, I started to fall back. But, I didn't notice until I saw three or four kids in front of me, some even on their third turn!
>
> Then, I decided to give up, and I realized I ought to give up. But I knew I would regret it later.

Then, pointing to another item on the chart, I asked the writers, "Did you write with true, exact details? Right now, find a particularly nice detail in the writing you did today, and share it with your partner." After a minute of talk, I said, "Isaiah found a lot of details in his writing. Let's listen to it and see if we agree that he has written with true, exact details." *[Fig. X-3]*

> I looked inside the tank. There he was, Hissy, my beloved pet snake. I looked at my mom eagerly. The moment I had been waiting for was almost here. The time to take Hissy out of his tank. I watched excitedly as my mom took Hissy out. I held out my hands. They were a little shaky but I was still excited. Mom gave Hissy to me.

"Isaiah, you have definitely zoomed in on one moment, and you stretched the moment out so much that I feel as if I am right there with you, leaning over the tank." Then

Then, I decided to give up, but realized I ought to give up. But I knew I would regret it later.

The 400 Meter
Jake

I sat behind the bleachers, waiting for my race to be called.
"2nd and 3rd graders, please line up by the entrance," the announcer said.
Just like last time I thought. We always go there.
Quickly, I jogged to the asphalt by the start point.
When it was my turn, I leaned foward. I was ready for the gunshot.
BANG! the gun went off, and I did too.
For the first ½ second, I stayed in position by Daniel Fabrezio. This time I'm going to win, I know I will.
Then, I started to fall back. But I didn't notice until I saw 3 or 4 kids in front of me, some even on their 3rd turn!

Figs. X-1 and X-2 Jake

Beginning
I looked inside the tank. There he was, Hissy my beloved pet snake. I looked at my mom eagerly. The moment I had been waiting for was almost here. The time to take Hissy out of his tank. I watched excitedley as my mom took Hissy out. I held out my hands. They were a little shaky but I was still excited. Mom gave Hissy to me. I could kind of tell we shared the same feeling. I just wanted to be with Hissy. We belonged with each other. We were really best friends. I sat down on the floor, still holding Hissy.

Fig. X-3 Isaiah

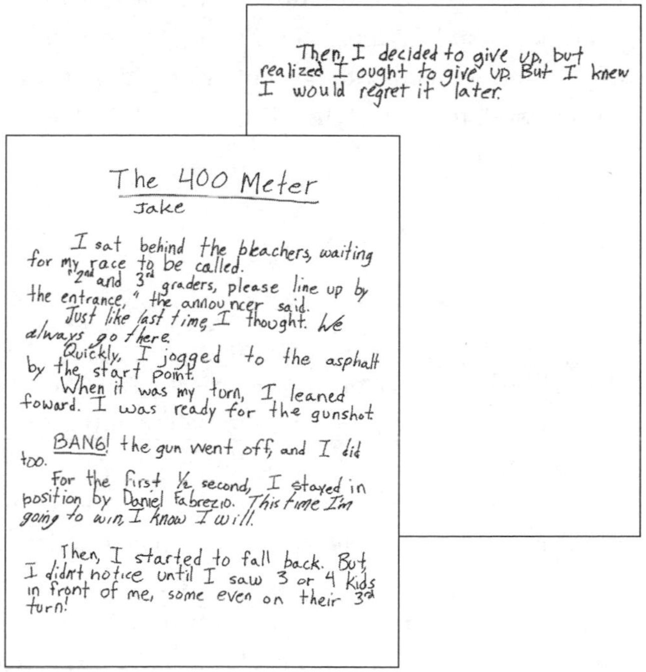

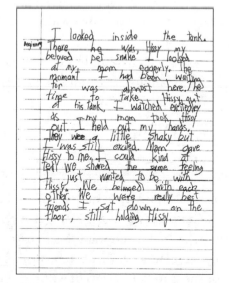

I asked the class, "Do you think Isaiah wrote with true and exact details?" When children confirmed that he'd done this, I said, "As you continue working tomorrow and for the rest of your life, remember to keep these qualities of good writing, as well as this sequence of writing work from your checklist, in mind."

⊙ HOMEWORK *Writing Every Night* You've graduated. We've only been together for two weeks but you've already been through one whole writing cycle, and you're already acting as job captains for yourselves, deciding what writing work it is that you need to be doing. The time has come, I think, for you to have your own time, away from the classroom, when you can decide what you need to do as a writer and then do it.

So I've made a writer's notepad for each of you, and every day after school you'll have a chance to gather an entry or two in your writer's notepad. Bring those entries to school because when it comes to choosing a seed idea, you may decide to select an entry that you wrote when you were in your own home space, giving yourself a job to do.

All the writers I know have little spirals tucked in their pockets or purses, and they're always ready to write. I once sat in a school with a gigantic hospital across the way. As I watched, I saw a window on the fourth floor open, and suddenly a telephone was flung out the window! I had my notepad there and recorded the whole episode.

It'll definitely be important to carry your notepad with you—and definitely have it in school every day.

⊙ TAILORING YOUR TEACHING

If your students could be more productive and focused during writing workshop . . . you could show the children how to use the Monitoring My Writing Process checklist as a guide for making plans. Remind them of the chart and show an example of how one child filled it out. Then the class can work on helping that classmate come up with plans for what she might work on today. And if you want this to become one of your rituals, you could end the lesson by saying, "So remember that before a writer starts writing, the writer often takes stock of where he or she is in the process of writing. The writer often gives himself or herself a little self-assignment. So every day for the next few days, anyhow, before you start writing

Eventually, you'll want to instruct students to tape or paste the pages from this portable notebook into their more permanent writer's notebook so that all their writing will be available to reread and glean from.

would you take a look at your progress through the writing process, as recorded on your chart. Let that help you make plans for your work."

If your students need help to make plans that are more closely related to their needs as writers . . . one way you might build upon this lesson is to have children assess themselves as writers, making goals and giving themselves assignments. "Today I want to teach you that another way in which you can become more independent is by looking over your writing and thinking, 'What am I doing that is working well?' and 'What do I need to work on more as a writer?'" You might then demonstrate how you look over your writing with those questions in mind. You will want to mimic the types of things you would like your students to notice as they self-assess. For example, "I have used two of these strategies on the chart for coming up with ideas. I've written about a special person, my sister, and I've written about a special place, Aunt Rose's house. And I've written them as stories. But one thing I am noticing is that sometimes I forget to use punctuation. Also, none of my stories seem to be very long." Show children how this self-assessment leads you to decide on the work you need to do next, recording it in an assignment box you made in your notebook.

ASSESSMENT

When you collect your children's finished first-draft stories, remember that you can choose the lens through which you want to look at that writing. You *can*, if you want, search your children's writing for flaws. You can point out errors, bemoan misspellings, list areas of weakness. But if your role is to help your children grow as writers, you would be wise to consciously and deliberately put those lenses aside and look, instead, with an eye toward celebrating growth.

Look for ways in which your instruction seems to have made a difference—even if the result isn't perfect yet. Has the writer begun the story with dialogue? Started close to the action in a zoomed-in, focused way? Retold the event step-by-step instead of summarizing it?

Look for approximations of higher-level work, and for evidence of risk taking. Cultivate the habit of celebrating the shaky steps writers take en route to new prowess. Pay attention to evidence that children have taken your instruction to heart and tried to use your guidelines as they write. The resulting texts won't be perfect—but even at this early point in the year, they should provide evidence that your writers are growing and your teaching is making a difference.

You will also want to pay attention to the children who seem to be made of Teflon™—all of us have those children, especially at the start of the year. When you find a writer of any ability level to whom your teaching never sticks, you have a choice. You could push the writer out of your mind. But the wiser decision is to let that writer become your teacher.

Speculate over what could be going on for the writer, and try to discover why your teaching has not taken hold for this individual.

Your children's work can give you feedback on your teaching—imagine getting feedback without an administrator or staff developer even coming into the room, without a letter in your file! What a gift! But for this to happen, you need to get out of the mind-set of blaming the child. If you see that your teaching hasn't made a dent for a particular child, you need to resist the impulse to regard this as the child's problem. Instead, see the evidence as providing a window on *your teaching*, not on the child's capacities. And do this without putting yourself through a guilt trip—which should be easy since it is still the start of the year!

Try to remember right now that your job is to be an avid learner of teaching. So yes, look for affirmation that you have made a difference, but expect and search for evidence that all is not perfect, too. Your teaching can't possibly be perfect—you don't yet know your children—and in the end, your real challenge will be to teach in ways that enable all your children to learn. I am reminded of a comic strip I saw once in which a little boy confides to a friend that he taught his dog to whistle. The friend is impressed and astonished, but then the little boy reminds him, "I said I taught him to whistle—I didn't say he learned to whistle!"

Learning to write, like learning to teach, doesn't happen overnight. Let yourself become a student of your students.

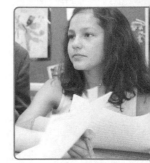

TIMELINES AS TOOLS FOR PLANNING STORIES

IN THIS SESSION, YOU'LL TEACH STUDENTS THAT WRITERS CAN USE TIMELINES TO PLAN AND STRUCTURE THEIR NARRATIVES.

GETTING READY

- Instructions on chalkboard telling children to bring their writing folders (containing writer's notebook and notepad) and sit with their partners in the meeting area
- Monitoring My Writing Process checklist on chart paper
- Story from your own childhood (plan parts for timeline)
- Idea for shared class story (event class experienced together)
- Two leads for your story (one using dialogue, one with an action)
- See CD-ROM for resources

You may find it surprising that the children are suddenly done with one piece of writing and back at the rehearsal stage. It's true that we've skipped revision altogether, and begun a second piece. I chose to do this because I think that at this stage, children need more practice planning and drafting narratives than they do revising them. I think the opportunity to cycle through the process again right away, this time accumulating new strategies and knowledge for each phase, is an important one. Before long children will have written two narratives, and then I'll ask them to select their best, and revise and edit it.

So this session returns to rehearsal, reminding children of what they already know about collecting and selecting entries, then adding a new technique that can accompany or replace storytelling as a way for children to plan the whole flow of the story. Specifically, in this session children learn to draft timelines as a form of planning their pieces, revising those timelines by thinking about where, in the sequence of events, their story really begins and ends, and thinking also about other options for where it could begin and end.

This session helps writers learn they have choices not only about what they will write, but also about how they will write. Many children assume that writing true stories means the writer acts as a stenographer, recording what actually happened. In this session, children learn that writers need (at the very least) to decide where in the sequence of events they will begin their story. By showing children that writers experiment with different entry points into the sequence of events, you give children a concrete tool for planning and revision. You can also teach them to look at what they've written and ask, "Are all the dots on my timeline crucial to the main story?"

Children learn that they can weigh different ways a story can start; they can tell the story aloud one way—and soon they're ready to scrawl a draft, writing fast and long.

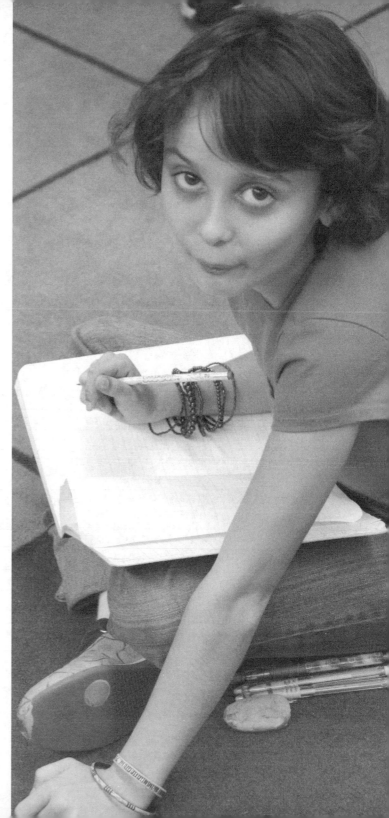

MINILESSON

Timelines as Tools for Planning Stories

CONNECTION

Summarize the work children did yesterday in the previous session to provide context for today's lesson.

"In the previous session, you all acted as job captains, deciding what it is you, as writers, need to do. Some of you are still finishing your first story, but most of you gathered entries for a new story yesterday, and chose a second seed idea. Some of you storytold that new idea or tried writing different leads for it. Please keep track of what you've done on your writing process checklist." I pointed to the one on chart paper to remind them.

Monitoring My Writing Process	First Piece	Next Piece
Gather entries		
Select and develop one seed idea		
Storytell to rehearse for writing		
Read published writing that resembles what I want to write		
Draft leads—try action, dialogue, setting		
Choose paper, plan story across pages, copy lead		
Write draft with each part on a separate page		
Reread and revise for clarity		
Draft endings—try using important actions, dialogue, images, or reminders of the whole story		
Revise and edit more now or decide to wait until later, or not to revise		

COACHING

This could easily have been preceded by a minilesson that reminded children of all they have already learned to do. Such a minilesson would have entailed re-visiting charts and reminding children that when they want to begin a new piece, they use their repertoire of strategies to gather entries, then reread those entries looking for a seed idea. The minilesson could have allowed time for children to storytell their stories. They'd then be even more ready for this new session.

By citing the variety of choices children have made, you accentuate the options open to them.

Tell children you will teach them another strategy for developing a story idea: making timelines.

"Today I want to teach you another technique narrative writers sometimes use to imagine how a story might go and to get ready to write a draft. We sometimes make timelines of the story we want to write. This helps us organize our writing because the timelines can help us remember what happened first, then next, until the end of the story."

TEACHING
Demonstrate the strategy of developing an idea by making a timeline with your own writing idea.

"Have you ever followed a diagram to build a model? As writers, we sometimes make ourselves a pattern, a plan, before we write and then use that plan to help us know how to write our drafts. When we are writing a narrative, one way to make a plan is to write a timeline."

"Yesterday, when we were collecting entries for our second story, I wrote one about walking home in a rainstorm and another about a bumblebee I rescured from a rain puddle. I think I'll try developing the latter entry into a story—it's a small story, but I think I can make it big."

"I don't know how to start though, so making a timeline could help me plan. Watch how I make a timeline for the story I've chosen so you can do this too, when you need to." I drew a horizontal line on the chalkboard.

"Let me see, what happened first? I had lunch." I wrote "Lunch" near a dot at the beginning of my timeline. "Then I grabbed a frisbee and went out to toss it around." I added "Brought frisbee to yard" near a second dot. "I threw the frisbee." I wrote "threw frisbee" by a third dot, placed a bit farther along the line. "It landed in a mud puddle." I wrote "Mud puddle" and explained, "You'll notice I write just a few words on each dot of my timeline, and that each dot represents a new action. I noticed bees swarming around the frisbee and one bee buzzing and swimming across the puddle. It looked like it was frantic, like it was drowning." I labeled another dot "Bee drowning," and then I described bringing a stick near the bee, letting it climb up the stick to my hand—only to sting me. Before I was done, I'd added "Rescued bee," "Bee stung me," "Stepped on it," "Ran away," and "Got frisbee" onto my timeline.

You'll see that I use this story for a few days of this unit. When planning a minilesson, you will want to ask yourself, "Which piece of writing will I use for the Teaching section of my minilesson?" and "Which piece of writing will I use for the Active Engagement section?" Frequently, as in this session, we will thread two or three pieces of writing throughout a unit of study. Kids benefit from using the same text over and over because it is familiar. If the whole text is new to kids, they appropriately focus on the content and other aspects of the story—their attention is diffused.

Notice that the writing I have done is as brief as possible. I try to be a minimalist for several reasons: I don't want to suck the energy out of the room by going on and on about my own stories. As often as possible, I want the children's stories to fill the air in the classroom. Also, children can become overwhelmed when the teacher writes on a much more sophisticated level than they can. And finally, the bare-bones quality of this writing allows me to return to it later to demonstrate revision by stretching out the details, reworking the plot line, and adding what I was thinking and feeling.

By this time, my timeline looked like this:

```
↑  Lunch
•  Brought frisbee to yard
•  Threw frisbee
•  Mud puddle
•  Bee drowning
•  Rescued bee
•  Bee stung me
•  Stepped on it
•  Ran away
↓  Got frisbee
```

"Do you see how making a timeline helps me set the parts of my story in order? When I write, I can use my timeline to remind me to tell what happened first, second, next, and after that."

ACTIVE ENGAGEMENT

Set children up to try the strategy you've taught. Recall an event the class experienced together; help children make their own timelines of that event.

"Let's try making a timeline together. I'm thinking we could practice by making a timeline of when that dragonfly flew into our room—remember him?"

"With your partner, say how a timeline could go of the other day when the dragonfly flew in while we were reading. Tell what happened first, then second, then third, and so forth. For now, use your fingers as dots on a timeline." The children talked to their partners. I listened, jotting notes.

Convene the class. Share what you overheard individuals doing in a way that allows you to reiterate the steps you hope all children will follow when making timelines.

After a minute, I asked for the children's attention. "I heard some ideas for our timeline dots. Carl, you said the first dot would be, 'We were doing math.' So I'll make 'Math' our first dot." I wrote "Math" on a new timeline on the board.

"Olivia, you said, 'We were listening to a story when Jonathan saw the dragonfly.' I'm going to make that into two dots because first we were listening to a story, *then* Jonathan saw the dragonfly and called out, didn't he?" I started to write "We were listening to a story." Then I pointed out I could abbreviate that phrase as "Story" and wrote just that instead.

You'll notice that I use just a word or two for each dot of the timeline. Each dot on the timeline represents the next action. For now, the personal narrative I am writing and expecting kids to write consists primarily of a character progressing through a series of actions (a plot). If your kids are writing at a more advanced level, you might include dots that represent smaller actions. By leaving these out, however, I have set myself up to add them later. Notice that I begin the timeline before the story really starts, with lunch, and end it with other bits that could be extraneous. I am deliberately messing up, setting myself up to demonstrate how writers revise timelines in order to focus their stories.

Your teaching will have more meaning for you if you use a story from your own life, though we've deliberately chosen a story that could be yours in case you don't think of one.

You will create a wonderful sense of community as you mine the true dramas of your class, using events you experience together as the raw material for minilessons such as this. If your ceiling falls in or a mouse runs across the floor during reading time, take secret pleasure in these mini-disasters because each will make a great story!

I deliberately started this second timeline with a dot (and an event) that are irrelevant to the main story. This will again set the stage for a subsequent mid-workshop teaching point.

It is not an accident that I almost wrote this bullet to represent two linked events. We try to embed little tips into our demonstrations, and one way to do this is by deliberately making the mistakes that kids are apt to make and then self-correcting them, saying aloud why the correction is preferable.

"What should the next dots be, Sam?"

"Add the part about Jonathan seeing the dragonfly. And then tell that it landed on the rug and we were totally silent."

"And then?"

"You started to read *The Lion, the Witch and the Wardrobe*."

"And then?"

"And it listened to Chapter six before it flew out the window!" As the children recalled the episode, I added to the timeline until the completed version looked like this:

Math

Story

J. saw dragonfly

Landed on rug/silent

Read Chapter 6

Flew out

It is great to weave a love of literacy into as many stories as possible. I'm always trying to send subliminal messages to kids.

"Did you see how we took a tiny event that happened to us and we remembered the story, then made a timeline that helped us retell what happened first, next, and then next? The timeline can help us organize our writing because we will tell the story of what happened first, then second, then next."

Some writers will make timelines that are overly full because they write every last bit of the story on it. These writers write a full sentence beside each dot. Teach these children that when writers make timelines, we just jot a quick word beside a dot, using that word later to spark a detailed memory.

LINK
Compile the new list of strategies students have learned for developing their seed idea before drafting.

"Let's go back and add, 'Make a timeline' to our Monitoring My Writing Process checklist. And after you have found your seed idea for your second story, try planning it by making a timeline. In the end, this might be something that really works for you—in which case you will do it often—or it might not work for you. But for this cycle through the writing process, give it a try. Making a timeline shouldn't take more than a few minutes. When you've finished making it, you know other ways in which writers get ready to write. You can try writing different leads, or you can storytell your draft to yourself over and over, thinking, 'How can I tell this story really well, even better than last time?'"

Because the concept of a timeline is a rich one, you may want to support this across your day. For example, children may also learn that readers notice the major events (the important dots) in the timeline of a story, and can retell a story by recalling those events in sequence. Of course, if you have a flow of the day chart or a daily agenda, these are timelines of a sort and you'll want to point this out to children.

WRITING AND CONFERRING

Writing Timelines: Predictable Problems

During writing time today, you'll want to convene small groups based on the assessments you made when you studied children's notebooks and specifically their timelines. You will probably have some children who do not really understand the nature of timelines. They may not grasp that the line represents the passage of time, that the dots signal events or actions, or that their job is to write only a word or phrase alongside each dot, something that is a reminder of the much more detailed story they will eventually write. You can probably gather all the children who are confused about timelines and show them that your flow-of-the day chart in which you overview the day's agenda is already a timeline of their day. They could work with you to make another timeline – perhaps of that day's start of school. They could also make a timeline of a well-known story such as *Owl Moon*. As you work on one of these shared timelines, you can tuck in little pointers and show the group that timelines are tools for telling or retelling stories. You will want to take the time to teach this organizational tool because children will need it throughout the year.

Your children's timelines will also sometimes reveal problems with their personal narratives. Some children will still not have zoomed in in a manner that allows them to retell an event with detail. You may decide to let this go, for now, especially if these are writers who struggle. Many children find it easier to write about an adventure-filled day than to write about a single episode. On the other hand, you may want to help your writers focus—and it's vastly easier to help them now, before they begin their drafts, rather than later. These writers are sometimes reluctant to focus for fear their narratives will end up being too short, so you may need to help writers understand that once they've narrowed themselves to a small number of dots, they can expand their timelines and eventual drafts. Prompts that help

> **MID-WORKSHOP TEACHING POINT** **Resetting the Tone** "Writers, can I have your eyes and your attention?" I said, waiting an extra-long time and sweeping the room with my eyes to convene children. "Writers, I need us to gather now in the meeting area because we need to have a serious conversation." Once children had gathered, I said, "Lately you've been restless and distracted. When I look around the room, instead of seeing you pulled intently towards your paper, I see many of you leaning back in your chairs as if you're just slopping some dots onto the page. You are missing the entire point of timelines, because timelines are meant to be tools of thought."
>
> "Let me explain. Pretend you have a very generous grandmother and she asked you to mail her your birthday list. I know for sure you wouldn't just slap any ol' word onto a page and mail it to her. You'd do a ton of thinking in order to produce even one word on that list, and equal thinking for the next item on the list. Making timelines requires the same sort of dedication, the same level of attentiveness, because each dot represents a whole scene in the story you'll eventually write, and it represents a writer's choice."
>
> "So our classroom needs to become a place where writers can focus. We're going to institute a system of silent work places. If any one of you needs help from a partner, the two of you can go to one of the two conferring stations I've set up on the margins of the room. There are only two of these, however, because I'm going to be admiring the ways in which you're able to help yourselves."

writers do this include, "Can you think of exactly what you did (or said, thought, felt) at that moment?" Or, "Show me, act it out." "Say out loud the exact words you said." This type of guided practice usually helps the child to "write in the air," so you will want to follow up by prompting the child to start putting the new timeline on paper.

Some children may write feelings and thoughts on dots in the timeline, not understanding that each dot represents a new event or a new moment in time. You might see one dot labeled, "I peeled all the bark off the tree" and the next dot, "It was a long piece" and next, "It was fun." You could help such a writer by teaching her to make a movie in her mind of the event, starting at the very beginning and slowly moving through it, writing down dots and labels for every key scene in the movie. What would the scene be for "It was fun"? Was it a big smile on your face? Was it a look of concentration? The action of smiling or looking serious is what should be written on the timeline's dot, if there is going to be a dot for that part.

If any of these issues are troubling a sizable portion of the class, you will want to address them in a mid-workshop teaching point, or even during the next minilesson.

You can anticipate that many children will finish work on their timelines fairly quickly (this doesn't mean the timeline will necessarily be an effective one), so you may move quickly toward your mid-workshop teaching point. In it, you lay out further work that your children could do once they feel as if they've finished with their first timeline. However, another alternative is to not rush towards this particular Mid-Workshop Teaching Point, and to instead convene the class and remind writers that whenever they're 'done' they need to function as their own job captains.

In a conference you can use the work of one child to show other children examples of the way work can progress quickly from a list of story ideas *[Fig. XI-1]* to timelines *[Fig. XI-2]* and then on to a draft *[Fig. XI-3]*.

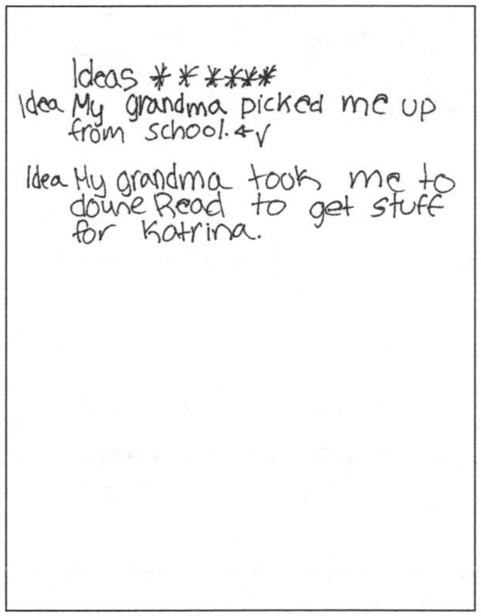
Ideas *****
Idea My grandma picked me up from school. 4√
Idea My grandma took me to doune Read to get stuff for Katrina.

Fig. XI-1 Sophie lists possible stories she could write about her grandmother.

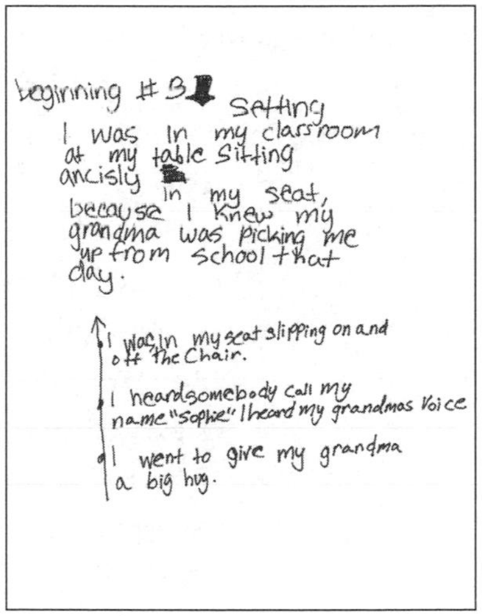
beginning #3 Setting
I was in my classroom at my table sitting ancisly in my seat, because I knew my grandma was picking me up from school that day.
I was in my seat slipping on and off the Chair.
I heard somebody call my name "Sophie" I heard my grandmas voice
I went to give my grandma a big hug.

Fig. XI-2 Sophie makes a timeline for the story she's decided to tell.

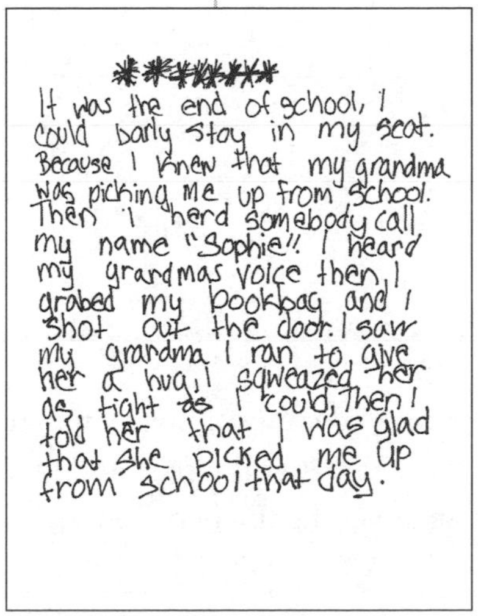
****
It was the end of school, I could barly stay in my seat. Because I knew that my grandma was picking me up from school. Then I herd somebody call my name "Sophie"! I heard my grandmas voice then, I grabed my bookbag and I shot out the door. I saw my grandma I ran to give her a hug, I sqweazed her as tight as I could, Then I told her that I was glad that she picked me up from school that day.

Fig. XI-3 Sophie's first draft

SHARE

Revising Timelines

Convene writers. Celebrate that they are imagining various starting points for their narratives.

"Writers, earlier this year you planned stories across your fingers and across the pages of booklets. Today you learned that you can also plan stories as we plan our school day— by recording a timeline. The important thing to realize is that timelines are meant as quick ways to jot some notes—and they are meant as tools for revision."

Explain that timelines can be used to help writers focus and revise our writing before it is even written. Give an example.

"Timelines give us a way to revise our stories before we've even written them. Let me show you what I mean," I said, turning to my timeline. "After I have made a timeline, I reread it and think, 'Are all the dots on this timeline important to the real story I want to tell?' Sometimes I cross out parts of a timeline that aren't that important. Watch me as I reread my Bee timeline and reconsider which parts are important to the story I want to tell."

Lunch
Brought frisbee to yard
Threw frisbee
Mud puddle
Bee drowning
Rescued bee
Bee stung me
Stepped on it
Ran away
Got frisbee

"I'm realizing that if I want to zoom in on the most important part of my story, I can cross out the part about lunch. It doesn't really matter to the story." I crossed out that event on my timeline. Then I held my pen poised over the final dots on my timeline. "I'm not

Timelines are amazing tools for teaching children that they can take control of their writing. It's easy to feel that the way writing is on the page is the only way it could be—after all, there it is. The choices writers make are easier to see when children learn to manipulate timelines.

sure how to end the story. Running away and getting the frisbee doesn't really relate to the bee part. I might want to end the story with me stepping on the bee. But that is an angry ending. Is that what I want? I'll have to think about that some more and try to remember more about what happened. I want to think more about what the important thing is in my story."

Ask children to consider revising the timeline of the class' story.

"Right now, would each of you think about our class dragonfly story? Look at the timeline—are there any events on this timeline that are *not* important to the heart of the story?" I waited half a minute, giving children time to do this. "Give me a thumbs up if you see some dots we could take out of our timeline."

```
↑
•  Math
•  Story
•  J. saw dragonfly
•  All saw
•  Landed on rug/silent
•  Chapter 6
•  Flew out
↓
```

Naomi suggested, "We don't have to keep the part about doing math because it doesn't have anything to do with the dragonfly."

"That's smart! So let's cross off the first event—Math—and we could just keep going, asking, 'Is there anything else on our timeline that isn't part of the real story?' And then we'd cross it out if it's not."

Remind children they can use this strategy on their own.

"So, writers, whenever you are working with timelines, look back and think, 'Is every dot on my timeline important for the main story I want to tell?' Your story will get better if you cross out unnecessary dots. Often, the first few dots on your timeline, and sometimes the last ones as well, aren't essential to the story. A writer I know said, 'If you are writing about a waterfall, start when you can just hear the falls ahead of you.' So if you are writing about rescuing a drowning bee, start just a bit before you extend a helping hand."

I added very obvious bits into my timeline which aren't integral to the story I'm writing. I did this deliberately, in order to make the point. Because the example is an obvious one, it's all the more likely that children will grasp the lesson. I generally find that I make my point best in minilessons when I'm not subtle in the least.

Later in this series, we'll teach writers that story mountains are a more sophisticated way to plan the plotline of a narrative. The big difference between a story mountain and a timeline is that in the former, the writer makes a decision over what to highlight.

Whatever children suggest in terms of revising timelines can work, of course, since the point is that timelines can be revised. Whether the decision of what to revise is the best or not matters little.

HOMEWORK *Storytelling from Timelines* Tonight, at home, use your timeline to jog memories of the sequence of your story. Storytell this new piece of writing in preparation for drafting it tomorrow.

Remember, the story about a drowning bee will not sound like this: 'Lunch, brought frisbee to yard, threw frisbee to puddle . . .'

When you storytell or write a draft from your timeline, don't just read the labels off the dots! Instead, look at a dot, and then tell a whole story that goes with that one dot. For example, the first dots of the bee timeline say, 'lunch' and 'brought frisbee to yard.' The story that goes with those dots may start like this:

> After lunch I grabbed my new frisbee and went to the yard. The sun
> was shining bright. "See you later, Mom," I said, and ran through
> the back door, letting it bang shut.

The dot says "frisbee" but the story will contain not only this, but other details I recall:

> I threw the red frisbee up into the sky. It flew up, up, up, rebounded
> off the garage door and then . . . it landed with a plop in a mud
> puddle right next to the sticker rosebush. Surrounding the muddy
> frisbee was a swarm of buzzing bees.

Remember Robert Munsch's advice and storytell your story several times, to yourself and to others. Use the dots as a guide, but say a whole lot for each dot. Add to the story in ways that aren't on the timeline. Make your stories sound like the stories we read in books—and tomorrow, you'll have a chance to write them on the page.

Notice that I am tucking a cautionary note into my teaching. This cautionary note comes from prior experiences doing this work with children. I'm presenting an extreme version of what not to do.

If you want to raise the stakes of children's storytelling, ask them to try to tell their story in such a way that the story commands attention. It's likely that your child will need to recruit an audience. While she washes the dishes, a student might say to her father. "Can I tell you the story of a memory I have?" The father will agree and as the story starts, he may listen politely. But if the storyteller succeeds, she will draw the father in to really, really listen. Ruth Sawyer, author of The Storyteller, *writes: "I have never told a story that I have not wondered if this were not after all the supreme test of the art: To command attention, not trade on mere willingness of others to listen. To take the center of the marketplace, or a table at the inn, and, whether by the sharing of great adventure or taking the gentle road of fancy, be able to lift the soul with exaltation or move it with amazement. To hold 'children from play, and old men from the chimney corner'—nothing short of this, I take it, can be called storytelling" (1942, p. 71).*

If your students are new to timelines and tend to include too many items or too many details . . . you could make and talk through a timeline of a class event like a birthday celebration or trip. You can highlight the brevity of each label on the timeline and highlight also that each dot represents a step forward in the sequence of events.

If your students have experience with timelines . . . you could show them how to angle the timelines in ways that help to get to the heart of their story. Writers can make different timelines of the same event, depending on what they decide they want to show. For example, if you wanted to show that a class visitor was greatly anticipated, your timeline might start before the visit and convey the class' excitement—one dot might represent the narrator peeking into the hall to see if the visitor was approaching yet. On the other hand, if you wanted to show that the visitor brought odd animals with him, the timeline might start as the visitor entered the room carrying a wriggling bundle.

If your students could use more support in using timelines effectively . . . you might create a minilesson in which you ask children to join you in studying timelines that other children have made, noticing their different choices and the effects these choices might have on the stories. They might notice the following:

- Some label each dot with a word, some with a sentence
- Some are interesting just by themselves, some seem flat already
- Some start with a small event, some start broad
- Some have a lot of cross-outs, some are untouched

If your children already know how to make timelines and want other tools for planning their narratives . . . you could teach them that writers keep in mind the kind of text we'll be writing, and use our knowledge of the genre in which we're writing to help us prepare for drafting. This means that when children know they're writing narratives (or stories), it's helpful for them to think in advance about their setting, their characters, and their plot. Children can be reminded to use all they know as readers of stories to guide them as they plan the stories they will soon write.

COLLABORATING WITH COLLEAGUES

Sometimes people ask me for advice on using these units of study. They want to know whether it's important for a group of teachers to read through an entire book or series of books before launching the work in classrooms. They have questions about whether it's best for a teacher to hold the book in his or her lap while teaching a minilesson, or to let the particular words slip away in favor of teaching the big ideas of a minilesson.

I believe there are many right answers to these questions. As the song goes: "Different strokes for different folks."

But there is one right answer that I believe pertains to all of us, and this is it: Our teaching will be immeasurably deeper and richer if we do the work ourselves in the minilessons we plan to give to children, and then refer to our own writing and learning from those minilessons as we teach them to our students.

In many schools, one teacher agrees to read ahead in a unit of study, and during grade-level meetings, this teacher gives a very abbreviated version of an upcoming minilesson to the group of teachers. Then for a few minutes—even just five minutes works—the room is quiet as everyone does a tiny bit of fast writing. The pieces we produce are written on topics we're willing to share with our children, and they are abbreviated—which works perfectly for minilessons.

When teachers write together, we experience firsthand what it is we are asking children to do. When we're asked to make a timeline of a small moment in our lives, we'll find ourselves confronting all the questions that children will confront. Do I label each dot with a word? A phrase? How small are the steps I take through an event?

The fact that we write ourselves will have giant payoffs, but the conversations we have with our colleagues as a result of the writing will be even more powerful.

Finally, let me emphasize that the children need to know that you and the other teachers are learning this work alongside them. Roland Barth, the author of *Improving Schools from Within*, recently reminded Teachers College Reading and Writing Project principals that schools need to be places where everyone's learning curve is off the charts. "Write down the areas in which you find you are learning, learning, learning," he said to principals. After giving people a moment to record, he pressed further. "Here is the question: Who knows about this learning you are doing?" Barth's point was that in schools, those of us who are called upon to mentor children need to be very public about our learning. So strut your stuff!

IN THIS SESSION, YOU WILL SHOW
CHILDREN THAT WRITERS CAN
DEVELOP SEED IDEAS BY CHOOSING
ONE DOT FROM A TIMELINE AND
EXPANDING THAT EVENT INTO A
NEW TIMELINE.

GETTING READY

- Instructions on chalkboard telling children to bring their writer's notebooks and sit with their partners in the meeting area
- Sample second timeline made from one dot of first timeline, written on chart paper
- See CD-ROM for resources

TIMELINES AS TOOLS FOR DEVELOPING STORIES

Writing is a powerful tool for thought because it allows us to put our words, our thoughts, onto paper. Then we can hold our thoughts in our hands, and we can think about our thinking. In this minilesson, you'll teach children that once they've jotted a timeline of their story onto the page, that graphic organizer can become a tool for thought. They can look at what they've written and ask, as they did in the previous session, "Are all the dots key to the story I want to tell?" They can also think, "Which dots are so important that I should expand them?"

Eventually, children will learn that in order to decide where and how they will start and develop a story, they first need to decide what their story aims to show. For now, however, it is enough for children to realize that writers have choices. Whereas many children have assumed that writing true stories means telling what happened, children will go away from these two sessions aware that writers can select just one part of their story, just one dot of a timeline, and expand that single dot into a timeline, a story, of its own.

By showing children that writers not only eliminate unnecessary dots or actions, but also add actions that are important, you will give children a practical introduction to revision. For now, you spare them the work of writing a sequence of long drafts, and yet you still give them an experience in thinking, "How else could I have written this?"

Your children will think through different ways their story could start. They will tell the story aloud one way and then another. Soon they'll choose one and scrawl out a draft, writing fast and long.

MINILESSON

Timelines as Tools for Developing Stories

CONNECTION

Remind writers that making timelines can help them plan and draft stories.

"Yesterday we learned that writers can get ready to draft stories by making timelines to lay out what happened first, next, and next. In the process of trying to remember everything that happened, some of you came up with so many dots! Jonathan had eleven! Remember that we also learned we can look back at our timelines to cross out parts that are not important."

"We also learned that writers sometimes try starting the story at one dot on the timeline, then we try starting at another dot. Writers ask ourselves, 'Where, in a sequence of events, is the best place for me to start my story?'"

Name the teaching point. Specifically, tell writers that they can zoom in on just one dot of a timeline, expanding that single dot into a timeline of its own.

"Today I want to teach you that as writers, we revise not only by eliminating dots that seem unnecessary to the timeline, but also by adding dots, expanding the most important events."

TEACHING

Show children an example of a timeline that has been made from a small part of another timeline.

"I noticed that Sasha found that by zooming in on the important part of her story, she ended up with just one dot on her timeline! Sasha started out with a timeline with seven events on it. She ended up deciding that none of them were important except one: 'We twisted and spun on swings.' Then Sasha did something that all writers sometimes do—she made a second timeline out of that one dot since it was the most important part, the part she wanted to focus on! To do this, she made a movie in her mind of what happened inside that one dot. Here's the new timeline Sasha made out of 'We twisted and spun on swings.'"

Got on swing

Tried to touch leaves

A girl beside me tried to do it too

Bumped each other

Her name was Lizzie

We laughed

"Can you see how Sasha took that one event and really thought about exactly how it went, and made a new, more focused timeline out of it? That is the strategy you can try when you need to get to the heart of your story before you draft."

ACTIVE ENGAGEMENT
Ask children to try this new strategy for developing a seed idea.

"Open up your notebooks to the timeline you made in the last lesson. Find one important dot on your timeline, just like Sasha did. See if you can zoom in on that one dot and make a movie in your mind of what happened inside that single moment. Try to remember the tiny little actions in it." I gave the children a few minutes to read over their timelines and to choose an important dot to expand upon.

"Partner 1, please tell partner 2 the story of just one dot on your timeline. Tell the story so your partner can make a movie in his or her mind of your tiny actions." The children did this.

"I heard many of you remembering more small events by zooming in on one dot on your timeline and replaying that one small moment of your story like a movie in your mind. Yazmin, will you please share what you discovered when you tried to do this?" [Fig. XII-1]

"I remembered lots more about my reading buddy being restless." Yazmin pointed to his next finger. "He started fidgeting and pulling up grass." Yazmin pointed to a new finger. "Then he rolled back and forth. He even tried to run off." Pointing to yet another finger, Yazmin said, "I had to jump up and bring him back to our reading spot."

"Wow, Yazmin, it sounds like you could turn that one dot into four more dots on your timeline. Now that you know you can do this with this one dot, you'll realize you could do the same thing with other dots. So you'll need to look back at your original draft of a timeline and think again about the story you want to write. What's not important in that story and can be deleted? What is important and can be expanded? Writers fiddle with our timelines as a way to weigh possibilities for our drafts."

Be sure that children don't get the idea that the timelines are important as products. They are only important as tools for revision, as a shortcut method to weigh alternatives.

I usually don't have children practice on their current writing work in this way because this often doesn't leave any work for them to do when they go off to their seats to write. But today I thought that by having the children try to zoom in on one existing dot during the Active Engagement, they would be more likely to go back and make revisions they might not otherwise make on their timelines. Notice that I ask partner 1 to do this work, and partner 2 to listen. Another day, these roles will flip. Both benefit from this tiny interlude of closer practice—and from the brevity of the minilesson.

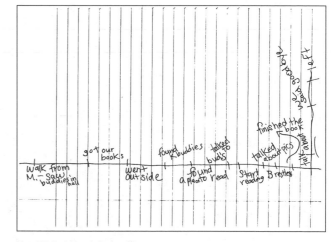

Fig. XII-1 Yazmin's timeline

LINK
Remind children that after they select a seed idea, they have a repertoire of ways to begin developing that idea.

"Writers, you have learned that after a writer decides on a seed idea, there are some things the writer can do to get ready to draft. Today you can choose from all those things. You may decide to make and rethink your timeline, eliminating dots that don't really go with the story and expanding dots that are especially important. You may decide to storytell your stories and to use storytelling as a way to get a new trajectory on your story. You can experiment with different leads, trying out a lead that begins with a small action, then trying one that begins with dialogue or with the setting. Of course, you can also try leads that start at different places in the timeline. I can't wait to see the choices you make during today's writing workshop!"

Ideally, when we send kids off to do their work, we want to remind them that they can draw on what they learned earlier in the year as well as on what they learned today. This is a nice link because it reminds writers that they have choices to make and lots of work to do. As often as possible, I try to use the link as a time to reference and revitalize classroom charts that spell out strategies I've taught earlier in the unit and in the year.

WRITING AND CONFERRING

Getting a Good Start

You may question whether timelines really merit two full days of minilessons and mid-workshop teaching points, and my answer is a resounding yes.

One reason timelines matter is that your children are probably still more willing to do initial revisions, revising leads and timelines, than final revisions, producing a sequence of full drafts. Because they are still fairly inexperienced writers, your students probably can't yet entertain and discard a whole sequence of ideas simply by mulling over their plans. Timelines, like leads, allow children to make their abstract plans into a concrete object—manipulating that concrete timeline makes it easier for them to rethink those abstract plans.

But the other reason to work on timelines for several days is so you can keep children working productively while at the same time stalling them from drafting until you can confer with each of them! That way, you can help them get this next piece of writing off to the best possible start. Just because children are working on timelines does not mean you need to focus on timelines as you confer. Instead, I suggest you study the child's writing, look over and listen to the child's plans, and decide how you can help the child have as successful an experience as possible writing the upcoming piece.

If the child is not yet writing about a tightly focused event, you will have time to intervene. Rely on the standard questions: "Of all the things that you did while at your grandma's, what's the one particular event that you most remember?" "How did that start?" "What exactly were you doing at the start?"

If the child you are conferring with did, in her last piece, focus on a specific event, and if she did seem to make a movie in her mind and retell the story as she recalled it, you will very likely find that the previous draft is detailed and lively but that the story is swamped by dialogue. Danielle's draft is typical of the personal narratives I saw in those New York City schools where writing workshops had only recently been instituted.

MID-WORKSHOP TEACHING POINT · *Choosing a Starting Moment* · "Writers, can I have your eyes and your attention? Let me stop you for a minute. Wow! It's so quiet in here, another dragonfly might come for a visit!"

"I want to show you one more way in which I use timelines to help me get ready to draft. Remember how, during our first piece of writing, we spent time trying out different leads? Well, writers not only weigh different ways to word their leads, we also consider different times in the sequence of events to start with. Watch how I try this out, asking myself, 'When, in a sequence of events, do I want to start my story?'" I pointed to my bee timeline, at the dot labeled "Mud puddle," and said, "I could start then." I voiced that lead:

> I stood beside the mud puddle, staring at my brand-new frisbee that lay in the center. "I'll get you," I said to the frisbee, but then I saw a buzzing swarm of bees circling it.

Then I pointed to a later dot, and said, "Or I could start it when I got a stick to rescue the bee."

> I nudged the bee gently with my stick. It climbed onto the stick unsteadily, clinging to the bark. Then it inched up and up, away from the muddy water, higher and higher, toward my finger.

"I bet I could even start my story with this dot—'Rescued bee'."

> "I can't believe it!" I thought to myself. The wet bee was inching up my finger.

"Do you see how I looked at my timeline and experimented by beginning my story at different times in the sequence of events? Let's try that with our class story. Look over our

continued on next page

Danielle is in fourth grade, but she is an inexperienced writer. Still, this first story of hers shows evidence of instruction: it is focused, chronological, detailed, and includes direct dialogue. In fact, the draft reads like a soundtrack of a film, without any actions!

When I conferred with Danielle, I celebrated the fact that she clearly has made a movie in her mind and recorded that movie [Fig. XII-2]:

> I was in the pool. Me and my sister was playing water fight so I was scared because I thought that I was going to drown so my sister said, "You are not going to drown. I got you. Don't worry I have you." So I said "Okay." She said, "Go on your back." I was telling my sister "Please don't drop me, please don't drop me," and she said "I'm not going to drop you. If you keep saying that I will drop you!". . . .

I pointed out, however, that because she knows the people, the place, and the actions, she only paid attention to the sound track in her movie. For the sake of her reader, she needs, in the next piece, to play that mental movie to record not only the dialogue, but also to tell who spoke, to tell how she spoke, and to tell what she did along with the dialogue, so that the next draft reads more like this:

> She said, "Go on your back," and she rolled my body over in the water. I held my sister's arm and yelled, "Please don't drop me!" with panic in my voice. . .

I could, of course, have suggested Danielle revise this piece so as to add the speaker, the speaker's intonations and actions . . . but it was just as effective for me to use knowledge gleaned from her last piece to set Danielle up for her next piece. And in this way, I gave her more confidence and energy for the writing ahead of her.

---

continued from previous page

timeline, think in your mind about one dot you could use as a starting time for a story, and say that lead in your head." I waited a half-minute. "Now try a second starting time, and a second lead."

Tashim said, "We could start it when we were reading and Jonathan saw a dragonfly."

Picking up a sheet of paper, I said, "So your story would go like this: 'When we were reading?'"

Giggling, Tashim said, "No. I'd write, 'We were so quiet, we could probably have heard ants crawling along the floor. Then our teacher stopped reading, and we were just about to say, 'Don't stop! It's the most exciting part!' But she was looking at Jonathan because he was looking up at the top of the bookshelf where a dragonfly had landed. 'He wants to listen to the story,' he said'."

"That is so beautiful! There are also many other places in the timeline we could begin the story about the dragonfly. Writers, do you see that all of your stories can begin in different places? You can return to your own writing now."

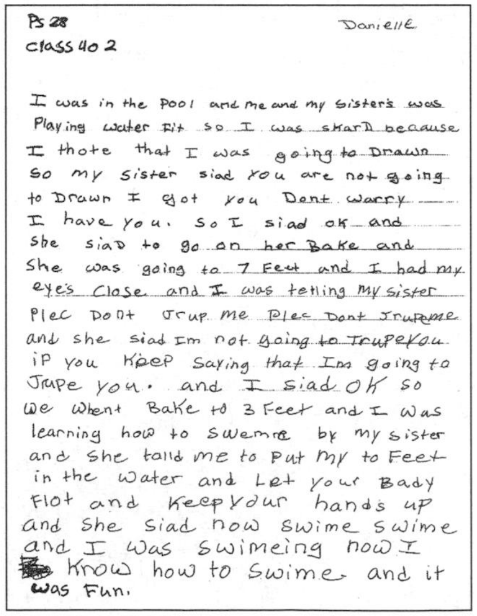

PS 28   Danielle
class 40 2

I was in the Pool and me and my sister's was Playing water Fit so I was skard because I thote that I was going to Drawn so my sister siad You are not going to Drawn I got you Dont warry I have you. So I siad ok and she siad to go on her Bake and she was going to 7 Feet and I had my eye's Close and I was teling My sister Plec Dont Jrup me Plec Dont Jrupme and she siad Im not going to Jrupeyou iP you Keep saying that Im going to Jrupe you. and I siad oK so We Went Bake to 3 Feet and I was learning how to Swemre by my sister and she taid me to Put my to Feet in the water and Let your Bady Flot and Keepyour hands up and she siad now Swime Swime and I was swimeing now I Know how to Swime and it was Fun.

Fig. XII-2 Danielle

SHARE

Planning and Goal-Setting

Explain to children that writers can keep themselves on course by making and sticking to plans and goals. Ask them to make some goals and plans with their partners.

"Writers, most of you have shifted from drafting to revising timelines and leads to beginning your draft, and that's great. When you write, you'll keep your timeline near you and it can act as a silent teacher, a quiet coach, reminding you of your hopes for this new piece of writing. Some people tie yarn around a finger to remind themselves of how they want to act. Writers have our own ways to keep ourselves on course, and one way we do that is to use plans. Timelines are a form of a plan."

"But you may want to give yourself other reminders as well, and you need to decide on the particular reminders you need. I told you earlier that you need to be job captains for yourselves, deciding when it is time for you to start this second piece of writing. Well, you also need to decide on a goal and reminders that will help you do your best work."

Explain that writers can make goals for themselves by looking at their past writing and deciding what to aim for in future writing. Share the story of one child who did that.

"You can glean those reminders from looking back on your first completed piece and thinking, 'What did I do in this piece of writing that I want to always do as a writer?' Then jot yourself a reminder on a sticky note, and put it beside you as you write. Perhaps you remembered to write with periods and capitals—well, you definitely don't want to go back to the old days before you did that! So write a reminder."

"Natalie realized by looking at her first piece that she wrote what one person said and the next person said, but her writing was like a sound track. It told what people said, but didn't tell the actions, their intonations, so she's written herself a note that says, 'Not just a sound track!'"

In other places in this series, you will have the chance to teach children that they can also form goals for themselves by aiming to work on certain qualities of good narrative writing, either qualities they name for themselves or qualities they pick from the class chart. Any of the class charts can become the spark for writerly aspiration, and future sessions in this series will offer you a place to explore this use of the charts more with children.

Ask children to get started on this work now, with partners.

"Right now, get with your partner. Look over each other's first pieces, and create together some goals for your future writing, starting with this next piece."

HOMEWORK *Collecting Words* This year we are going to travel on a journey through language, and our souvenirs will be words. We are going to collect words like a tourist collects postcards in order to remember all our new experiences with language.

After you leave school today, listen for words that catch your attention. You may overhear a conversation where someone uses a phrase that strikes you as special. Jot it down in your notepad. As you are reading, pay attention to any words that you can practically taste. Write them down in your notepad. Pay attention to words, savor them, then use them.

From this day forward, gather words that seem to be just right for saying hard-to-say things, words that are somehow remarkable, jot them down, and then we will try to use these words when we talk and when we write. We will begin to collect these words in our very own album.

TAILORING YOUR TEACHING

If your children are skilled at drafting and revising timelines for their stories . . . you may want to remind them that writers can plan other elements of a story in addition to the plot. For example, teach children that before they begin a draft, some writers take a few minutes to envision the place in which the story is set. Teach children that it helps to go back to the beginning of the story and to think, "Where was I exactly?" If the writer's first thought is a general one such as "I was in the park," teach the child that it is important to press on for more specifics, for example, "I was sitting on the bench under the giant willow tree in Central Park." Then you can teach children that writers sometimes take a second to sketch the place, and do so thinking, "What can I put in my story that will help readers see the scene clearly?" Of course, the challenge will be to paint the picture using not a drawing but words.

Words hold power, and the language we use and the way we use it often impacts our success and status in this world. Whether the language is academic or poetic, our students need constant exposure and encouragement in its usage. You can encourage this language study during your daily read alouds and throughout the day. Math, science, and social studies vocabulary sets also offer numerous opportunities to explore and celebrate words!

COLLABORATING WITH COLLEAGUES

In the New York City school district, leaders sometimes conducted school "walk-throughs." Often a team consisting of the superintendent, the principal, and assorted other people in power would walk in and out of every classroom in a school, sampling bits of data. In one room they might ask to see the teacher's records of reading assessments, in another they might look closely through a randomly selected child's work. In some rooms, they might stay five minutes and in other rooms, much longer.

Sometimes, in the wake of these walk-throughs, harsh mandates and memos would go out. Sometimes the walk-throughs added to a climate of mistrust between schools and their leadership.

New York City's current deputy chancellor, Carmen Farina, has instituted a different kind of school visit. She calls these *Glory Walks*. "Show me what's working, or almost working, in this school," she says, and uses her visits as a time to celebrate, to study characteristics of successful practice and to spread success stories.

After Carmen visits a school, she invariably talks about that visit with everyone she meets with over the next few days, always sending others to see and emulate what she most admires. Schools that have never been regarded as exemplary are suddenly hosting visitors, displaying what it is they do well.

Word has spread through New York City. This is a place where good work is often recognized and celebrated. Walk-throughs are often now *Glory Walks*. Morale is rising, efforts are redoubled, and schools are improving.

Keep this message in your mind as you study your children's work. Look at the children who've never been regarded as mentors and models. What can you see in their work that you can glory in? Can you find ways for unlikely children to be touted as teachers and asked to help others?

Try learning from Carmen Farina's model. People work harder and grow faster when we are seen and our work is recognized.

IN THIS SESSION, YOU WILL TEACH CHILDREN THAT WRITERS REPLAY LIFE EVENTS TO HELP OURSELVES WRITE IN WAYS THAT LET READERS FEEL THE EXPERIENCE.

GETTING READY

- Instructions on chalkboard telling children to bring their writer's notebooks and sit with their partners in the meeting area

- Examples of memories that have been seared into your mind—big and small

- Chart paper and markers

- Qualities of Good Personal Narrative Writing chart

- Example of paragraph formatting on chart paper

- Two drafts of a child's writing, one without paragraphs, one with, copied onto transparency or chart paper

- Overhead projector and marker

- Copies of a child's writing with paragraphs indicated by boxes (one copy per partnership)

- Copies of a story retyped with no paragraph formatting at all (one copy per child)

- Tool containers on each table with sharpened pencils (for use during share)

- See CD-ROM for resources

WRITING FROM INSIDE A MEMORY

Yesterday your children tried one timeline and another, and you helped them to feel the elasticity of their plans for their narratives. Today you'll teach towards an almost opposite goal. Today's session aims to help children understand that in order to write an effective narrative, after weighing possible plans, a writer commits himself or herself to one trajectory and then relives that story, holding onto the unfolding storyline with the same rapt attention that a reader might give when lost in a book.

The fiction writer, John Gardner, has pointed out that when reading, we first see letters on the page. But soon we are seeing not ink marks on a page but a train rushing through a Russian countryside or rain pelting down on a ramshackle house. "We read on, we dream on," he says.

But here is the secret. Readers can read words and see a train hurtling through the Russian countryside or rain pelting down on a ramshackle house if first, we as writers have seen those scenes. We must first write, seeing not words on the page but the events of our lives. We see these events, relive these events, so that readers can, in turn, do the same.

If you don't actually do this work on the page, do it in your conversations with friends, and notice yourself doing it. The other day my husband brought me to the window to look out at what had been a small garden and was now a patch of scorched earth. "You know what happened?" John said, and launched into this story. "Matt told me that every spring, he burns his dead plants, and new growth shoots up," he said. "So I brought out the garden hose and left the water running into the lawn, just to be safe. Then I took a match and set fire to the dried grasses we used to have in the center of the garden. It smoldered. I wondered if it would catch fire. I blew on the sparks. Then I glanced away. Out of the corner of my eye, I saw an explosion of fire. The whole garden was wreathed in flames. I grabbed for the hose, but the little stream of water seemed like nothing! I thought the house was going to burn down!" As John retold the escapade, he relived it in Technicolor and I, in turn, felt as if I had been right there with him. For both of us, the story made our hearts leap. I didn't tell him the whole event was great for my book!

MINILESSON

Writing from Inside a Memory

CONNECTION

Put today's work into the context of the writing process as a whole so that children can see the writing cycle of rehearsing, drafting, revising, and editing.

"We've talked earlier this year about the fact that writers don't just sit down in front of a blank sheet of paper, pick up a pen, and write. Instead, as writers, we live in a way that gets us ready to write. We first see possible stories everywhere and gather entries, then we select an entry that we believe particularly matters, storytell the story to our friends and ourselves, and draft and revise timelines of the story sequence. We often explore different leads and plan how our story will lay out across pages in a booklet or down the page in paragraphs."

"And then the day comes when we write a whole draft. As you know from earlier in this unit, we usually write fast and long. While we write, we try to keep our minds on our subject."

Name your teaching point. Specifically, tell children that writing involves reenacting their own experiences.

"Today I want to teach you that writing personal narratives well involves reliving episodes from our own lives."

TEACHING

Point out to children that we all have memories that are seared into our minds forever. Give examples.

"Writers, I'm sure that for every one of us, there are moments in our lives that are seared into our memories forever. For me, one of those is the time I heard that a second plane had just flown into the World Trade Center towers, and all of a sudden the awareness flooded into me that this was not an accident. I can close my eyes and relive where I was in that moment, what I heard on the radio, what I thought, what I looked at, what I said, what I did. I can, and I do, go back to my experience of that event and replay it."

"As a writer, I have come to realize that I can go back and relive not only the traumatic, life-changing events, but also little moments that for some reason have mattered to me. I do not know why I remember the story of saving that drowning bee. Maybe I feel like my

COACHING

So far this year, children have inched along through the writing process. In this Connection, I'm helping them to look back over the terrain they've traveled as if they're finally standing on a hilltop, surveying the route they've traveled. By helping them trace the path they've taken, I'm teaching towards independence. I want them to understand that whenever they write, they'll make a similar journey. It is important, then, that they see all the steps of the process as a single trail of work.

In order to teach children ideas that are deeper than the usual ones, you'll want to revisit content you have talked about earlier, layering the content with new insights and interpretations. Ideas grow like onions, in successive rings of thought.

We teach not only explicitly but also implicitly. By treating a little story about a bumblebee with such respect, I hope to convey to children that gigantic life issues can be contained in the seemingly mundane details of life.

whole life has been about trying to give folks who are drowning a stick to hang onto—I don't know. But I do know that when I wrote that story, I could feel again the wash of pride when that little bee climbed higher and higher up my stick, safe at last. And I know when I wrote that story, I can feel again the sudden throb in my finger as that bee turned on the very hand that had rescued it."

"Whenever I write a personal narrative, I relive my own experiences. Remember my story about Dad coming in to that basketball game? That was almost forty years ago but right now, I can still hear Dad's booming call, 'Lukers!' and the blood rushes to my face all over again. The truth is, I am not totally sure Dad really called out 'Lukers' that night. He called me that a lot, but did he holler that across the gym? I don't really know. When I write, I bring all the memories to my pen, and I imagine what probably happened. When I write, I remember an afternoon from years and years ago, and I reenact it in my mind."

"And the experiences that we remember and relive become all the more intense and searing and beautiful because we are living through them a second time, a third time."

Demonstrate to show that you write by reliving.

"Let me show you how I go about doing this kind of writing, and then we'll try it together. I'll never forget the day when Jeremy came running into the class with a cricket— that's the topic I've chosen to write about for now."

"I'm going to close my eyes and really put myself back into that memory. I remember exactly where I was, over here. And I remember it was hot out and I was feeling sticky. Now I'm going to look through the same eyes I had then and see what I see and hear what I heard then and write it! If I can't remember something, I'll picture how it might have gone and write that."

I stood at the easel, copying something out of a book.

Then I paused, reread, and crossed that out. "I want to be more detailed about what was going on before Jeremy interrupted me."

I stood at the easel, trying to hold <u>Peter's Chair</u> open with one hand while I copied the lead with the other.

The juxtaposition of these distinct stories is no accident. By showing children that there are many episodes in our lives that for some reason are seared into our memories, I emphasize the power writing has to imbue small moments with meaning. It is through writing that we discover the particularities of how and why moments matter.

Notice that when I write in front of children, I generally work on just a tiny excerpt of text. I think aloud, letting children in on the thoughts as I weigh them. I deliberately show myself struggling in ways that resemble the struggles children also encounter.

"I could include the lead I was copying but that's not the main story. Instead, I want to get to the main event."

> I stood at the easel, trying to hold <u>Peter's Chair</u> open with one hand while I copied the lead with the other.
>
> Suddenly I heard a commotion behind me and turned to see Jeremy, who was holding a cricket.

I paused, and reread, testing what I'd written against my true recollection of the scene. "No, I didn't know at the time that he was holding a cricket. Let me stay true to what I knew at that moment."

> I stood at the easel, trying to hold <u>Peter's Chair</u> open with one hand while I copied the lead with the other.
>
> Suddenly I heard a commotion behind me and turned to see Jeremy, who had his hands clasped as if in prayer. A circle of kids gathered around and Jeremy opened his hands so a few kids could peek in. "What is it?" I asked.

"Did you see how I recreated the event in my mind, then wrote it, trying to stay specific, detailed, and true to the unfolding story?"

I've chosen to write this sequence of tiny drafts because I want to highlight that it is very important for the narrator in a personal narrative to stay inside a specific perspective. If I'm standing at the easel, copying from a picture book and a child approaches me, I'm not apt to discern instantly that the child is holding a cricket!

I tuck a lot of teaching into this demonstration. I model envisioning, adding specific details, getting to the main event, replaying the episode, and slowing down the key part. I also demonstrate how I work through these predictable problems. I think, I write, I cross out, and I try again. This is what I want students to do as they write.

ACTIVE ENGAGEMENT

Ask kids to try the strategy you've introduced. In this case, have them relive an important moment from the day before and write it down as they lived it. Then share one child's writing as an example.

"To practice, think of something important that happened to you yesterday. For now, maybe you want to recall a time when you entered or left a place, as the sequence of events should be clear. For example, recall how you entered the lunchroom and found a seat, or how you left school at the end of the day and boarded the bus. Some small episode. Now remember how it started. Where were you? What did you do? What did you say? Thumbs up if you can recall what you did and said."

Watch the way I move kids quickly past topic indecision, shepherding them along so they have a moment in mind and can proceed to learn from my pointers on how to write about that moment.

When most thumbs were up, I said, "So, quickly, scrawl that small moment down in your notebook, just as I wrote mine on the easel. Imagine yourself right inside the story. Stay detailed, specific, and true to the story. This is just an exercise; you won't actually regard this entry as a draft to develop."

After a few minutes I asked children to share what they wrote with partners, and I listened in.

"Listen for the details in Ellie's try-it." *[Fig. XIII-1]*

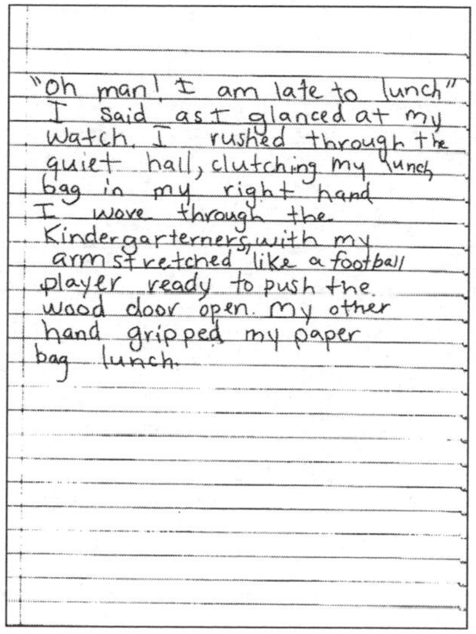

> "Oh man! I am late to lunch," I said as I glanced at my watch. I rushed through the quiet hall, clutching my lunch bag in my right hand. I wove through the kindergarteners with my arm stretched like a football player ready to push the wood door open. My other hand gripped my paper bag lunch.

"Do you hear how Ellie got right inside the moment and wrote thoughts from her head at that moment and wrote the things she saw at that moment? She was really reliving it as she wrote, wasn't she?"

LINK
Remind writers of all you've taught so far about the qualities of good personal narrative writing, adding this new one aloud.

"Before you get started, writers, will you think for a moment about the work you will do today? There are probably some of you who began your draft yesterday and have decided you're going to start over, revising like writers revise, so that you really live inside your story. Some of you haven't yet begun your draft. Remember that you are job captains for your own writing lives. I can't wait to see what you decide to do today."

As the year unfurls, there will be more and more times when you ask children to stop and jot in lieu of turning and talking with partners. This is the first such time, and you may need to take special care to help children realize that they're simply creating a tiny exercise-text. You aren't looking for a class full of lunchtime or bus line publications!

Fig. XIII-1 Ellie

Qualities of Good Personal Narrative Writing

- Write a little seed story; don't write all about a giant watermelon topic.
- Zoom in so you tell the most important parts of the story.
- Include true, exact details from the movie you have in your mind.
- Begin with a strong lead—maybe use setting, action, dialogue, or a combination to create mood.
- Make a strong ending—maybe use action, dialogue, images, and whole-story reminders to make a lasting impression.
- **Relive the episode as you write it.**

Keeping these charts alive in our classrooms is extremely important. It is not enough to simply hang charts on our walls and expect kids to look at them, let alone use them. The more a chart is referred to, the more likely it will be used by your students.

"And remember to relive the episode as you write it. This is how we make our writing intense and real."

WRITING AND CONFERRING

Conferring Effectively

By now, your kids are probably engaged enough in their writing that you can think less about simply getting them going and more about conferring well. As I have mentioned earlier, I recommend that teachers generally begin a writing conference by learning what it is the child has been trying to do as a writer. If we know the writer's intention, we can support that intention by equipping the writer to do what he wants to do, or we can explain why we think he should be aiming toward a different goal.

I recommend opening most writing conferences by asking, "What are you working on as a writer?" At first, children will answer by telling you about the topic. If the child does that, ask a follow-up question: "And what exactly are you trying to do as a writer? What strategies have you been using?" Sometimes you will need to show the child the sort of answer you have in mind. You can do this by looking over the child's draft and then answering your question yourself, saying, for example, "It looks like you have been experimenting with different leads, and some include dialogue, some include the setting. Is that right?"

Once you and the child have established whatever it is that the child has been trying to do, I recommend saying to the child, "Can you show me where you have done that?" Then I look at what the child has already done and as I look, I am trying to think of what I can compliment. I try to compliment something that I hope writers will do another day in another piece, which means I need to find something transferable. "I love the way you told where you were when you were bowling," I said to one writer. "Always remember that it is smart to bring out the setting for your story like you did just now." In a writing conference, after I've complimented the child, I tell the child that there is one thing I'd like to teach. Then I name the teaching point and teach it, just as if this were a brief minilesson.

Before any one day's writing workshop, it helps to anticipate the sort of things you might find yourself

---

MID-WORKSHOP TEACHING POINT   *Paragraphing*   "Writers, can I have your eyes and your attention? Today I want to remind you that writers are always working on more than one thing. While you are reliving your life, reexperiencing an episode, you also need to keep an awareness in your mind that paragraphing matters, just like punctuation matters. Words can be like books—I bet you agree with me that when every inch of a bookshelf space is crammed with books and you can't see how they are organized, it's hard to appreciate any of them. We pass them by."

"On the other hand, if a bookstore has its books nicely grouped—a round table featuring a selection of mysteries, a special shelf of biographies, and a display of store favorites—and if each of these groups is set out carefully with space around it, then it's easier to take the books in, to decide which ones to read."

continued on next page

teaching. Your list of possibilities will be cumulative, and will pertain to many days. For now, your list of possible teaching points for a conference might look like this:

- Writers focus on small incidents.
- Writers envision, then storytell, rather than summarize, starting by telling a small action that we did at the start of the envisioned story.
- Writers write with specifics; so that instead of saying "I played a game," the writer names the game.
- Writers include exact speech.
- Writers spell word wall words correctly.
- Writers punctuate as we write.
- Writers write with paragraphs.
- Writers sometimes pretend to be strangers, rereading a draft for the first time and thinking, "Can I follow this? Does it all make sense?"
- Writers sometimes recruit readers who can tell us places where our draft is confusing.
- Writers try to solve our own problems, inventing solutions rather than simply lining up behind the teacher.
- Writers begin their stories with a small action, with dialogue, or with the setting.
- Writers stretch out the important sections of a story.

continued from previous page

"Writers, we need to make sure people's eyes don't fly right past our words and our ideas like they fly past books when they are crammed too close together with no organization! Group your thoughts and your writing. The micro-event that happens first in your story and that is represented by the first dot on your timeline is probably one grouping, one patch of words. After you write about that first micro-event, indent the next line, moving those words far in from the edge of the page to signal readers that this is a new group of thoughts—a new paragraph. You've seen how this looks in books, and you may have been doing it already yourself. Here's what a new paragraph looks like in handwriting—see mine here on the chart paper? From now on, as you write, chunk your story into paragraphs. And for now, mark a box around the sentences that you think go in a chunk. When you make the next draft, you can put in the paragraphs. We'll talk more about this at the Share. Okay, writers, back to work!"

SHARE

Paragraphing

Convene writers. Tell the story of one child's writing in a way that demonstrates how that writer decided to use paragraphs.

"Writers, you all are doing smart, intense work reliving parts of your lives and writing it down from your insider's perspective. And I am really pleased that you are keeping one eye on your content and one eye on your paragraphs. Earlier, Abraham reread his story about his cat, Ginger, and realized that his story had different sections in it, almost like different chapters. I'll show you how he added a code that signified a new paragraph. This is what he'd written," I said, reading from my chart paper copy of his story:

> Ginger stretched out on the carpet and yawned. I scratched behind her ears and she leaned her head into my hand. She purred. My mom was in the kitchen baking cookies. She was singing a Spanish song. She always sings when she's in the kitchen.

"Abraham realized that his piece really had two parts: one about his cat and one about his mom," I said, and added the paragraph sign at the appropriate place. "Abraham was really smart because when he saw he had two topics, he paused and thought, 'If I have two topics, does this mean I have two stories? Or do they really fit together into one small moment, just not in one paragraph?' In this instance, he decided they belong in the same story because they are both parts of a longer story about Ginger eating one of his mom's chocolate chip cookies and getting sick. On Abraham's second draft, he'll leave a bit of white space between the first message and the next bit. That will give us, as readers, a chance to get ready for content that is a little bit new."

> Ginger stretched out on the carpet and yawned. I scratched behind her ears and she leaned her head into my hand. She purred.
>
> My mom was in the kitchen baking cookies. She was singing a Spanish song. She always sings when she's in the kitchen.

I selected an example that isn't subtle, and abbreviated it for this purpose. Minilessons aren't times to be subtle—the message goes by children too quickly.

Paragraphs are more important than many people realize. When children learn to paragraph as they write, they are on their way towards internalizing the importance of structure in writing. If a child who is writing a narrative knows that each new step forward in time probably merits a new paragraph, this internalized feel for how writing goes will nudge the child to expand on rather than simply mention each incident. The child will know that writing in one–sentence paragraphs is not a reasonable option.

"In Abraham's story, the need for a new paragraph came from a new subtopic, but sometimes the need for a new paragraph comes because time has moved forward, and sometimes it comes because a new person is speaking."

I'm mentioning things in passing that could easily be developed more fully!

Set children up to practice what you've taught. In this case, help them practice thinking about how to group sentences to alleviate dense, unbroken text.

"Right now, I'm going to give each set of partners a copy of Michela's draft. You will see that she is working on paragraphs, so she has boxed her story in ways that reflect the paragraph divisions she thinks will work. Each time she makes a new paragraph, would you and your partner think, 'Why does she think this is a new paragraph? Is it that time has moved forward? Is there a new subtopic? Is someone new talking? Has the story turned a corner?' Work with your partner to decide and jot the reason for the new paragraph beside the paragraph box that she made. There may be places where you disagree with her judgments. If so, write, 'We disagree because . . .' alongside the box and mark the text the way you would paragraph it." *[Fig. XIII-2]*

Alternatively, I could have shown children a teacher-written draft and said, "Would you and you partner help this author paragraph this piece? Tell each other your reasons for recommending she make paragraphs where you think they belong."

<u>Getting ready to go to California</u>

"Beep, Beep, Beep" the alarm clock went off. It was 4:00 in the morning.

"Go, Go, Go!" I screamed.

We peeled off our pajamas and jumped into our clothes as fast as we could.

"Get the toothbrushes, get the suitcases!" yelled my mom.

"Get the entertainment, get the extra pillows!" bellowed my dad.

"Where's my cell phone?" screamed my sister.

"Get everything!" I yelled.

"Honk, Honk!"

"The car service is here," I said, hitting my head with my palm.

We bolted out the door and slammed it behind us.

The car door opened with a creak and we hopped inside.

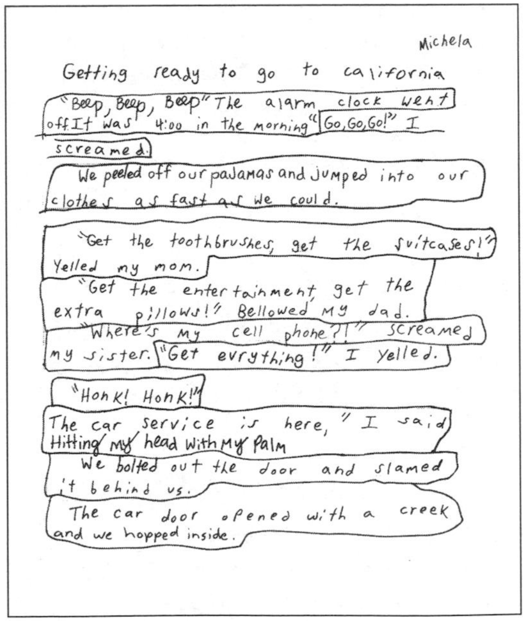
Michela
Getting ready to go to california
"Beep, Beep, Beep" The alarm clock went off It was 4:00 in the morning" Go, Go, Go!" I screamed.
We peeled off our pajamas and jumped into our clothes as fast as we could.
"Get the toothbrushes, get the suitcases!" Yelled my mom.
"Get the entertainment get the extra pillows!" Bellowed my dad.
"Where's my cell phone?!" screamed my sister. "Get evrything!" I yelled.
"Honk! Honk!"
The car service is here," I said Hitting my head with my palm
We bolted out the door and slamed it behind us.
The car door opened with a creek and we hopped inside.

Fig. XIII-2 Michela

As the children read and marked the paragraphs in Michela's draft, I listened in. "Writers, I heard you doing some smart work as you read Michela's draft. You noticed lots of reasons for using paragraphs. Some of you noticed reasons for paragraphing we haven't even mentioned yet! Remember from now on as you write, to use these reasons to group your thoughts in paragraphs."

HOMEWORK *Paragraphing Text* Writers, I've typed up a short picture book for you with no paragraphs in it at all—I took them out! I did that so we can all experiment together with ways to make paragraphs. Tonight, read the entire excerpt first to get a sense of the story. Then, think about how paragraphs could best help this story make sense and have an effect on readers. When you decide the places you think make the most sense to paragraph, will you jot a note alongside it explaining the reason you paragraphed there? Tomorrow when you come to school, you and your partner can compare what you did with each other and then we can look at the actual book and discuss what the author chose to do. Then you'll have more thinking to draw from as you paragraph your own writing.

TAILORING YOUR TEACHING

If some of your students try to make a movie in their mind of the memory they want to storytell, but when they close their eyes, they say they don't see anything . . . you might want to try leading those students on some guided imagery practice. Begin by asking the group of children (or the child) to get comfortable and close their eyes. Then, ask the children to imagine they are somewhere you know they can picture like a park or a beach. At first, be very specific with the words you use to describe the place. You might say, "You are heading toward the ocean, but first you have to walk through the beach grass and climb up a giant beach dune. Your feet feel heavy and for every step you take, you slide back a step or two. At the top of the hill, you are surprised to see another dune." In later days when you practice guided imagery with the students, you can be less exact, removing a bit of the scaffolding. You might say, "You are heading to the ocean. Notice what is under your feet. How do you feel?" Your specific language in the beginning days of guided imagery practice will not only help children grow an image in their minds, it will also help them see ways to put together words to make images. After several sessions of guided imagery, some students may be ready to lead the guided imagery sessions themselves. Of course, getting images in their minds is only the first step to writing from within images, and in a fully constructed conference or minilesson you'll need to help children transfer what they've learned under your guidance to their own writing. "Remember how you closed your eyes and pictured yourself walking on the beach when we practiced guided imagery?" you might ask. Then, "Try that same process now. Where were you when this memory begins? Put yourself there and take a few steps, just like we did at the beach. Tell me what is happening. . . ."

You can use any short picture book for this exercise. We've sometimes used an excerpt from Bill Cosby's The Meanest Thing to Say.

> One day, a new boy, Michael Reilly, came into our class. It didn't take long for him to start trouble— just until recess.
>
> I walked to the basketball court with my friends— Andrew, José, and Kiku. My cousin, Fuchsia, was waiting for us. She's in a different class.
>
> José was dribbling when Michael showed up.
>
> "I know a better game," Michael said. "It's called Playing the Dozens. You get twelve chances to say something mean to a person."

ASSESSMENT

Earlier I emphasized the importance of trying your hand at the work you are asking children to do. Frankly, I want you not only to experience what it's like to write, I also want you to experience the rush that comes when you see your own writing improving. There are a few minilessons in this series that have special power to lift the level not only of the children's writing, but also of your own—so let me channel you towards them.

First of all, you do need to keep in mind that adults, like children, usually reach first towards big watermelon topics and that our writing will be light years better if we instead write about a tiny seed story.

The paradox, however, is that it is much easier to write well if we select a story that matters to us. So you will find it helps to use a strategy like recalling a person you care about (I'll take my son, Miles, for example), and then listing tiny 30-60 minute vignettes that you recall involving that person. I'd steer you to select a small moment that has seared itself into your memory. For example, I won't forget being at the beauty parlor, seeing my cell phone vibrate on the hair dresser's counter and thinking, "Who would call me now?" I picked up the phone, and it was a policeman saying, "Your son has been in a bad accident."

You'll have your own small moment; it needn't be a traumatic one but you will write the narrative more easily if the moment is one that you recall with crystal clarity. Those moments are, I believe, already congealed into coherent stories in our memory banks, and so when we write the story,

relive the story, those moments are easy to capture on paper.

Finally, I'd give yourself today's minilesson. It is very likely that when you first write the story you've selected, you stand outside the story, discussing it, rather than reliving it. A teacher I know wrote her first draft like this:

> After I got home, I went into the house and I could tell something was wrong. I realized the painters had painted the wrong wall!

After taking in the minilesson, she rewrote her draft doing her best to stay inside the story as she wrote it:

> I drove up the driveway, then stopped the car. Putting my keys into my bag, I thought, "I'm going straight to bed." But when I entered the kitchen, something seemed wrong. I stood in the doorway, letting my eyes scan the room. The oven was fine (no fire). The counters. Then my gaze fell on the wall, and for a moment I just stared. "What the . . ." I thought.

After going through the process of writing and then revising based on the minilesson she was about to teach, she felt much more equipped to help children do the same writing work.

WRITING IN PASSAGES OF THOUGHT:

PARAGRAPHING TO SUPPORT ELABORATION

IN THIS SESSION, YOU'LL SHOW CHILDREN HOW WRITERS CAN BRING OUT MORE OF THEIR STORIES BY WRITING WHOLE PARAGRAPHS FROM SINGLE KEY SENTENCES.

GETTING READY

- Instructions on chalkboard telling children to bring their writer's notebooks and sit with their partners in the meeting area
- Sample of a first draft, a child's or your own, with numbers inserted to indicate where the writer decided to elaborate (on chart paper or overhead transparency)
- Second page on which the numbered inserts are written (on chart paper or transparency)
- Sample of another child's writing that needs elaboration, for use as a class text (one copy per partnership)
- Example of another child's writing that illustrates elaboration
- Tool container on each table with sharpened pencils
- See CD-ROM for resources

One of the first essential skills to teach *writers is the skill of elaboration. Inexperienced writers tend to write in what Mina Shaughnessy (1977) calls "sentences of thought" instead of "passages of thought." They write one sentence when a more skilled writer would write three sentences, or ten.*

When a child writes, "I sat on the bench at the ball game. Then the game started. The first player made it to first base," we need to teach the child that the draft would be much stronger, the reader could more easily put herself in the narrator's place, if the child wrote two sentences for every one. "I sat on the bench at the ball game. It was still damp and the water soaked through my pants. Then the game started. People stopped talking and started watching. . . ." As humans, we need help empathizing with others—generally, the more we know about others, the more easily we can see ourselves in them and can put ourselves in their shoes. We need to teach our writers how to say enough to help the reader feel the person in the story.

Elaborating is important for more pedestrian reasons as well. The New York Times *recently showcased research that showed that by considering length alone, one can accurately predict the score a student will receive on the new writing component of the SAT exam. The longer the answer, the higher the score. The Educational Testing Service, the designer of the test, has hastened to challenge that claim, but the research stands. On standardized tests, length matters. Elaboration matters.*

I believe that one way to help children develop the habit of elaborating is to encourage them to think and write in paragraphs rather than sentences. If children begin to group their thinking in clusters of sentences, whole passages of thought, rather than in smaller clusters of words, they will draw more language, more thoughts, out of themselves and onto the page. Used in this way, paragraphing is not an afterthought or a postwriting organizational structure.

MINILESSON

Writing in Passages of Thought: Paragraphing to Support Elaboration

CONNECTION

Celebrate that your children are writing from inside their stories and not summarizing them from a distance.

"Writers, I love the way you are reliving parts of your life and writing down what it was like as though you are right in it all over again! Carl knew he wanted to write about his first checker game, so he made a tiny thumbnail sketch on his paper to remind himself of the topic for that page. He *could* have written, 'My opponent and I sat down and began to play.' Instead, what Carl did was he sat back and closed his eyes and really transported himself back to that moment. Then he played a movie in his mind of what happened at the very start of the checkers game, and then he told the story as though he were right there doing it all over again. Listen:" [Fig. XIV-1]

> At my first game of checkers I sat down on my chair. I was getting ready for my match. I took a deep breath. I rubbed my hands together. Then I had my eyes glued to my opponent like I was going to murder him. He sat down with me. We started to shake hands to one another. I said may the best man win. My opponent had a strange little smile on his face.

"Many of you, like Carl, are taking the time to relive the moments you are writing about, and that's great for your writing!"

Create the context for today's lesson. Point out to children that many of their paragraphs are tiny, a signal that their texts are underdeveloped.

"Yesterday, you were not only reliving your stories, you were also starting to chunk your stories into parts that go together and parts that need a little space between them—you were making your writing into different paragraphs. What I learned yesterday as I watched you work is that right now, the way you are writing, a lot of you have zillions of tiny paragraphs! Now, on the one hand, that's wonderful, because that means you have zillions of small, step-by-step actions, and narrative writers all wish to spell out the small steps in a progression! But, on the other hand, it's almost always true that your paragraphs deserve more than just one quick, thin sentence in them. Probably, each new micro-moment in your story needs more words and sentences."

COACHING

I am always pleased when minilessons dovetail together as this one does with others around it. This minilesson extends the Teaching Share from last session and leans towards the minilesson in the next session.

It makes sense that children will need additional scaffolding to have success with what we teach. So, in this instance, you'll tell children that when their writing involves lots of tiny paragraphs, this is a signal that they need to elaborate more. Teach them that at the very least, elaborating means writing two sentences instead of one.

> CARL
>
> MY FiRSt gAME of CHECKERS
>
> AT MY FiRSt gAME of CHECKERS I SAt DOWN ON MY CHAiR. I WAS getting READY foR MY MATCH. I took A DEEp BREATH. I RUBBED MY HANDS together. THEN I HAD MY eyes glued TO MY oppeNET LiKE I WAS goiNg TO MURDER HiM. HE SAt DOWN With ME. WE STARTED tO SHAKE HANDS to oNE ANOTHER. I SAiD MAY THE BEST MAN WiN. MY oppeNET HAD A STRANge LittlE SMiL E oN HiS fACE.

Fig. XIV-1 Carl

Name your teaching point. Tell children that tiny paragraphs signal a need for elaboration.

"Today I want to teach you that when your piece has lots of tiny paragraphs, this is a sign that you need to elaborate more. It means you need to say more about a topic, a moment, a scene before you move to the next paragraph. It's great to elaborate in your first drafts as you write, but you can also go back to a complete draft and realize there are places where you need to say more."

We can learn some qualities of good writing from the expert authors who write books on the topic—but some of the lessons that will matter for children will come simply from looking at children's work and thinking, "What next step might I suggest for this writer?"

TEACHING

Spotlight one child's revisions in a way that illustrates elaboration.

"Let's look today at Michela's writing and let her teach us. Yesterday, we looked at how she boxed her writing into paragraphs. Remember how she found she had lots of one- and two-sentence paragraphs in her story? After Michela realized this, she inserted little numbers in her draft where she thought she could say more, and then on another sheet of paper, she wrote those numbers and additional sentences that could elaborate on her initial writing. Michela realized that in her first draft, she tended to write conversations but not actions or descriptions. In her revised version, she wrote not only what people say but also what they do, and she described the scene. This is her first draft with numbers inserted wherever she added more text:" *[Fig. XIV-2]*

I like using Michela as an example because her original draft isn't especially developed or strong, and yet she does an extraordinary amount of work on it. The model, then, conveys to all children that this work is doable.

Getting ready to go to California

"Beep, Beep, Beep" the alarm clock went off. It was 4:00 in the morning. *1 "Go, Go, Go!" I screamed. *2

We peeled off our pajamas and jumped into our clothes as fast as we could.

"Get the toothbrushes, get the suitcases!" yelled my mom. *3

"Get the entertainment, get the extra pillows!" bellowed my dad.

"Where's my cell phone?" screamed my sister. "Get everything!" I yelled. *4

"Honk, Honk!" *5

"The car service is here" I said, hitting my head with my palm.

We bolted out the door and slammed it behind us. *6

The car door opened with a creak and we hopped inside.

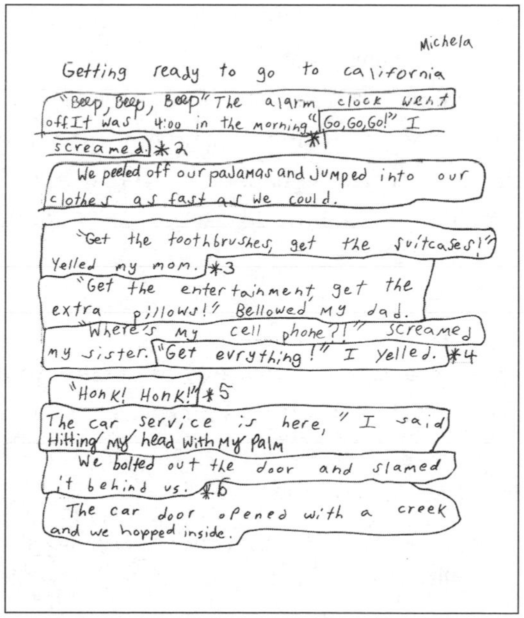
Michela

Getting ready to go to california

"Beep, Beep, Beep" The alarm clock went off It was 4:00 in the morning "Go, Go, Go!" I screamed *2

We peeled off our pajamas and jumped into our clothes as fast as we could.

"Get the toothbrushes, get the suitcases!" Yelled my mom. *3

"Get the entertainment, get the extra pillows!" Bellowed my dad.

"Where's my cell phone?!" screamed my sister. "Get evrything!" I yelled. *4

"Honk! Honk!" *5

The car service is here," I said Hitting my head with my Palm

We bolted out the door and slamed it behind us. *6

The car door opened with a creek and we hopped inside.

Fig. XIV-2 Michela

"Her next page (on which she'd written the inserts) looked like this." *[Fig. XIV-3]*

1. You'd think we would be exhausted but . . . we ran around in circles, trying to figure what to do.

2. Our birds whistled to cheer us on, saying "Run, run, run."

3. I was shoved into the small wooden bookcase as my sister ran to get the toothbrushes and suitcases.

4. It was a mad, mad house. Every which way people bumped into each other struggling to get ready. When we were finally ready we all plopped onto the couch. I let out a loud sigh and closed my eyes for a quick rest.

5. Suddenly the house was in motion again.

6. We ran down the dark, deserted street toward the blinking taillights.

Debrief. Extrapolate principles that can be deduced from the one example. Explain that writers can often see how to elaborate by looking for what they have left out of stories.

"In her next draft, Michela will intertwine the original draft and her inserts. Some of you may decide you need to do similar work to expand your paragraphs and to be sure readers really can picture the events in your narrative. If you aren't sure what to add to your paragraphs, it can help to think, 'What have I put into my story? What have I left out?' Good stories usually have actions, dialogue, descriptions, and thoughts. When you reread your drafts, think about which elements of successful narratives you have already incorporated into your draft, and which you might still want to add."

Active Engagement

Set children up to practice the strategy on a class text with partners.

"Remember Jake's story? Let's practice elaborating by pretending Jake's story is our story, and thinking, 'How could the paragraphs be a little longer?' Let's just look at the start to his story." *[Fig. XIV-4]*

I sat behind the bleachers, waiting for my race to be called.

"Second and third graders, please line up by the entrance," the announcer said.

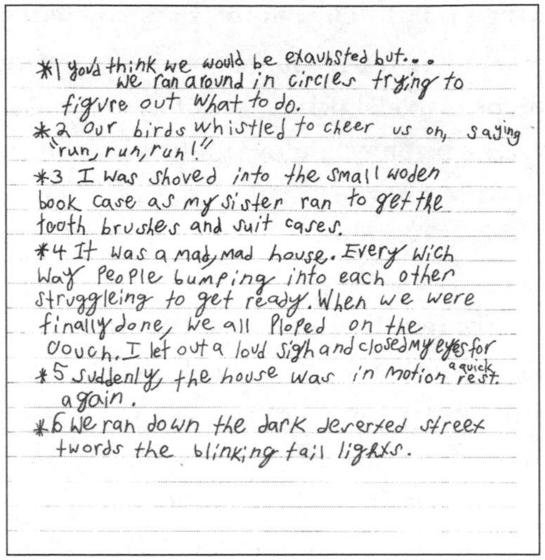
*1 you'd think we would be exaubsted but...
we ran around in circles trying to
figure out what to do.
*2 our birds whistled to cheer us on, saying
"run, run, run!"
*3 I was shoved into the small woden
book case as my sister ran to get the
tooth brushes and suit cases.
*4 It was a mad, mad house. Every wich
way people bumping into each other
struggleing to get ready. When we were
finally done, we all ploped on the
couch. I let out a loud sigh and closed my eyes for a quick rest.
*5 suddenly the house was in motion again.
*6 We ran down the dark deserted street
twords the blinking tail lights.

Fig. XIV-3 Michela

Your revisions will be more effective if they are informed by self-awareness. It is extremely telling to look at your own writing asking, "Do I include actions? Dialogue? Thoughts?" Most of us have ways we tend to write and we use those tried-and true-ways often.

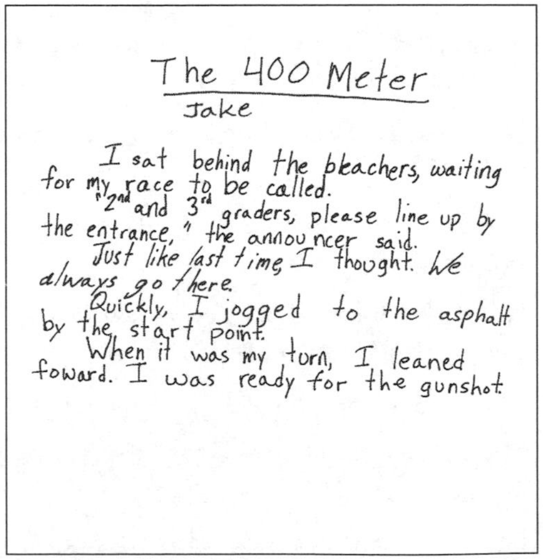
The 400 Meter
Jake
I sat behind the bleachers, waiting for my race to be called.
"2nd and 3rd graders, please line up by the entrance," the announcer said.
Just like last time I thought. We always go there.
Quickly, I jogged to the asphalt by the start point.
When it was my turn, I leaned foward. I was ready for the gunshot

Fig. XIV-4 Children practiced elaborating by trying to do so with Jake's lead.

"Would you and your partner read over this draft and think, 'What element of effective narrative does Jake tend to exclude in his story? Does he include dialogue? Small actions? Thoughts? The setting?' If you can figure out what is usually not there in his draft, then you know one way to elaborate on the draft. Please tell your partner what the writer could add."

After the children worked in partners for a bit, I reconvened the group. "Christina thought that Jake didn't include a lot of setting, so she and her partner invented ways he could add it. Christina especially added the setting in places where the paragraphs were a bit too short to be very meaningful."

> I sat behind the bleachers, waiting for my race to be called. All around me, kids stood about wearing the colors of their school. The sun was hot.
>
> "Second and third graders, please line up by the entrance," the announcer said. From all parts of the crowd, kids separated from their friends and started to go toward the gate.

Joseph waved his hand. "We thought he could include what he was thinking, like wondering if he would win or not."

> I sat behind the bleachers, waiting for my race to be called. I wondered if all my practice would pay off. I wanted to win.

LINK
Restate today's lesson in a way that helps children see how to use it today and every day. Here, remind children that when they need to elaborate, they can think of what types of information are missing and add them.

"When you go off to write today and every day, remember you can elaborate on your sentences and paragraphs by adding actions, dialogue, descriptions, and thoughts, just like we did here together with Michela's and Jake's drafts. If you have zillions of tiny paragraphs and realize you need to elaborate, start today by rereading your draft and asking yourself, 'What have I put into my story? What have I left out?' Then you can mark where you want to add parts and write them into the next draft."

Someday, you'll want to help children cull through all the details they could add to choose the most meaningful ones— leaving the others behind. Someday, you'll explain to children that authors include (and exclude) different kinds of information for different reasons—dialogue has its place and time, as does description. For now, we want to banish kids' censors and loosen their inhibitions about writing. To write well, kids first need to write voluminously, not worrying whether the writing is marvelous or not.

WRITING AND CONFERRING

Focusing on English Language Learners

As these first few weeks of school fly by, you are quickly coming to know each one of the children who comprise your diverse classroom community. One of the things I love most about the writing workshop is the time I have to confer with each of these unique individuals. Conferring gives me the time to teach in a highly customized manner. One group of children who require this customized teaching are those whose first language is not English. In New York City these children are called English Language Learners (ELLs).

A single description cannot adequately represent this diverse group of learners. Each English Language Learner is different and will need a different kind of attention. We must take care not to assume that because these children share a designation, they also share strengths and weaknesses. Thank goodness for the writing workshop—a time in the day when the bulk of instruction is responsive and based on assessments.

When studying ELLs, it is helpful to understand that many grammatical errors are due to assumptions the children make about English based on their native language. English doesn't work in the same manner as many other languages and this causes children confusion. In Spanish, for example, the adjective follows the noun, so the child says "la casa blanca," not "the white house." If a child whose first language is Spanish writes "the flower blue," we can acknowledge that if the child were writing in Spanish, this would be perfect, but in English, the words are sequenced differently.

MID-WORKSHOP TEACHING POINT *Answering Readers' Questions* "Writers, can I have your eyes and your attention? I was just conferring with Simeon, whose writing the teachers and I examined earlier this month (see Session VI). Simeon discovered a way to elaborate by thinking about questions the reader might have and adding the word *because* to expand and clarify what he was saying. First he wrote this sentence." [Fig. XIV-5]

> When I went in everybody looked and laughed at me.

"Then he thought about the reader. Would the reader understand why everyone was laughing at him? So he went back and added the word *because* and that pushed him to say more."

> When I went in everybody looked and laughed at me because I was covered with mud.

"Sometimes, when you are reading your writing, think about your readers' possible questions, like Simeon did, and try to answer them. One way to do this is by adding *because*. We make things clearer by answering questions like why, what, who, or when."

Simeon

One day it was a rainy day and I had on a pink tuxedo and it was my cousins wedding so I was so exited I ran to her I was like are you exited I said yeah she said so I ran to my dad and then I fell in the mudd and I was messed up so I got so mad that I felt to hit some body when I went in every body looked and laued at me I was so scared that she might not want me to carry the rings

Fig. XIV-5 Simeon

Another area that will improve a child's writing as well as his comprehension is language and vocabulary development. Expanding a child's vocabulary will help the child elaborate, make a text cohesive, and communicate complex ideas. For example, when Ahra first wrote about a thunderstorm, she wrote with the basic facts only. *[Fig. XIV-6]*

> One night when I went to sleep, I heard a thunderstorm. I saw a lot of rain. I thought it was a hurricane. When the storm came I hide under my blanket all over again. Finally, the storm has cleared.

When I conferred with Ahra, we brainstormed words and phrases that come to mind when we think of a thunderstorm: loud, boom, pow, like fireworks, hard rain, dark, wind blowing, hot, humid, lightning bright as day, trees swaying back and forth. She then sketched a quick picture of the scene, labeling the picture with the English words that I helped her access. The labeled sketch, then, functioned as a personal word-bank when she shifted from sketching to writing. Ahra's text was vastly richer as a result, but more importantly she devised a strategy she can use again when she writes. She learned she can brainstorm or research words she may need before she starts writing *[Fig. XIV-7]*.

> It was a hot and humid night. I went to bed around 7:30 pm. It was dark in my room. My grandma was sleeping in the bed next to me. The wind started to blow as hard as a hurricane.
>
> I got out of my bed and looked out my window. I saw the trees swaying back and forth like they were dancing. Then the lightning started. The lightning made the sky look like it was daytime. Then came the thunder, BOOM! POW! which sounded like fireworks. Then it started to rain, which sounded like a waterfall. I started to get scared.
>
> I hid under my blanket. I was so scared. I started to shiver and I screamed. My grandma said, "Don't worry. It's okay."

Once I help equip a child with some tools of language that enable her to tell a story more fully, I can move to support the child with some of the smaller words and sentence-level details. By focusing on one or two things at a time, I can push a child toward becoming a more successful writer.

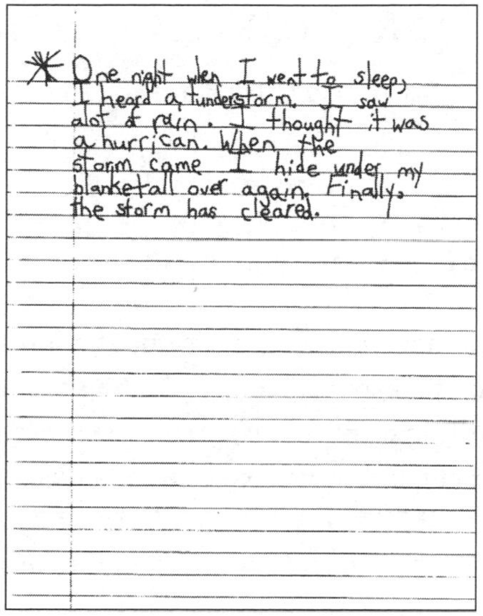

* One night when I went to sleep, I heard a tunderstorm. I saw alot of rain. I thought it was a hurrican. When the storm came I hide under my blanketall over again. Finally. the storm has cleared.

Fig. XIV-6 Ahra

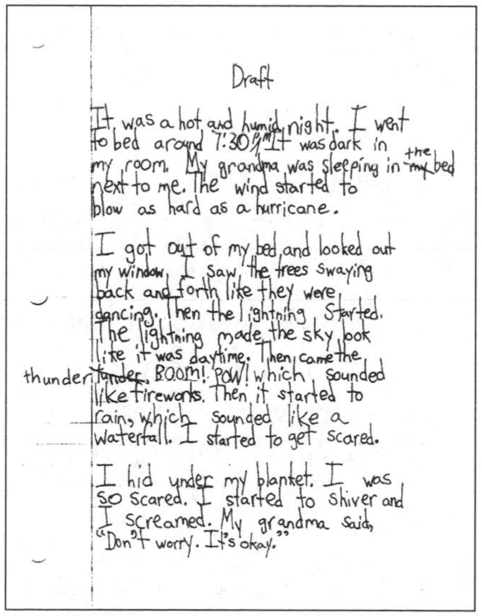

Draft

It was a hot and humid night. I went to bed around 7:30 pm. It was dark in my room. My grandma was sleeping in the bed next to me. The wind started to blow as hard as a hurricane.

I got out of my bed and looked out my window. I saw the trees swaying back and forth like they were dancing. Then the lightning started. The lightning made the sky look like it was daytime. Then came the thunder. BOOM! POW! which sounded like fireworks. Then it started to rain, which sounded like a waterfall. I started to get scared.

I hid under my blanket. I was so scared. I started to shiver and I screamed. My grandma said, "Don't worry. It's okay."

Fig. XIV-7 Ahra

SHARE

Listening to Elaboration

Remind children of the day's teaching. Invite them to share their work with a partner. Share one example of elaboration. Remind children to try this whenever the context calls for it.

"Writers, can I have your eyes and your attention? Many of you tried to elaborate on your sentences and paragraphs today by adding actions, dialogue, descriptions, and thoughts. Your writing seems to be growing before my very eyes. Nice work."

"Take a moment and show your partner a place where you elaborated on a sentence or a paragraph." They did. "Writers, let me share with you what Cameron did to expand upon his story about the tennis match. When Cameron reread his story, he decided to revise it. He added numbers into his draft as we saw Michela doing earlier, and then on another page wrote text he'd like to insert. *(Fig. XIV-8)* For example, he wrote a #1 beside:"

> I looked towards Cafelnnacaulf from the front row. He tossed the ball into the sky and I kept my eyes focused on the ball, as the racket smashed the ball I thought it must have been going 100 mph, because it landed in the box.

Revision *(Fig. XIV-9)*:

> It hit the cushioned wall. It came hurling toward me and the speed decreased slowly but surely by about 60 mph.

"Writers reread their writing thinking about the reader. Then they add to places where they want the reader to see and feel exactly what they did, just like many of you are trying to do. Remember to elaborate on your tiny paragraphs in any of the ways we learned today whenever you need the reader to really be there!"

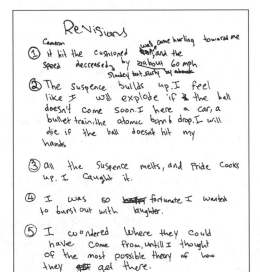

Fig. XIV-8 Cameron's first draft

Fig. XIV-9 Cameron's revision

HOMEWORK *Building Paragraphs, Elaborating on Each Sentence* I was in the convenience store last night and the store was offering several "2 for 1" specials. "Buy two bags of chips for the price of one." "Buy two deodorants for the price of one." I liked this idea. It made me think of our writing. What would happen if every sentence offered the same "2 for 1" deal as my local convenience store? How would that work?

If we start with one sentence from our fire drill story, "We got to the second floor at the same time as the first graders," can we get two sentences out of that one image? "Some of them looked nervous and they were very quiet!" You might elaborate on that sentence in a different way. Think about our talk, what we saw and heard, and what we felt and thought, because this is one way to elaborate on stories.

For homework, return to some of your one-sentence notepad entries and try to elaborate on them using the strategies you have learned so far. We have learned that writers can elaborate on a sentence by adding specific actions, dialogue, descriptions, and thoughts. This evening try elaborating on your single entries using the same strategies.

TAILORING YOUR TEACHING This session is an important one to revisit throughout the year, no matter what genre is being studied. After you have read through your students' drafts, you will have a better sense of their understanding, not only of paragraphs, but their methods of elaboration. Most children tend to find and use one favorite way to elaborate, like adding dialogue.

If your children tend to overuse dialogue as a method of elaboration . . . you will want to follow up this session with a lesson on how to balance the actual talk included with actions and internal thinking. You can point out what you have learned about what they have tended to put in and what they have tended to leave out.

"Writers, yesterday as I was conferring with all of you, I noticed that many of you have tried to elaborate by adding dialogue. And that is definitely one way to elaborate. But we also want to make sure we keep a balance and use dialogue where it will have the biggest impact and support your meaning. Today I am going to teach you that you can also elaborate by adding actions." Then you can use a text like Julie Brinckloe's *Fireflies!* to show how she surrounds her dialogue with lots of actions that show the reason for the dialogue. Ask children to practice by finding places in the class story where they can add more actions that will help create a clearer picture in the reader's mind. Suggest that this is something they can do anytime they want to elaborate on one of their sentences or paragraphs.

You need to remember the importance of helping children speak in paragraphs, rather than in short phrases or single sentences. We often settle for the first words a child expresses. Just think how much more we might hear by simply asking each child to say more. Of course we will want to teach some explicit strategies for elaboration, such as remembering exact actions, dialogue, descriptions, and thoughts. But by helping children speak in paragraphs rather than short expressions or individual words, we help increase not only their fluency but their confidence as well.

MECHANICS

During the time in your day set aside for mechanics, you will want to show children how they can use their writer's notebook as a place to practice and get control over whatever you've been teaching them. So if you have taught them ten high-frequency words, you can ask children to reread the entries they've written since the beginning of the year, double-checking that they have spelled those word wall words correctly.

You will have a handful of children for whom the word wall words are No Big Deal. You'll want to gather these strong spellers and tell them that you know that often the work you teach the rest of the class during mechanics time will be easy for them. Ask whether they are game to do some advanced work, working together in a small group. They will probably be thrilled at the suggestion.

If you are working with the rest of the class on spelling, you may suggest that your strong spellers reread their own writing to check for spellings they think may not be right (they need to learn to ascertain this for themselves) and then bring their writing to someone. While most of the class is looking at *because* and discussing what they notice about how it is spelled, these strong spellers can do similar work with their words. While most of the class takes a spelling quiz on Fridays, the strong spellers can figure out how to quiz each other.

Meanwhile, you will have some children who do not even find it easy to spell the word wall words correctly as they write. Teach these children that when they come to a stopping place in their writing, it is helpful to

reread it, and to choose the lens they will use to guide their rereading. (Sometimes they need to reread simply to regain momentum and remind themselves of what they have written so they can add on. If that is their goal, it is fine for them to overlook misspellings as they reread.) Sometimes they will want to reread to check their spellings. Teach children to mark—to underline or circle or leave a marginal dot—words they believe may be misspelled.

A child may think that twenty of his words are misspelled, but it is not reasonable for that child to look up twenty words per page in the dictionary! So don't suggest that once a child has marked a word as "probably wrong" she necessarily needs to fix it. It is very important for children to get better at simply sensing when a word isn't right. This, in and of itself, is a very helpful skill because that child can then work on that spelling if the writing will be public and accuracy therefore matters. But I do suggest asking children to repair the spellings on any word wall words that they've misspelled. Make sure that even your most struggling writer knows how to use the word wall as a sort of enlarged dictionary.

You do not need to wait until the child is officially editing a piece for publication before asking the child to repair his or her misspellings of word wall words. Your goal is to have children spell those words accurately and automatically whenever they write them, so at any point in the writing process you can remind children to double-check that they have done this.

DEVELOPING THE HEART OF A STORY:
REVISION

IN THIS SESSION, YOU WILL TEACH CHILDREN THAT WRITERS REVISE BY ASKING, 'WHAT'S THE MOST IMPORTANT PART OF THIS STORY?' AND DEVELOPING THAT SECTION.

GETTING READY

- Instructions on chalkboard telling children to bring their writer's notebooks to the meeting area
- Sample draft of a child's piece of writing that needs revision, written on chart paper
- Guest speaker—the child whose piece needs to be revised (prepare the child ahead of time so the child knows what to expect)
- Child's version of the class story you used in the timeline session, written on chart paper
- *Shortcut* (Donald Crews)
- Scissors and tape
- Chart paper and markers
- See CD-ROM for resources

The day the very first copies of my book The Art of Teaching Reading *arrived, a few teachers were beside me watching while I, with trembling hands, opened the box and brought out one copy of the book. My hand ran over the glossy cover with delight. I clasped the book against me, loving its heft. "I can't imagine you wrote all those words!" one of the teachers said. I remember thinking, "If she only knew." The words that I held with such pride were just the tip of the iceberg. In making that one book, I had written hundreds of thousands of words that no one would ever see. When people build houses, they fill a truck-sized trailer with the rejected materials. When I write, I need one of those trailers parked next to my desk.*

In life, I go through my days knowing that the work I do will go into the world, good or bad, as it is. In life, I can't take back my words. As I move through my days, if I am clumsy or hurtful or obscure, I can't rewind and make myself into a more agile or lucid or savvy person. I can't call back a speech I have given, a workshop I have led, a meeting I have facilitated, a conversation I have participated in. But I can call back my writing, and I can take whatever I've done and make it much, much better. Revising my writing (and in doing so, revising myself) is a great and powerful opportunity. Revision is my favorite part of the writing process. It is pure pleasure to be able to stand back, scan what I've written, and think, "How can I make my best work better?"

Children, however, often come into our classrooms dreading revision. We cannot tarry a moment, then, before inviting children to see revision in a whole new light. In this session you let children know that revision begins with selection. Writers reread and say, "This is my best work." We revise because the work merits the compliment of revision. And then revision itself is all about giving a piece of writing the respect, the listening attention that will allow that piece to become even stronger. The most important thing I do when I revise is to find the life in my piece, and create space for it. I say, "This is beautiful." When children see their own work become dramatically stronger through revision, sermons on the importance of revision are not necessary. That is our work in today's session.

MINILESSON

Developing the Heart of a Story: Revision

CONNECTION

Remind writers of the work they've been doing; rally their energies toward revision.

"Writers, you have been using timelines to develop your ideas, you have been paragraphing and elaborating on each paragraph, you've been experiencing the writing process that writers go through with every piece. Now many of you are about to finish drafting your second story. When writers have a collection of drafts, writers often look over the drafts of several stories (you have two) and select the best piece to really delve into and revise."

"I talked to a few of you earlier today about revision and I learned something surprising. I learned some of you don't like to revise! Some of you actually think of revision as something you have to do when you aren't writing well enough! So today I want to set you straight. When your writing is lousy, you throw it out. When your writing is alive and beautiful and full of potential, you revise it. Revision is a compliment to good writing!"

Name the teaching point. In this case, tell writers that revision is not about fixing errors; it is about finding and developing potentially great writing, sometimes by adding more to the heart of the story.

"More specifically, I want to teach you today that revision is about finding and developing the potential in your piece. This means, first of all, that when we revise, we return to drafts that seem promising to us. So today you'll reread both the stories you've written and decide which one has special promise; that will be the piece you revise and publish."

"And then, once it is time to settle into serious revision, you again need to reread, asking, 'Which section of this do I think works especially well?' That is, after looking for the piece that is good enough to revise, you look for the *section* that is the heart of it!"

"Usually in any story, there will be a part where the readers should pull in to listen— the part that really matters, the heart of a story. And one important thing we can do when we revise is find the heart of a story and develop it further."

"So revision is not about cleaning up messes; it is about finding and developing powerful writing, and one way we develop writing is by adding more to the important parts of the story."

COACHING

Stories often begin by setting a character into a setting and in a sense, this minilesson (like so many others) establishes the setting, the content, for today's teaching. If your students seem to have no resistance around revision, you will not want to begin the minilesson this way. If they have no reason to have reservations about revision, why offer them any? On the other hand, if you know there is resistance to revision in the air, acknowledging it may be the best way to begin.

In the K-2 Units of Study, *the fourth unit is* Revision *and the unit starts with me asking children if they are very proud of the piece they just published. After children respond with the resounding 'yes.' I tell them, "Because when writers really like a piece of writing, we revise it." In that unit, children not only revise their recently published piece, they also go back and scour their folders for other pieces "that are good enough to be revisited."*

TEACHING

Spotlight what one child did in a way that illustrates the teaching point. Retell the story of the process.

"Yesterday, Gregory did some powerful revision work. I want to tell you the story of his revision because some of you may want to follow his example. When I pulled my chair alongside Gregory, he'd already written a quick draft about the day he learned that his fish, Al, had died. I told him that what I usually do after I've finished a draft is reread it, thinking, 'What's the most important part of this story? What's the heart of this story?' So Gregory reread his draft. I copied it onto chart paper so you can see it." *[Fig. XV-1]*

> Al is Dead
>
> Dead. Ever since I had fish, I had Al: the best algae-eater in the world. Once I heard he was dead, I did not cry. I just was still. Then I asked, "Where is he?" My dad said, "In the trash." I asked to see him. I saw it was true. My dad put him back. For a second, I thought, then I said, "We can give him a funeral." My dad looked doubtful for a minute but I picked him up and said, "He was special." Then I cried. Al was gone.

"Gregory reread his story, looking for what he thought was the heart of the story; then he motioned to a line in the middle of the draft: 'I asked to see him. I saw it was true.' Gregory said, 'That's the most important part. That was the saddest part.'"

"Gregory," I said. "After I find the most important section in a story, I cut my page apart like this." At this point I started cutting the chart-paper version of his story into two at the place he'd identified. "Then I tape a lot more paper into that important section of the draft." I taped a half page of chart paper into his story. "Then I reread up to those blank lines, and try to make a movie in my mind of exactly what happened. And I write the story of that moment, trying to tell it with more details." To get Gregory started, I read his draft aloud to him, stopping at the section he'd identified.

Then I imagined aloud what Gregory might say for just another sentence or two, trying to give him an idea for what I meant by stretching out the important part. "I walked over to the trash can and looked in. I saw . . ." Then I said, "Take it, Gregory."

" . . . lots of trash . . . "

"Be exact. What exactly did you see? If you can't remember, make it up," I said, and repeated what I'd already said to give him a new jump start.

By now you have seen that there are several common methods you can use in the teaching component of a minilesson. You can write publicly or bring in writing you have done at home. You can tell children about a published author's process or show the author's work. You can reenact a conference you had with a child, or you can retell the story of a child's process. Another option is to invite the child to be a guest speaker, telling the class what he did to make his writing better. Knowing this list of options should enable you to invent minilessons more easily, and to realize that you could teach the same content about writing in any one of many different ways. In this Teaching component, I retell the story of one child's process of revision.

Notice that I copied this story onto chart paper for the purposes of this minilesson.

This draft is a great favorite of mine. Read it aloud well. Your children should get goose bumps!

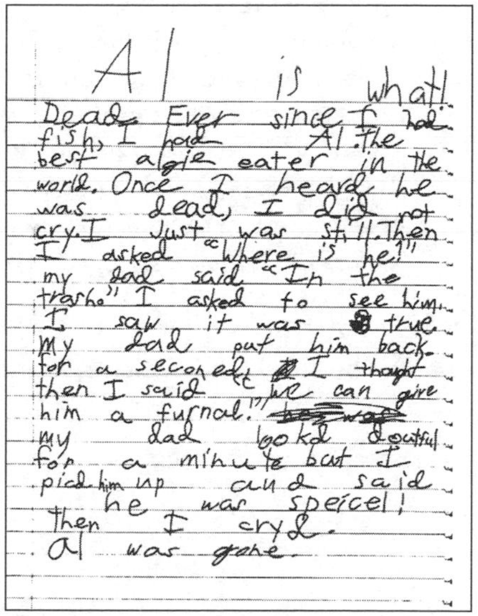
Al is what!
Dead. Ever since I had fish, I had Al. the best algie eater in the world. Once I heard he was dead, I did not cry. I Just was still. Then I asked "Where is he!" my dad said "In the trash." I asked to see him. I saw it was true. My dad put him back. for a seconed I thought then I said "we can give him a furnal!" my dad lookd doutful for a minute but I pick him up and said he was speicel! Then I cryd. Al was gone.

Fig. XV-1 Gregory

Gregory reiterated the last line of the story and then added on to it.

"I walked over to the trash can and I opened it. I looked in and saw . . . wet paper towels, orange peels, and a pile of coffee grounds."

"Keep going. What exactly did you do?" I said.

"I picked up Al."

"Be exact. What *exactly* did you do? What did you say?"

"I flicked off the coffee grounds, and said, 'Al, I'm gonna miss you.'"

Debrief. Point out what the one child did to find and develop the heart of his story.

"Class, do you see what Gregory did? He reread his story, determined that this part about looking in the trash can and seeing his beloved fish was the heart of the story, and then he added a chunk of paper right at that section of the story. He went back, recalled exactly what happened, and wrote that section with much more detail:"

First draft

> Dead. Ever since I had fish, I had Al: the best algae-eater in the world. Once I heard he was dead, I did not cry. I was just still. Then I asked, "Where is he?" My dad said, "In the trash."

Inset added to the second draft

> I asked to see him. I walked over to the trash can and I opened it. I looked in and saw wet paper towels, orange peels and a pile of coffee grounds. I picked up Al. I flicked the coffee grounds, and said, "Al, my friend. I'm gonna miss you." My dad put him back. For a second, I thought, then I said, "We can give him a funeral." My dad looked doubtful for a minute but I picked him up and said, "He was special." Then I cried. Al was gone.

"Today you'll want to look at the two stories you have now written in rough draft form. Decide which you like best—which is worthy of revision. Try this revision strategy once you have selected the story you want to revise. Reread your story, find the heart of it, and then develop that section of your text."

Details are magic. These details transform this story. Notice that my interjections are lean. I do not want to overwhelm his story. But my prompts are calculated. I shift Gregory from generalizations to specifics of what he saw, what he did, what he said.

When I debrief, I try to describe the actions a writer has taken that are transferable to another day, another piece. I describe what the writer has done in a step-by-step manner, because this is meant to serve as a how-to text for the class.

By explaining that every child in the room can follow in Gregory's path, finding the heart of a story and expanding on it as Gregory has done, I show children that Gregory's work is replicable and worth replicating—and it is! This revision strategy has proven to be accessible and powerful.

ACTIVE ENGAGEMENT
Set children up to do similar work on the class story.

"Let's practice it. Let's revisit our class story about the dragonfly and develop the heart of it. I've written a version of that dragonfly story on this chart paper. Would you each pretend it is your personal story and reread it, trying to find the heart of it? Then think how you could tell that one part with more detail. Let me read it aloud."

> We were so quiet, we could probably have heard ants crawling along the floor. We were barely breathing. Then our teacher stopped reading, just for a minute, and we were just about to say, 'NO! Don't stop! It's the most exciting part!' But she was looking at Jonathan because he was looking up at the top of the bookshelf where a dragonfly had landed. 'He wants to listen to the story,' we said.

"Tell your partners where the heart of this story might be for you. Make a movie in your mind of what happened at that part and tell your partner how you'd stretch that part out. Write it in the air with details." I gave them a few minutes to do this.

"Okay, writers, can I have your eyes and your attention? Most of you felt that the heart of this story was right at the end, when the whole class saw the dragonfly. If we hadn't spotted our unexpected visitor, the day would have been like any other. I heard lots of you adding details to embellish (that's a word for 'add on to') that part," I said, and began to write what I'd heard them say. "Milan, you said this:"

> The dragonfly was perched on the highest shelf.

"Jonathan, you added this next bit."

> It was purple and green.

"What else could we add?"
Ahra dictated, "It twinkled like tinfoil."

I nodded and transcribed as directed. Then I said, "I think we should tell what we did. Did we say something or do something?"

"The dragonfly was so beautiful that we all gasped," Sam said. I added this and then read the entire story aloud again, starting from the very beginning:

Of course, there is no one right answer to the question "What is the heart of this story?" If children choose a part and have reasons for their choice, they could certainly take the story in that direction. Theoretically, it could be valuable to let children discuss their decisions about which part is the heart of the story. But for now, you will probably decide to keep the minilesson as lean as possible.

I love this revision strategy because essentially we are asking children to do what they've worked hard to learn to do—make a movie in their mind, telling the story in a step-by-step way. But now they're doing this to expand a moment within the moment. They should have a lot of success with this.

When I say, "Write in the air" I am asking children to dictate to a partner the exact words they would write if they were writing instead of talking. I take some time to explicitly teach children what this injunction means.

We were so quiet, we could probably have heard ants crawling along the floor. Then our teacher stopped reading and we were just about to say, "Don't stop! It's the most exciting part!"

But she was looking at Jonathan because he was looking up at the top of the bookshelf. We all followed her gaze and there, perched on the highest shelf, was a green and purple dragonfly that twinkled like tinfoil. It was so beautiful that we all gasped. "He wants to listen to the story," we said.

We are not obligated to include every child's suggestion every time. If we elaborate on the heart of this class story with empty words and cumbersome phrases, the whole lesson falls flat. If children can feel the story improve, if they can feel that this kind of revision helps, then they will be drawn to the strategy. If you worry that the suggestions for revision of the class story that kids make won't be strong, ask them to turn and talk with their partners about what they'd add. Walk among them, listening in for suggestions to take. If there are none, let that inform your teaching for tomorrow! In the meantime, make up great suggestions yourself!

LINK

Summarize the lesson in a way that directs children through the steps of using this strategy.

"Writers, you really revised this story! You reread it, found the heart of it, and added more to the part where readers should really sit up and take note. That's what writers do all the time when we revise! You can do that every time you have a really deserving draft in front of you. I can't wait to see how you stretch out the heart of the story you pick to revise—if you decide you need to do that!"

Remind children to be job captains for themselves.

"Once you decide on your best story, remember that you need to be job captain for yourself, and figure out what jobs you need to do to make your story the best in the world. You may decide to divide it into paragraphs if you haven't done that already and to use codes—perhaps numbers inserted into the text—to help you elaborate by writing two sentences instead of one. You may decide to find the heart of your story, and then make a movie of it in your mind, adding details to stretch it out. You may have other ideas for how to make this story so, so much better. We'll be revising for a few days and editing. Then we will have a gigantic Author Celebration in which we publish the best of our two stories. Okay, writers, get going."

Notice that in this minilesson, as in most minilessons, I leave children aware of their options for the day ahead. Just because I've taught something in a minilesson doesn't mean everyone must spend the workshop doing the content of that day's minilesson.

WRITING AND CONFERRING

Getting Children Off to a Strong Start

In today's minilesson you sang praises to revision, but the real sales job will need to occur now, during the work session. Today your children will reread their two stories and choose the one they like best. Once they've made a choice, affirm their decision. "I can tell this story is really important to you, isn't it?" you can ask. You may not be able to discern this from what's on the page, but clearly the writer has weighed in on this story. Then help each writer decide what he or she wants to do to revise. Many children will decide to locate the heart of their stories, and to use all they know about writing strong narratives to stretch out this section. When you talk with children, you can make this revision much more powerful if your conferring is informed by two principles.

The first is this: if the writer can determine what it is she really wants to say in a piece, then this decision needs to steer her efforts to elaborate. This means that it helps if you ask, "Why do you think this is the story you decided to write? What do you really want to say to the world through this story?" You can help a writer realize that her story about bees descending on a class picnic is really a story about a week when everything seemed to be a disappointment. Alternatively, the same sequence of events could really be a story about how three best friends make even a class picnic into an adventure. In a conference, you can show a child that the same story can be told in different ways. Once a writer has decided what he or she really wants to say, this decision can inform the writer's choice of where and how to elaborate.

A second principle is this: everything you know about effective stories can inform your conferring. For example, you know that stories have settings. If a child seems at a loss for how he could improve a draft, you could always point out that he is writing a story, and, like the stories read during reading workshop, his story needs to have a setting. Similarly, the child might consider the characters in his story. Has he made them seem real?

The results of this revision work are often amazing, and children feel this when you read what they've written. The author thinks, "Wow! I wrote that! It's really good!"

> **MID-WORKSHOP TEACHING POINT**   *Inserting Paper to Help Revision*   "Writers, can I have your eyes and your attention? As I watch you work today, cutting your draft apart and adding more space into it, I am reminded that writing is more like playing in clay than inscribing in marble. You are all realizing that drafts can be cut and spliced. Ellie did something smart. She realized that she didn't like her lead sentence, so she wrote a new lead and taped it on top of the old one! And Isaiah realized that he needed to expand not just one section of his draft (the heart of it) but also another section where things weren't that clear. So he sliced open his draft in two different places, inserting some extra paper into both spaces."
>
> "I want to remind you of another system for making drafts malleable. Remember how Michela put little numbers into her draft and then, on another sheet of paper, wrote what she wanted to add next to that number? You can do something similar, if you want."
>
> "Okay, writers, you can return to your work now."

SHARE

Expand Key Sections by Bringing Out the Internal Story

Highlight a child who took the minilesson to heart. Tell the story of that child's work in a way others can learn from.

"Writers, today many of you tried to find and develop the heart of your story. Let me show you how Michela stretched out the important part of her story. First she wrote her story step-by-step. Listen to this first version." *[Fig. XV-2]*

First Version

> It was the night before Halloween, my Mom comes in the door. "Mommy, Mommy, Mommy," I shout. I run to her giving her a hug and a kiss. Then I notice she's carrying a little tiny brown box. "Pitter pat, pitter pat." Something's moving around inside of the box! I squeeze her arm. "What is it Mommy, what is it?"* My mom slowly opens the box as if she was afraid something would pop out. I peer into the box. An animal with black beady little eyes, a small orange beak and a pair of wings looks up at me with its head cocked to one side. "It's a bird!" I shout. "A bird?" My sister Alex comes running. She peers into the box. "He's sooo cute," says Alex. "What should we name him?" I ask. "I've got the perfect name, we'll name him Twinkle." Twinkle whistles. "Then Twinkle it is!" says Alex. Then we hurry off to bed and go to sleep dreaming of our new pet.

"Then Michela realized she'd rushed past an important part—the suspense of opening the box. So she rewrote that section of the story, using a star as a code to show where she'd add the new section. What I want you to notice is that Michela stretched out the important section of her story by telling not only what she and her mother did, but also what she thought. This is an important strategy writers use often. We don't only tell the external story,

Fig. XV-2 Michela

the sequence of actions that can be plotted on a timeline. We also tell the internal story, as Michela does in this instance. Listen for how she shows what she thought as she stared at the box in her mother's hands:" *[Fig. XV-3]*

> What could be in that box? I wondered.
>
> "Pitter pat, pitter pat!" a noise came from the box.
>
> "Pitter pat, pitter pat!" There it was again for a second time. Something was moving inside that box." Maybe there's a monster in there!" I thought. "A mini one!" I started backing away slowly.
>
> "What's in the box, Mommy?" I asked. "A monster?"
>
> "No, no," said my mom.

"This is such important work that, writers, I'm going to ask you to take out a sheet of paper and write just the heart of your story on that paper, telling what you did in small steps, and telling also the internal story, as Michela taught us to do. And for the rest of your life, always remember that writers write not only the external but also the internal story."

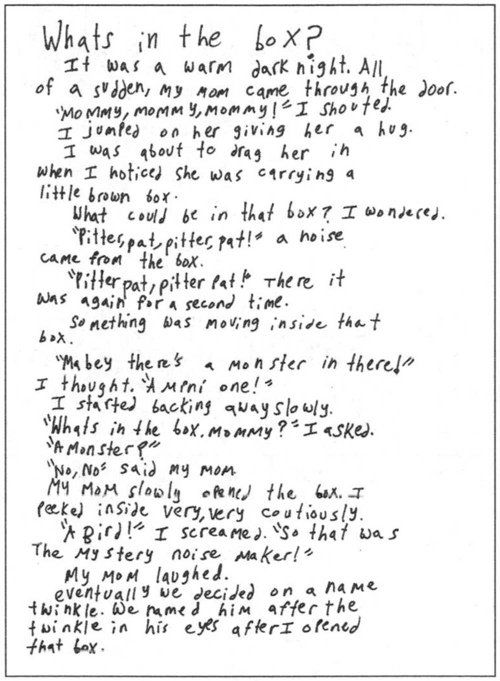
Whats in the box?
It was a warm dark night. All of a sudden, my mom came through the door.
"Mommy, mommy, mommy!" I shouted.
I jumped on her giving her a hug.
I was about to drag her in when I noticed she was carrying a little brown box.
What could be in that box? I wondered.
"Pitter, pat, pitter, pat!" a noise came from the box.
"Pitter pat, pitter pat!" There it was again for a second time.
Something was moving inside that box.
"Mabey there's a monster in there!" I thought. "A meni one!"
I started backing away slowly.
"Whats in the box, Mommy?" I asked. "A Monster?"
"No, No" said my mom.
My mom slowly opened the box. I peeked inside very, very coutiously.
"A Bird!" I screamed. "So that was The Mystery noise maker!"
My mom laughed.
eventually we decided on a name twinkle. We named him after the twinkle in his eyes after I opened that box.

Fig. XV-3 Michela's Insert

HOMEWORK ***Bringing Out the Internal Story*** Writers, in another few days we will hold our first Author Celebration of the year. You could say that we are approaching our first deadline, then. For me, however, the word *deadline* is all wrong. When I know I need to hurry and make my writing ready for publication, I feel as if I've been given not a *deadline,* but a *lifeline.* Tonight is one of your last chances to add more to the heart of your story, so spring to life! In your writer's notepad, take time to try one final, best-in-the-world draft of just the heart of your story.

Take a key moment in the story. Begin by timelining that episode on the page or across your fingers or in your mind. The manner in which you do this doesn't matter, but it does matter that you recall the step-by-step, moment-by-moment sequence of events. Now recall how the story started. Where, exactly, were you and what, exactly, were you doing? Make a movie in your mind and record the start—write what you said, what you did. Then continue writing the movie as it spins out in your mind, but this time remember to use words that access the internal as well as the external story. Write, *I thought . . . I noticed . . . I remembered . . . I wanted to say . . .*

Bring this to school, of course, and you'll have a chance to insert it into your draft.

TAILORING YOUR TEACHING   As publication day comes closer, you'll find yourself wanting to shoehorn in all the lessons you haven't yet had a chance to teach. It's probably wiser to remember that you have an entire year ahead of you, and many of those lessons are probably best reserved for a later unit of study. For now, you may want to shift towards teaching children that the rhythm of writing changes when we can see a publication date around the next bend. For one thing, writers become readers, rereading our own work and asking, "How will someone else read this?"

If you decide to teach children to anticipate their readers' responses and to revise accordingly . . . you may want to tell children that as publication date nears, writers need one thing more than anything else. We need the gift of an honest, attentive reader, one who will truly listen to what we have written and who will help us understand places in our text that are confusing, places where the reader goes, "Huh?" These very special readers need to be honest, but also supportive. Don Murray, my writing teacher, once summed up the role of a writing partner this way: "Above all, the writer needs to leave wanting to write." So listen and ask questions, yes; listen and convey when you are a bit confused, yes; but communicate also that you are dying to understand this writer's very important content.

MECHANICS

At this early stage in the school year, we need to determine our priorities regarding the conventions of written language that we will teach our children. High on my list would be conveying that conventions matter enough that children should take the extra ten seconds to stick a period at the end of what they believe to be a sentence, and should recall, for just a second, that *said* and *say* are the same words, really, and that the spelling of *say* is a good reminder that *said* contains the vowel *a*.

But while I'm playing Tough Guy Enforcer with bottom-line mechanics and spelling expectations, I also want to demonstrate that as a writer, I'm ravenously hungry to learn interesting and wonderful ways in which other writers use the conventions of written language. I want to model that sometimes I read a sentence that an author has written and I just gape over the sounds of it, and the punctuation that created those sounds.

Crews' story *Shortcut,* which opens with some inventive and effective punctuation, is a perfect place to begin. Ellipses aren't threatening to anyone. Children haven't usually been subjected to years of drills on ellipses, or seen their papers scrawled with red because they've gotten ellipses wrong. So marvel at the ellipses at the start of Crews' story:

> We looked . . .
> We listened . . .
> We decided to take
> the shortcut home.

Invite kids to join you in speculating over why Crews decided to use ellipses. How would the story have been different had he written it like this: "We looked. We listened. We decided to take the shortcut home"?

I'm not sure there is a right answer to that question. I suspect that in this instance, the ellipses represent time going by, and they convey that the children stood still on the train tracks, looking and listening, for a long time. They deliberated. Had the text not had those ellipses, I think I'd imagine the children took a quick, fleeting look up and down the tracks and, after seeing and hearing nothing, made their decision.

Then, too, I love thinking about why some of Crews' paragraphs are longer and some are incredibly short. While the children did lots of things, simultaneously, as they walked down the tracks, Crews' writing looks like this:

> We laughed. We shouted. We sang.
> We tussled. We threw stones.

When the sound of the approaching train makes time freeze and hearts stop, Crews' paragraphs (and pages) are incredibly abrupt:

> "I HEAR A TRAIN!"
> Everybody stopped.
> Everybody listened.

If you invite children to speculate with you why Crews varied his paragraph length or used ellipses, children will have their own theories. That's great. There is nothing magical about my theory. But I suspect there will be something magical about asking children to study the ways in which an author has used punctuation and paragraphs artfully. Your real goal is to change children's concepts of themselves and of the conventions of written language so that they are thinking, "I'm the kind of person who needs to understand how writers use punctuation to create effects in their stories." My hope is that this change in perception can matter more than you might dream possible.

GETTING READY

- Instructions on chalkboard telling children to bring their writer's notebooks and sit with their partners in the meeting area
- Editing checklist for each child
- Chart-sized editing checklist
- Example of writing that needs editing to make more sense (written on chart paper)
- Qualities of Good Personal Narrative Writing chart
- Tool containers on each table containing colored pens or pencils
- See CD-ROM for resources

USING EDITING CHECKLISTS

When I was in school, if there was any instruction about editing at all, it had the tone and purpose of correcting faults. I knew that at some point I'd let go of my writing and it'd come before the teacher who would scrutinize it, line by line, red-marking each flaw and error. Frankly, I always felt as if it was me, not my writing, that my teacher would scrutinize.

This part of writing made me feel naked and exposed, judged and humiliated. I wasn't alone in these feelings. Mina Shaughnessey, author of Errors and Expectations, writes that for many people, "Writing is but a line which creeps across the page, exposing all that the writer does not know. Writing puts us on the line and we don't want to be there."

In this session and in this series, we approach teaching children to write conventionally and to edit their writing in the same way in which we teach children to do anything as writers do. We rally children to care about this important aspect of writing, we induct them into the role of being writers who do this sort of work, and we demonstrate strategies that are doable and worth doing.

Just as children in this unit learned a rudimentary sense for the essentials of narrative writing and were empowered to use that introductory knowledge with independence and confidence, so, too, in this session, you'll hand over to children a very rudimentary understanding of how writers edit our rough drafts. Watch to be sure that your instruction gives children roots—and wings.

MINILESSON

Using Editing Checklists

CONNECTION

Create a context for today's lesson by talking about self-help books that fill bookstores and top best–seller lists.

"Writers, I thought about you last night when I stopped at the bookstore (I only have one book left in the pile beside my bed, so I needed to replenish the pile). At the bookstore, I noticed a rack of best-seller books and it was full of what I call self-help books: *How to Become a Millionaire, How to Win Friends and Influence People, How to Start Your Own Company.* I started to realize that it's human nature to want texts in our lives that can act as personalized coaches, whispering bits of advice to us. And I realized that you and I as writers have our own miniature library of self-help texts, and those are our charts."

"Today, I want to give you one more self-help book. It's time for one of my favorite parts of the writing process: editing. And you all deserve to have a self-help text that can act as a personalized coach, whispering bits of advice to you."

Name your teaching point. Specifically, tell children that writers use editing checklists to remind us of strategies we can use to edit our writing.

"Specifically, I want to teach you that most writers rely on an editing checklist—either a concrete physical list or a mental one—and each item on the checklist reminds us of a lens we can use to reread and to refine our writing. If we have six items on our checklist, we're apt to reread our draft at least six times, once with each item as our lens."

TEACHING

Tell children they each have a personalized editing checklist. Demonstrate how to read through a draft, using an item on the checklist as a lens.

"You'll see later that I've put an editing checklist inside each of your writing folders, and you'll see that the lists are somewhat personalized so they can each function as a personal coach. But every editing checklist will contain some shared items, so let's look at one of those shared items. I want to show you how writers use an item or an editing checklist as a lens, rereading the draft through that lens."

"Every writer's editing checklist always says something to the effect of 'Read your writing to be sure it makes sense to strangers.' I'm a lot older than you, and yet, in all these years, that first

COACHING

Did you notice that in this Connection, I bypassed the usual process of contextualizing today's session by recalling previous learning? If you did notice this, it suggests you are internalizing the architecture of minilessons. But of course you'll also want to remember that our teaching needs to be shaped to our specific purposes. And today, it didn't seem necessary to go backward before going forward.

Name_____ Date_____		
Title: _____ Unit of Study: _____		
Reread your writing carefully. Put a check √ in each box under "Author" as you complete each editing item. Once all the boxes are checked, give this editing checklist to the teacher for the final edit.		
Editing Checklist	Author	Teacher
1. Clarity - Read, asking, "Will this make sense to a stranger?" Find confusing spots and rewrite to make them more clear. Note places where you stumble as you reread and revise to make them easier to read.		
2. Punctuation - Read, paying attention to the actual road signs you've given readers. If you followed the punctuation as you've written it, will the piece sound the way you want it to sound? Have you guarded against sentences that run on and on? Have you punctuated dialogue?		
3. Spelling - Do your words look correctly spelled to you? Circle ones that feel as if they could be wrong, try them again, get help with them. Check that the words on the word wall are correctly spelled.		
4. Paragraphs - Narrative writers use a new paragraph or a new page for each new episode in the sequence of events. Do you paragraph to show the passage of time? Do you also paragraph to show changes in who is speaking?		
Optional Items:		
Punctuation		
*For strugglers...*Have I written with periods and capital letters? Do I avoid using 'and' or 'so' to scotch tape lots of short sentences together into one run-on sentence?		
*For more experienced writers...*Have I used complex punctuation and varied sentences to help readers read my story with expressiveness and in a way that creates the mood I want to create? Have I used a mentor author to give me ideas for new ways to use punctuation to create a powerful effect in part of my story?		
Spelling		
When tackling long and challenging words, have I tried to record every sound I hear in the word? Have I used what I know about how other words are spelled to help me spell parts of the challenging word? Have I reread my spelling and circled the parts of a words which I think could be wrong? Have I used spellings I know (and especially those on the word wall) to help me tackle words of which I'm unsure?		

Fig. XVI-1 Editing Checklist (see CD-ROM Resource List)

item has never left my checklist." Referring to a chart-sized editing checklist that contained only two items, I read the first item: "Read, asking, 'Will this make sense to a stranger?'"

"To check for sense, I pretend I know nothing about the topic or the writer. I pick up the paper and start reading, and as I read, I watch for places where I go, 'Huh?' I mark the places that cause some confusion. Later, I go back and rewrite those places so they're clearer. I also mark places that are for some reason hard to read correctly. Writers have a saying, 'When you falter—alter!' If I stumble as I read something or need to reread to figure out what a part is saying, then I figure the section needs more work."

"Let me show you what I mean by showing you a draft that one of my students from last year wrote." I revealed a chart-paper copy of a child's story. "Follow along while I read just the start of Esther's story. We'll pretend we're Esther, and we're using the first item on our checklist to prompt us to reread the draft, checking for sense. See if you find yourself going, 'Huh?' We'll want to come back and clarify those confusing places." [Fig. XVI-2]

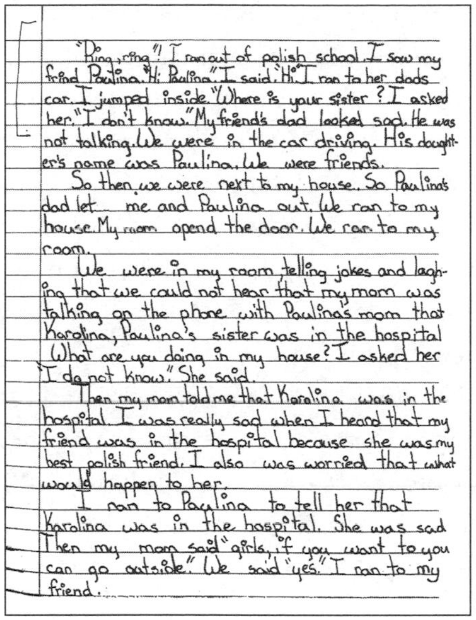

> "Ring, ring!" I ran out of Polish school.
>
> I saw my friend Paulina. "Hi Paulina," I said. "Hi." I ran to her dad's car. I jumped inside.

"Hmm . . . I'm a little confused. I understand the words, the vocabulary, in this story, but if I try to make a picture in my mind of what's really happening, I can't do it. Why is she jumping inside her friend's car?"

> "Where is your sister?" I asked her. "I don't know." My friend's dad looked sad. He was not talking. We were in the car driving. His daughter's name was Paulina. We were friends.

"Now I'm even more confused . . . and if I was Esther, I'd want to clarify so no stranger would read this and go, 'Huh?'" Then I said, "Writers, in Esther's case, she'd been trying to do exactly what we taught her, writing her story step-by-step—but she'd written her piece in such a step-by-step manner that we couldn't understand the big things that were happening. So she went back and clarified:"

> "Ring, ring!" The bell rang, telling us we could leave the Saturday Polish school. So I ran out to the street to find Paulina's dad because he drives me home. I got in the car and noticed Paulina's sister wasn't there. She was always there. . . .

Fig. XVI-2 Esther

Your intonation should suggest this is already confusing.

It was as if, instead of saying, "I picked the flower," Esther had written, "I leaned down. I put my fingers near the flower's stem. I squeezed them. I pulled up . . ." but she hadn't made it clear that she was describing picking the flower! In instances such as this, if you can figure out the intelligence behind students' errors, you can help them enormously. Esther was following my instructions to a T—and going overboard doing so. This happens with nearly every lesson we teach—children often overuse the teaching of the minilesson when they try it for the first few times. Embrace their enthusiasm even as you help them see the teaching in its proper perspective.

"Writers, did you see that I took the first item on the checklist and acted as if it was a personalized assignment? I read, using that item as a lens, and then I did the work that item led me to do. Then I moved on to the next item on the checklist. On all our lists, this item says, 'Check the punctuation,'" I said, gesturing towards the second item on an enlarged list on chart paper. "So I reread a whole other time, and this time I pay special attention to the road signs that tell us how to read. Sometimes I see that I've left out periods, and my sentence goes on so long I forget what the beginning was. So I repair that. If I have dialogue, I check to make sure I have the punctuation that shows the reader that people are talking and these are their exact words."

"The third item that I put on everyone's checklist is spelling," I said, gesturing to this item on the enlarged chart. "To check my writing for misspellings, I read it very slowly, looking at each word. Does each word look right? If I get to any that I think might be wrong, I circle that word and then go back and check. To check words, I ask someone, look at our word wall, or find them in a dictionary or other book."

Using a different color pen or pencil, or one with a special flair to it, can be a tool that inspires editing: a fancy editing tool can spark kids to make changes just for the thrill of using it—especially when it comes to adjusting spelling and punctuation.

ACTIVE ENGAGEMENT
Ask children to read through their drafts with their partners, focusing on one item on the editing checklist.

"Writers, right now, with your partner, let's work with the next item on that checklist." I gestured to the chart and read aloud, "Make sure your paragraphs work the way you want them to in your story. Partner 2, will you spread out your draft and will the two of you read it, checking paragraphs together? If you both find a way the paragraphs could be better for the story, make sure you mark that spot, and maybe make a note in the margin about what needs fixing. Okay, go ahead." The children worked for a bit on that item from their checklist before I interrupted.

At some point, the children will need to assess their writing and decide which editing tasks in particular they need to add to their own editing checklists. The checklist is also a place you can add items you and the child discuss in conferences and strategy lessons. This is another way to help hold the child accountable for all the teaching to date.

LINK
Remind children that they can use this strategy forever when they write.

"Writers, I hope you've learned that editing checklists, like self-help books, can function as personalized coaches, giving us a to-do list. Today, find the editing checklist in your writing folders and use each item as a lens. Reread with that lens, and do the refinements that work prompts you to do. Later today and tomorrow, you can start your final draft and from this day on, always remember that whenever you are going to put your writing into the world, you need to edit it very carefully so that the people reading it will see exactly what you intend for them to see. So when you get started on this important editing work—your last chance to make the writing as perfect as you can get it—you can always use a checklist to help you remember the areas to consider carefully. Someday, you will have used a checklist so often that you won't need it on paper; you can use it right out of your mind!"

WRITING AND CONFERRING

Focusing on Tenses and Pronouns

Two areas where children can easily help themselves in the editing stage are tenses and pronouns.

As you confer with children, pay attention to the tenses they've used in their drafts. Sometimes children misunderstand what we mean by making movies in our heads and recording what we recall, and they write personal narratives exclusively in the present tense, almost as if the story is a caption to a movie. In the following draft, for example, John has tried to write in the present tense.

Lost Dog

My family, my cousin and I are driving home happily from lunch. As we get out of the car we notice the driveway gate is wide open. I find myself yelling, "Pepper, Pepper!" I'm looking everywhere in my green yard. I can't find my dog. My happiness turns into sorrow. Then my sorrow turns into cold tears that are dripping down my face.

In general, past tense is the usual tense used for storytelling. There are reasons why a writer might deliberately break stride and write about a past event in present tense, but that'd be an unusual choice. In the story cited above, the writer simply misunderstood the instructions and thought that when he was told to 'make a movie in his mind and record what happened,' this required present tense. His piece worked more easily when he was given permission to rewrite it in past tense:

My family, cousin and I drove home from lunch. As we got out of the car, we noticed the driveway gate was wide open. "Pepper, Pepper," I yelled. I looked everywhere in my green yard. I couldn't find my dog.

If you see a child trying to maintain present tense, you may want to help the child start the draft over again, this time writing in past tense.

Pay attention also to pronouns. You'll see that children often overuse he or she, and the reader can't keep track of the characters. Tell children that writers are careful to match pronoun references with proper nouns since the pronoun always refers to the person mentioned just before it. You could tell them that one way, then, to edit for clarity is to read while asking: "Is it clear who the character is in every part of my story?"

MID-WORKSHOP TEACHING POINT

Reading with Writing Partners "Writers, may I stop you for a moment? You're doing a great job finding places in your own writing that you can make better by editing.

"Right now, I want to teach you that after you have looked over your own writing carefully and edited it, you can also ask a writing buddy to look it over to see if they find other areas where editing would make the piece stronger. All writers have a friend who helps us edit, or we rely a lot on our editors who help us publish our poems and stories and articles. No one on this whole planet can see every opportunity to make something a little better by herself; we need another pair of eyes!"

"Please exchange papers right now and be another pair of eyes for your partners. When more than one person edits a piece of writing, it helps keep all the changes straight if you use different colored pens. So partners, choose a different color from what the writer used, and put on your best 'editing glasses'!"

SHARE

Preparing for a Celebration

Ask children to show each other what they've done, what they've learned, and what they've resolved to do next.

"Writers, would you gather in the meeting area?" Once the class convened, I said, "Writers, don't you love the days just before a holiday, when everything takes a special significance and special urgency? I love the prelude to Valentine's Day as much as I love the day itself. It's fun to make lists of what I need to do, to busy myself with preparations, to anticipate the actual day. I'm telling you this because today is the prelude to another sort of holiday—our first Author Celebration—and I love the quickening in the air as we ready ourselves."

"Tonight, I'm going to look over the drafts that you've edited today. I'll function as your copy editor. Every author sends his or her books to a copy editor who reads the manuscript over and makes added corrections."

"Tomorrow won't be a usual writing workshop because every minute of the day will be reserved for making final copies of our pieces."

"Before you leave your draft with me, take a few minutes to savor this special time. Meet with your partner and tell your partner what you did to make your story even better today, and what you learned as a writer that you'll carry with you always."

⊙ [HOMEWORK] **Preparing for the Celebration**   Writers, our first Author Celebration is just around the bend. Tonight I hope you will help with preparations for that event. You might think this means that I'm hoping you'll bake brownies or mix Kool-aid, and it's true that I want you to think about ways to make the occasion a special one. But the truth is that when a person writes, when we send our words out into the world, what we long to receive is not a brownie . . . but a response. One writer said that sometimes, authorship feels like tossing rose petals into a well and waiting, hoping to hear a splash.

You will probably be uneasy about the idea that publication day is just around the bend. "Shouldn't I send the drafts off to parents who'll type them?" you may ask yourself. It is true that the day is apt to arrive with some children who haven't finished their final draft. I strongly urge you to go forward anyhow. Children need to finish a unit and to celebrate the work they've done right then and there . . . not two weeks later when every loose end is tied up. You can celebrate the end of the unit—whether or not every detail is completely finished. Your real purpose in this celebration is closure on one unit, and a drum roll to the next. Your hope, too, is to make writing authentic for children by ensuring that they are writing for readers.

My mission today is to create a sense of occasion around the upcoming author celebration, and to be sure that editing takes on special importance because it is a way of preparing one's work to go out in the world.

I'll probably have a chance to look over and correct some children's drafts during today's workshop or during other portions of the day. If I've made corrections on some drafts, I'll certainly send those children home with encouragement to begin making their final copies at home.

Let's be sure that every writer in our community knows that someone has truly heard that writer's work, and truly recognized the time and care invested in that story. And who is in a better place to take notice of what a writer has accomplished than the writer's partner?

At our celebration, it will be your job to introduce your partner to his or her audience. You'll say to the second graders, "I want to introduce you to . . ." and then you'll say, "This writer is especially famous for her ability to . . . Notice the way she (or he) . . ." You will need to think tonight about your partner's writing, and try to use precise details to exactly name what your writer has done that is especially noteworthy. Keep what you write to yourself, just as you keep Valentines to yourself, until the 'Big Day' comes.

TAILORING YOUR TEACHING   One of the goals of this session is to encourage students to regard themselves as people who have important reasons not only to write well, but also to spell and punctuate well—they are writing for an audience who wants to know exactly what they are trying to get across! The editing work you focus on during this first unit of study will depend on the grade and the experience of the children you teach and on you, the teacher. You will want to consider how much time you want to spend on editing and how specific you want to be. You also want to remember to celebrate all that your children do know about language, conventions, and writing.

If your children need extra help to edit for spelling accuracy . . . you might begin a lesson in which you equate editing to getting dressed for a special occasion or celebration. You might say, "One way writers edit is that we check the spelling of each word. Writers ask, 'Does this word look right?' Then we either fix the word in a snap or we try out a few different spellings and choose one that looks right." Demonstrate how you read closely for spelling by pointing under each word, asking questions, and stopping when a word doesn't look right.

If your students need extra practice editing for spelling mistakes . . . you could use a child's piece of writing as a class text to work on editing together. In the minilesson you might say, "Let's practice together what it's like to edit for spelling. A little girl, Jenna, who lives next door to me asked if I could help edit her writing, so I figured we could all help her." Pass out a copy to each partnership along with editing pencils. "Working with your partner, read this excerpt of Jenna's writing very slowly and carefully, touching each word with your pencil. Ask yourself, 'Does this look right?' If you find a misspelled word you know in a snap, cross it out and write the correctly spelled word above it. Underline any words that don't look right, but you're not sure how to spell. Try writing those three different ways at the bottom of the paper and choose the one that looks right to you."

> I was running fast then I triped over something. I fell in the air. Ahh! I scramed. I was falling off the edge of the street. I was almost going to hit myself on the floor. I put my hands doun so I would not hit myself on the hed so hard.

You could harvest insights by saying, for instance, "Who found some words that were misspelled that you knew in a snap?" Or, "Who found a word that didn't look right, but was not sure exactly how the word was spelled?" Point out what they did. "You did a really good job editing this writer's story for spelling. Because you read slowly and carefully, touching each word with your editing pencil, you were able to catch and fix some of the misspelled words." Bring the lesson to a close by saying, "So writers, whenever you want to get your writing ready for readers, for an audience, you need to become an editor by checking your spelling and fixing anything that does not look right or sound right, just like we did here together. This will help your readers be able to read and enjoy your stories easily. And your stories will be ready for our publishing celebration."

ASSESSMENT

One day on my way home from work, I was listening to a radio interview with a famous visual artist. The interviewer was asking him how he kept himself on track through his starving artist days—the days when he was working well under the radar of gallery owners, art collectors, and paparazzi; the period when he was a bricklayer by day and a painter at night. "Did you ever consider just giving up?" she asked.

I remember the artist taking a few seconds to answer. He began by saying that although he often longed for an income that wasn't fraught with gaps and surprises, he always had energy and hope for his art. He said he had a variety of tricks to help him stay motivated and focused, even when an eviction notice had been slipped under the door. One of the most important things he did that helped him to keep moving forward as an artist was looking backward and taking time to reflect on how his art had changed. He said that looking back regularly through his body of work helped him to notice ways he'd grown, how he'd changed, and what he still needed to work on as an artist. For this painter, the act of reflecting was incredibly motivating.

Taking time to step back and reflect is incredibly important as we try to grow, no matter whether we're trying to become better painters, golfers, spouses, parents, cooks, teachers of writing . . . or writers. All of this suggests to me that it would be time well spent to tuck in opportunities for our students to step back and reflect on their work as writers.

It's important to consider, however, that reflecting on one's writing work isn't just about rereading old entries and drafts. The more important and challenging work of self-reflection requires naming what you see and considering its significance.

This first unit, then, provides a perfect opportunity to give students time to self-assess, to reflect on their work so far, and to answer questions such as:

- What do I notice about myself as a writer as I read through my work?
- How have I changed as a writer so far?
- What are three things I do well as a writer?
- What are some things I want to get stronger at as a writer?
- What is my favorite piece, and what are the things I love about it?

In some classrooms, teachers have students do this work during homework for a couple of days at the end of the unit. Then, in class, the students talk in small groups about their self-reflections as the teacher listens in on their conversations. If students write self-reflections, they will be powerful artifacts to accumulate over the course of the year and analyze at the year's end.

Although this self-reflection may benefit the student primarily, certainly we, as teachers, can use the responses to help us plan instruction. When we see that we have several children who feel strong at writing authentic, accurately punctuated dialogue, we can suggest those children become mentors to other children who may have a more difficult time with this. If we find that we have several students who say they still struggle with coming up with ideas for writing, we can pull these together for some small-group instruction. Assessment is one way to channel growth.

GETTING READY

- Empty bulletin board prepared to receive each child's writing
- Tacks
- Assorted stickers
- Juice and cups
- See CD-ROM for resources

PUBLISHING:
A WRITING COMMUNITY CELEBRATES

This first celebration of the year *is a momentous occasion for both you and your students! Your students have learned to work productively and independently, to use a repertoire of strategies to generate and develop ideas, and to be able to capture moments on the page, minding the conventions of standard English. This day is a celebration of a great accomplishment; your children are writers!*

Today your young writers will feel how their work can affect others; they will share compliments and celebrate each other's work. Some children will be astounded that they've made their classmates laugh; some will be shocked by the attention their words get from the others in the class. Most will be thrilled, as we all are, to feel that they have made something, an artifact that can stay in the world forever. Writing celebrations help our young students regard themselves as authors in a working, thriving community of other authors. In Ralph Peterson's brilliant book, Life in a Crowded Place, *he explains that celebrations contribute to our sense of belonging by helping us learn to focus on others and their achievements rather than just on our own (1992, p. 39). The gallery wall of writing you create today is an announcement to the world: "Look! Here we are all authors."*

Celebrations need to build in grandeur from the beginning of the year until the end. This first celebration needs to make your writers feel proud and strengthen their motivation for writing while still leaving room for fancier celebrations to come. As children's writing strengthens and deepens, so must the celebrations that honor that work. For now, plan to celebrate children's change into writers rather than celebrating exquisite writing. The truth is, the pieces of writing may yet be far from exquisite—after all, for many writers this may be their first time working through the entire writing process! Don't succumb to the temptation to postpone the celebration until the writing is fantastic, or until you've had time to work individually with each child until they've written something impressive. Let the children's finished work stand as examples of their best work to date. This way, the children, and all the grown-ups watching their development, can see their growth throughout the year more clearly—something they couldn't see if these first pieces are "propped up." This particular celebration is truly a lovely way to appreciate where children are and encourage their growth as writers from this day forth.

CELEBRATION

Start the school day by building up excitement toward the approaching celebration.

When the children lined up on the playground in the morning, ready to come into the classroom for the day, I heightened their excitement. "You all seem bursting with energy this morning," I said. "No wonder—it's our Author Celebration!" When children convened in the meeting area to review the schedule for the day, I said, "I know for certain what your first question will be: 'When will we have our celebration?'"

For the celebration, bring the guests into the classroom. As a welcome, describe a reading that you attended at the local bookstore. Explain the structure for today's celebration.

"This is a very special moment," I said once the little children, the class' younger reading buddies, had settled in the meeting area alongside my class. "Today we are gathering to celebrate that Room 203's children are truly becoming writers. Last Saturday, I went to a reading at our local bookstore. Lots and lots of people gathered in a corner of the bookstore, just like we've gathered in a corner of our classroom, and the author's writing partner, a person known as her editor, spoke first. She said, 'I want to introduce you to someone whose writing I know very well.' Then the editor went on to tell us what this writer did so remarkably."

"Afterwards, the author read her writing aloud, and we got a chance to ask her questions about her writing life, questions like, 'Where did you get the idea for your story?' or 'Who especially helped you to write this story?' or 'What did you learn from writing this?'"

"I'm telling you this because today we will celebrate your writing just as we celebrated that famous author's writing. In a few minutes, we will gather in one of our four corners (remember we gathered in a corner of the bookstore!) and then, in each corner, an author will take her place in the author's chair (you'll see I have one set up in each corner). The author's writing partner will sit beside her, and our reading will begin. First, the writing partner will introduce the author. You will read the introductions you wrote at home last night!"

COACHING

I know that it is not truly the case that every child in the class is beside herself with excitement over the fact that today is our Author Celebration, but I'm going to act as though, of course, children feel thrilled at the prospect of sharing their writing. At the start of the year, especially, we are building a culture in our classrooms, and the values of that culture make a very big difference. So I will do everything possible to be sure that this community is one that honors the written word, one that regards author celebrations as one of our most important occasions.

Younger children, not parents, are the audience for this celebration. At the start of the year, your emphasis will have been on helping children cycle through the writing process with independence. In order to be sure that your workshop is a productive one, one where children are able to carry on with independence, you will not have been able to coach and guide every writer about his final piece of writing. Chances are very good that some children will be publishing stories that are laden with problems. At this early stage, it is crucial that you accept that children's best work is worthy of celebration. You will have lots of time to raise the level of that work—for now, some children will publish stories that are still unfocused, underdeveloped, and so forth. For this reason, I suggest you postpone the celebration with the high-stakes audience until a bit later in the year. Meanwhile, this is a wonderful way to induct younger children into the writing culture of your school.

"Then, Authors, read your stories. When you have finished, please leave a little bit of time for silence. Let there be just a moment when no one speaks and everyone lets the story sink in. Then one of you can ask the writer a writing question—just one, for now."

When each member of each group has shared her piece and answered one question, ask everyone to gather in the hallway beside a shrouded bulletin board.

"Writers, the work that you shared deserves to be sent out into the world. At the bookstore, after the reading, the bookstore created a gigantic display of the author's work, and that made me realize we, too, needed a way to display your work. So you'll see," I dramatically pulled the shroud off a beautifully matted bulletin board, "I've created a special display case for your masterpieces!" I paused for the oohing and ahhhing. "Now, when I gesture to you, please say the name of your writing partner and that writer please come to me for some stickers to decorate your piece. Then you will hang your writing in our display case!"

In this fashion, one child after another was named, approached me for a few stickers, and then hung her writing on the bulletin board.

Here is Terrance's final draft: *[Fig. XVII-1]*

> "Matches!" I thought. I picked them up. I flipped them open and took out a match. "This is not right," I thought. "I'm going to do it anyway," I said. I rushed to my room to set a string on fire. I crawled under my bed. "No one can see me now," I thought. I set the string on fire. WOOOF!—the sheets burst into flames. "What's that smell?" Mom yelled! "Nothing," I said. That's when I heard running footsteps. The last step she took was to my room.
>
> She saw the flaming sheets. She ran to my room. She flipped the bed over. The flames burst into her face, almost leaving her hair like rice crispies. She backed away from the fire. I crawled out from under my bed! My mom ran to the bathroom. She got two big buckets of water. She threw the water on the bed to make the fire stop. But the fire was too strong to put out, so my mom called the fire department. They brought fire hoses and other materials. They put out the fire. Then I got on punishment for 4 months.

If possible, it would be great to station an adult in each of the four corners, though, of course, the grown-ups can also keep an eye on two corners at once. Your hope is that the author takes his place of honor, and the partner sits beside the author. The partner uses the class' attention-getting signal to ask for everyone's attention and waits (help them do this) until the group is focused and ready to listen. Then one partner begins, saying, "I'm proud to introduce you to my writing partner. I think Terrance has a special talent for conveying excitement . . . " Then the author reads aloud, and when the listening children hear evidence of what the partner described, the listeners signal with a quiet thumbs-up.

You may wonder what, exactly, the work looks like that children are pinning onto the bulletin board. Your first and biggest question is probably this: is the work totally correct? Although children will have devoted earnest effort to making their writing their best, and you will have had three or four editing conferences in which you teach three or four editing tips in relation to this one piece, there is no way every child in your room (or even most children in your room) will have been able to fully correct their own writing.

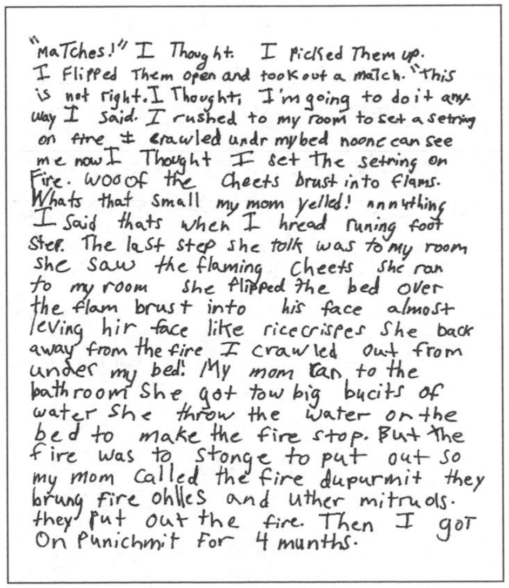
"MaTches!" I Thought. I Picked Them up.
I Flipped Them open and tookout a match. "This
is not right. I Thought, I'm going to do it anyway I Said. I rushed to my room to set a setring
on fire I crawled undr my bed noone can see
me now I Thought I set the setring on
Fire. WOOOF the Cheets brust into flams.
Whats that Small my mom yelled! annything
I Said thats when I hread runing foot
Step. The last step she tolk was to my room
She Saw the flaming Cheets She ran
to my room She flipped the bed over
the flam brust into his face almost
leving hir face like ricecrispes She back
away from the fire I crawled out from
under my bed! My mom ran to the
bathroom She got tow big bucits of
water She throw the water on the
bed to make the fire stop. But the
fire was to Stonge to put out so
my mom Called the fire dupurmit they
brung fire ohlles and uther mitruols.
they put out the fire. Then I goT
On Punichmit For 4 munths.

Fig. XVII-1 Terrance's final draft

Bask in the glory of progress as writers. Remind writers that a whole year for writing stretches ahead of them. Create time for children to compliment each other's writing.

"Writers, I need to tell you that frankly, I am incredibly excited because I listen to this writing and I think, "And this is still Unit One!" I know it will be an amazing thing to see how your writing gets even better. Maybe our last celebration better be at that bookstore . . . because look out world, here these writers come!"

"Before we end our celebration, could we hear from our young guests? Second-graders, what did you notice about these bigger-kids' writing? Will you guys turn and talk, and let's hear from our visitors, and learn from their observations." We heard from several.

"Writers and guests, before we go back to our other work, would everyone get yourself something to eat and drink, and let's have a party!"

Here is Olivia's final draft: *[Fig. XVII-2]*

The Place: the Finish Line

I held my sled in my hand tight. My heart pumped as me and Alejandra walked over to Balin. The words, "Balin, do you want to race?" wouldn't come out. Finally, they did. "Hey, Balin, do you want to race?" I said. "Sure, why not? On the count of three," was his response.

"I must have sweated buckets as we got our sleds in place. "1," said Balin. My heart pumped. "2," said Balin. I sweated ten buckets. "3," said Balin. I nearly wet my pants.

After three, we were off. It was going very smoothly and we were tied for the lead. Then suddenly me and Alejandra hit a big root and went in the air and landed with a plop, and slowed down. I wondered what we hit but reminded each other we had a race to finish.

So we dug our hands in the cold snow and pushed ourselves forwards. We tried and tried to win. But as we trailed behind Balin we heard him cheering, "I win! I win!" I reminded myself everybody's a winner.

If you are thinking that, for your children, the only way for the work to be absolutely correct is for you to correct it, and even retype it, then you need to know that you are in good company. All of us teach children with needs like that, and frankly, even grown adults rely on copyeditors. It goes without saying that although children devote earnest effort to making their writing their best, their texts will not be perfect.

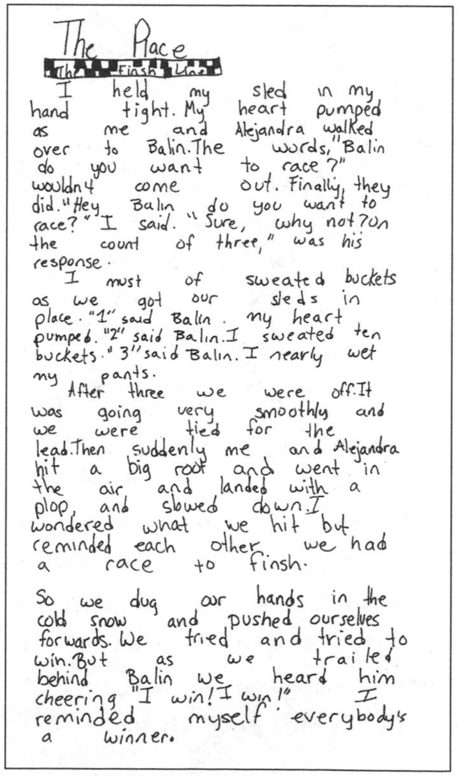
The Place
The Finsh Line
I held my sled in my hand tight. My heart pumped as me and Alejandra walked over to Balin. The words, "Balin do you want to race?" wouldn4 come out. Finally, they did. "Hey Balin do you want to race?" I said. "Sure, why not? On the count of three," was his response.
I must of sweated buckets as we got our sleds in place. "1" said Balin. my heart pumped. "2" said Balin. I sweated ten buckets. "3" said Balin. I nearly wet my pants.
After three we were off. It was going very smoothly and we were tied for the lead. Then suddenly me and Alejandra hit a big root and went in the air and landed with a plop, and slowed down. I wondered what we hit but reminded each other we had a race to finsh.
So we dug our hands in the cold snow and pushed ourselves forwards. We tried and tried to win. But as we trailed behind Balin we heard him cheering "I win! I win!" I reminded myself everybody's a winner.

Fig. XVII-2 Olivia's final draft

Here is Felix's final draft: *[Fig. XVII-3]*

It was a warm, sunny day. It was also the day before Easter, around the time for me to have lunch. Just me and my mom all alone in the car. She was driving somewhere, and I had no idea where.

"Hmmm, I wonder where we're going," I said in my head. I tried to think of something that I told her I wanted really bad, but I couldn't think of anything. So I just asked her.

"Where are you going?" I asked her.
"You'll see," she answered.
"Can you just tell me?" I begged.
"Nope," she said.
"Please," I said.
"No!" she said so loud she almost screamed.
"Fine," I said in an angry voice.

She drove up to some animal shelter.

"Yay! So what kind of animal can I get?" I said.
"A cat," she said.
"Yay! A cat. I love cats," I said happily.

So anyway we got out of the car and went into the animal shelter. I started walking down the aisles, and this one cat started staring at me and I started staring back. We were staring at each other for about 2 minutes. Then my mom saw me.

"Mom, watch this," I said. So my mom came over to see.
"Why don't you get that cat?" she said.
"Okay," I said.

So the person who worked took him out of his cage. The shelter worker gave us a box so I could carry him home on my lap. "Hmmm, now what should I name him?" I said in my head.

You will certainly want to have had editing conferences with children to improve their use of conventions in their writing. But, even if you have taught three or four editing tips in relation to this one piece, there is no way every child in your room (or even most children in your room) will be able to fully correct their own writing.

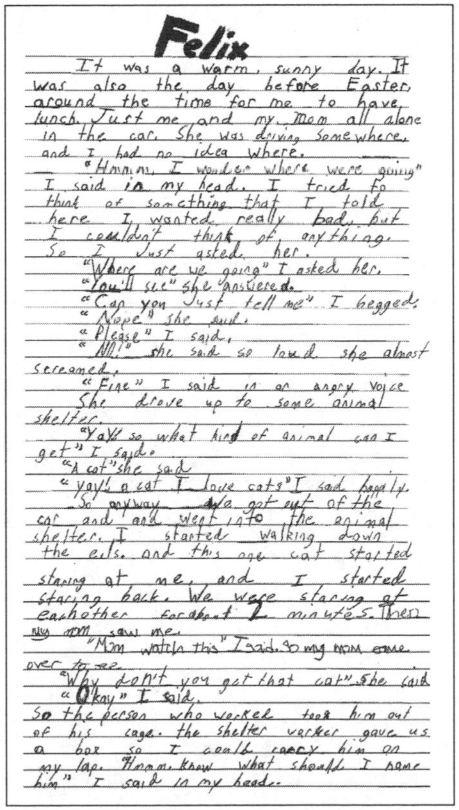
Felix
It was a warm, sunny day. It was also the day before Easter, around the time for me to have lunch. Just me and my Mom all alone in the car. She was driving Somewhere, and I had no idea where.
"Hmmm, I wonder where were going" I said in my head. I tried to think of something that I told here I wanted really bad, but I couldn't think of anything. So I Just asted her.
"Where are we going" I asked her.
"You'll see" she answered.
"Can you Just tell me" I begged.
"Nope" she said.
"Please" I said.
"NO!" she said so loud she almost screamed.
"Fine" I said in an angry voice
She drove up to some animal shelter.
"Yay! so what kind of animal can I get" I said.
"A cat" she said
"yay! a cat I love cats" I said happily.
So anyway we got out of the car and and went into the animal shelter. I started walking down the eils. and this one cat started staring at me. and I started staring back. We were staring at eachother for about 2 minutes. Then my mom saw me.
"Mom watch this" I said. So my mom came over to see.
"Why don't you get that cat" she said
"Okay" I said.
So the person who werkel took him out of his cage. the shelter worker gave us a box so I could carry him on my lap. "Hmm. know what should I name him" I said in my head.

Fig. XVII-3 Felix's final draft

Here is Gregory's final draft: *[Fig. XVII-4]*

Al is Dead

Dead. Ever since I had fish, I had Al: the best algae-eater in the world. Once I heard he was dead, I did not cry. I just was still. Then I asked, "Where is he?" My dad said, "In the trash." I asked to see him.

I walked over to the trash can and I opened it. I looked in and saw wet paper towels, orange peels and a pile of coffee grounds. I picked up Al. I flicked off the coffee grounds and said "Al, my friend. I'm gonna miss you."

My dad put him back. For a second, I thought, then I said, "We can give him a funeral." My dad looked doubtful for a minute but I picked him up and said, "He was special." Then I cried. Al was gone.

Here is Michela's final draft: *[Fig. XVII-5]*

GETTING READY TO GO TO CALIFORNIA

By: Michela

"Beep, beep, beep" the alarm went off. It was 4:00 in the morning. You'd think we would be tired but . . .

"Go, go, go!" I screamed.

We peeled off our pajamas and jumped into our clothes as fast as we could.

"Get the tooth brushes, get the suitcases!" yelled my mom.

I was shoved into the small, wooden bookcase as my sister ran to get the suitcases and toothbrushes.

"Get the entertainment, get the extra pillows!" bellowed my dad. I was yanked to the side to make room for my mom while she ran to get the entertainment and extra pillows.

"Where's my cell phone?" screamed my sister. I was pushed into the stereo as my sister grabbed her cell phone from the top of the CD rack.

"Get everything!" I yelled still rubbing my head from my past incidents.

It was a mad, mad house. We ran around in circles trying to figure out what to do, when finally we realized we were done packing. We all plopped on the couch. I let out a loud sigh and closed my eyes for a quick rest.

"Honk, Honk!" the car service is here.

We bolted out the door and slammed it behind us. We ran down the dark deserted street toward the blinking taillights.

The car door slowly opened with a creek and we hopped inside. We were on our way to the airport.

Fig. XVII-5 Michela's final draft

For more examples of final pieces, go to the CD-ROM.

You will decide, based on the expectations of your community, whether you need to go through and correct each piece, asking each child to recopy your corrections, or whether you can publish children's best work at this point in the year. I hope you can do the latter. If we are always propping children's work up so that it looks perfect, then how can we keep track of their development over time? How can we hold ourselves responsible for them learning to do significantly more on their own? If your school community has trouble with displays of imperfect work (they no doubt accept this for clay sculpture and portraits, but if they do not regard approximation in writing with equal trust), then I recommend moving the display case inside the classroom and perhaps titling it, "See Our Work In-Progress" or "Celebrate Rough Drafts and Revisions!"

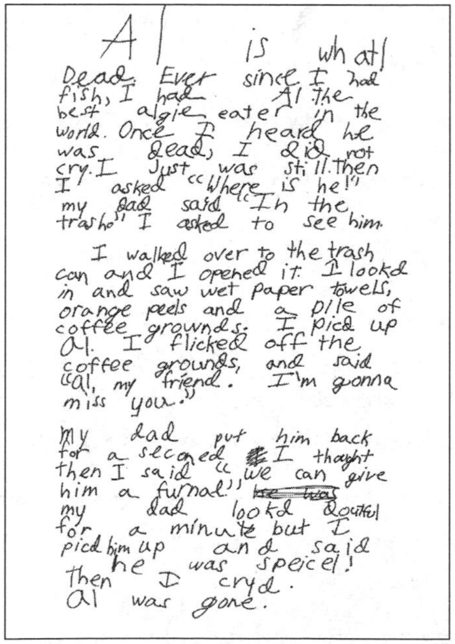
Al is what!

Dead. Ever since I had fish, I had Al the best algie eater in the world. Once I heard he was dead, I did not cry. I Just was still. Then I asked "Where is he!" my dad said "In the trash" I asked to see him.

I walked over to the trash can and I opened it. I lookd in and saw wet paper towels, orange peels and a pile of coffee grownds. I pick up al. I flicked off the coffee grounds, and said "al, my friend. I'm gonna miss you."

my dad put him back for a secaned I thaght then I said "we can give him a furnal" ~~he was~~ my dad lookd doutful for a minute but I pick him up and said he was speicel! Then I cryd. al was gone.

Fig. XVII-4 Gregory's final draft